Dr Alan Scott is a Fellow in the Department of
Religious Studies at Yale University.

OXFORD EARLY CHRISTIAN STUDIES

General Editors

Henry Chadwick   Rowan Williams

THE OXFORD EARLY CHRISTIAN STUDIES series includes scholarly volumes on the thought and history of the early Christian centuries. Covering a wide range of Greek, Latin, and Oriental sources, the books are of interest to theologians, ancient historians, and specialists in the classical and Jewish worlds.

ORIGEN AND THE LIFE OF THE STARS

A History of an Idea

ALAN SCOTT

CLARENDON PRESS · OXFORD

1991

Oxford University Press, Walton Street, Oxford OX2 6DP

Oxford New York Toronto
Delhi Bombay Calcutta Madras Karachi
Petaling Jaya Singapore Hong Kong Tokyo
Nairobi Dar es Salaam Cape Town
Melbourne Auckland

and associated companies in
Berlin Ibadan

Oxford is a trade mark of Oxford University Press

Published in the United States
by Oxford University Press, New York

© Alan Scott 1991

British Library Cataloguing in Publication Data
Data available

Library of Congress Cataloging in Publication Data
Origen and the life of the stars : a history of an idea
Alan Scott.
(Oxford early Christian studies)
Revision of thesis (Ph.D.)—Yale University, 1988.
Includes bibliographical references and index.
1. Origen—Contributions in cosmology. 2. Stars—Religious aspects—
Christianity—History of doctrines—Early church, ca. 30–600. 3. Powers
(Christian theology)—History of doctrines—Early church, ca. 30–600.
4. Astronomy, Greek. 5. Cosmology, Medieval.
I. Title. II. Series.
BR65.O68S39   1991   113'.092—dc20   90–26226
ISBN 0–19–826462–3

Typeset by Pentacor PLC, High Wycombe, Bucks
Printed by
Bookcraft (Bath) Ltd., Midsomer Norton, Avon

For my parents

ACKNOWLEDGEMENTS

This book is a revised version of my 1988 Yale dissertation, *Origen and Astral Souls*. I owe the new title (*inter alia*) to Bentley Layton. Many scholars have been very helpful to me in the course of this project, including Zlatko Pleše, Don Westblade, Frederick Norris, Elizabeth Clark, Wayne Meeks, Rowan Williams, and Henry Chadwick, as have the editorial staff at Oxford University Press. Thanks are due above all to my dissertation adviser, Rowan Greer. I hope my great debt to scholars such as Cherniss, Crouzel, Festugière, and Theiler (to name a few) is evident in the notes and bibliography. All errors are my own.

I am also grateful to my wife Violeta, who proofread the text, to Mr and Mrs Chan Kim Bing, to Mr and Mrs Henry Pierce, and to the Yale University Department of Religious Studies.

Many thanks to the following presses for their kind permission to quote translations from these works: Origen, *Contra Celsum*, trans. Henry Chadwick (Cambridge: Cambridge University Press, 1980); *The Testimony of Truth*, NHS 15, trans. S. Giverson and B. Pearson (Leiden: E. J. Brill, 1981); *Old Testament Pseudepigrapha*, ed. James Charlesworth (Garden City, NY: Doubleday, 1983); Origen, *On First Principles*, trans. G. W. Butterworth (Gloucester, Mass.: Peter Smith Publ., 1973), *Alexandrian Christianity*, trans. J. E. L. Oulton and Henry Chadwick (London: SCM Press; Philadelphia: Westminster Press, 1954); and various works of Philo, trans. H. Colson and G. H. Whitaker, in the Loeb Classical Library Series (Cambridge, Mass.: Harvard University Press, 1929–53).

CONTENTS

NOTE ON CITATIONS

Abbreviations follow those collected in the *Theologische Realenzyklopädie, Abkurzungsverzeichnis* (Berlin: Walter de Gruyter, 1976). In addition the following abbreviations are used:

B.	W. A. Baehrens
BG	Codex Berolinensis Gnosticus
CCAG	*Catalogus Codicum Astrologorum Graecorum*, ed. Franz Boll *et al.*
CIMRM	*Corpus Inscriptionum et Monumentorum Religionis Mithraicae*, ed. M. J. Vermaseren
CCel.	Origen, *Contra Celsum*
CH	*Corpus Hermeticum*
CMAG	*Catalogue des manuscrits alchimiques grecs*, ed. Joseph Bidez *et al.*
CS	Henri Crouzel/Manlio Simonetti
DDG	*Doxographici Graeci*, ed. Hermann Diels.
Dev.	Robert Devreesse, *Les Anciens Commentateurs grecs des Psaumes*
DK	*Die Fragmente der Vorsokratiker* (7th edn., 1954), ed. Hermann Diels and Walther Kranz
DL	Diogenes Laertius
DND	Cicero, *De Natura Deorum*
GCS	Griechische christliche Schriftstellern
K.	Paul Koetschau
Kl.	Erich Klostermann
LCL	Loeb Classical Library
NF	A. D. Nock/A. J. Festugière
NH	Nag Hammadi
NPNF	Nicene and Post-Nicene Fathers Series
P.	Erwin Preuschen
PAS	Joannes Baptista Card. Pitra (ed.), *Analecta Sacra*
R.	J. Armitage Robinson
Ra.	Max Rauer
RD	A. Rousseau/L. Doutreleau

SC   Sources chrétiennes
St.   Otto Stählin
TDNT   Kittel's *Theological Dictionary of the New Testament*,
          trans. Geoffrey W. Bromiley

With a few exceptions, I have used the Greek texts listed in the *Thesaurus Linguae Graecae*, ed. Luci Berkowitz and Karl A. Squitier (New York: Oxford University, 1986). When more or less the same text was available in the Loeb Classical Library, I used the text in that series. The most important example of this is Philo. All texts are given in translation. All unattributed translations are my own.

Following Whittaker, I refer to the author of the Didaskalikos as Alcinous rather than as Albinus. This does not affect any of my conclusions. I have not included any Mandaean sources, though much material presents itself, because of the dating problems associated with these texts. Marcel Borret, SJ (ed.), *Origène: Homélies sur Ézéchiel*, SC 352 (Paris: du Cerf, 1989), appeared too late for me to use.

INTRODUCTION

Origen is generally recognized as the most important Greek patristic writer and as one of the best thinkers early Christianity produced. Many early Christian writers were influenced by classical ideas, but Origen is remarkable both in the extent of his debt and in his ability to combine the inheritance of classical antiquity with an interpretation of Christian scripture. Others took over pagan ideas, but few used them so much, and perhaps none used them so well. The question of how Origen's appropriation of pagan thought should be understood is a long-standing problem, and continues to be a source of controversy among historians of the period.

In this century a number of scholars have emphasized Origen's debt to the Platonism of his own day and consider him a 'middle-Platonist'.[1] Discussions of Origen in terms of middle-Platonism have marked a real advance in Origen studies, for much of his work can be understood only against the backdrop of the interpretation of Plato which was current in the time between Antiochus of Ascalon (d. *c.*68 BC) and Plotinus (d. AD 270). And yet this is not a category into which Origen neatly fits. First, it is doubtful if, strictly speaking, there is such a thing as 'Christian middle-Platonism'.[2] Second, Origen, after all, regarded himself as an interpreter of scripture and not as a Platonist, and so he did not have any special obligation to stay within a particular philosophical school of thought. Like many Christian theologians he seems to incline naturally to Platonism, but he was widely

[1] Especially Hal Koch, *Pronoia und Paideusis*, AKG 22 (Berlin: Walter de Gruyter, 1932); recently Robert M. Berchman, *From Philo to Origen: Middle-Platonism in Transition*, Brown Judaic Studies 69 (Chico, Calif.: Scholars Press, 1984).

[2] See J. H. Waszink, 'Bemerkungen zum Einfluß des Platonismus im frühen Christentum', *VigChr* 19 (1965) 134 n. 10, and Heinrich Dörrie, 'Was ist spätantiker Platonismus?', *Platonica Minora*, Studia et Testimonia 8 (Munich: Wilhelm Fink, 1976), 523 n. 27. For an equally negative appraisal of middle-Platonism in Philo see David T. Runia, *Philo of Alexandria and the Timaeus of Plato*, PhAnt 44 (Leiden: E. J. Brill, 1986), 507–19.

read in the other main philosophical traditions as well. Further, it is important to note that Origen had extensive contact with Jewish apocalyptic literature and gnostic Christianity. To read him strictly in terms of any one of his interests and influences is therefore to give a skewed version of his work. Plato and contemporary Platonism have both influenced him, but only as part of a much broader picture.

Examining Origen's use of philosophy is a twofold process. One must consider the state of a given problem in Origen's own day. Sharply focused questions are easier to answer than blurry ones, and Origen lived in a time when philosophical questions were often in a confused state—the genius of his younger pagan contemporary Plotinus was that he was able to bring so much order out of so much chaos. Origen's task was further complicated by his interest in issues raised by Jewish and gnostic texts and by his desire only to use philosophy within boundaries established by scripture. He was not as successful as Plotinus in addressing the philosophical problems of his day, but this in part was because he was trying to do something which was much more difficult.

After clarifying a particular historical problem, one must examine the use Origen makes of this philosophical inheritance. It may be possible to discuss the ideas which have influenced Origen without considering the specific function of these ideas in his theology, but such an approach, for whatever it may tell us about Origen's milieu, will not tell us much about Origen. Like Philo and Clement, Origen certainly has been influenced by Greek philosophy, but his use of the philosophical tradition often transforms it into something new and original (which is why Porphyry accuses Origen, in contrast to Ammonius, of betraying his Hellenic education).

The present work investigates the view, common in antiquity, that stars have souls and the uses to which this belief is put in Origen's thought. There are many philosophical commonplaces which Origen takes over, but this idea merits closer consideration for a number of reasons.

First, Plato's teachings about the astral gods were of great religious importance, but were also highly ambiguous and troublesome. His successors put them in a number of new forms which were again both important and yet ambiguous and

troublesome. In Origen's day the problem of the nature and
religious function of the stars was universally recognized as a
major topic, but it remained without consensus in many key
areas. It was therefore ripe for speculation and representative of
the challenge Origen faced in bringing philosophy to bear on
problems of Christian theology.

Second, the place of the living star in Origen's thought has not
been treated independently since 1668 when Pierre Huet
included a brief section 'De Astris' in his monumental *Origeniana*.[3]
Origen includes speculations on the life and intelligence of the
stars in his discussion of several important theological issues.
Though it was routine for theology and astronomy to be
considered together in pagan philosophy, Origen was the first
Christian theologian to do so (aside from Christian gnostics, who
influenced him in this regard). Origen's speculations on the life of
the stars were formally anathematized in the sixth century,[4]
together with other, more familiar aspects of his cosmology, and
this rejection affected the way that astronomy was treated in
subsequent Christian theology.

Third, though questions about the souls of stars now look quite
whimsical, they were once seriously debated by philosophers. In
fact, discussions of the life of the stars were common in
Hellenistic schoolrooms.[5] Origen's ideas on the stars and their life
is part of a much broader philosophical tradition which is only
rarely mentioned in treatments of Greek philosophy. Though the
present work discusses the debates on the nature and function of
the living stars as background to Origen's thought, hopefully this
topic will also be of more general interest.

The aim of this book is to trace the rise and development of the
idea of living heavenly bodies and to see its use in Origen's
theology. The first part will deal with Plato's important speculations on this topic. A number of contradictions are inherent in
Plato's attempt to understand the religious importance of the
stars. Plato's successors, Aristotle, and the old Stoics took over
parts of this inheritance and set it in a new form, but did as much

---

[3] Reprinted in both C. H. E. Lommatzsch's and Migne's editions of Origen's
works. The section 'De Astris' is in Lommatzsch *Opera*, 23. 115–25; in Migne, *PG*
17. 973–80.
[4] *ACO* 3. 213. 27 f.; 4. 1. 248. 14–16.
[5] Aëtius *DDG* 274. 6 f.; 432. 6–8; Achilles *Isag.* 13 (40 f. Maass).

to complicate the problem of the stars' place in a philosophical cosmology as to solve it. The view of the classic philosophical schools (aside from the Epicureans) was that the heavenly bodies were alive, but the way that this was true and the significance of this life was unclear.

The second part will consider the ways in which these problems continue and become more complex in the early empire period, which is the time of Origen's immediate intellectual predecessors. Confusions about how to talk about the stars continue and are evident in Philo, whose ideas on the heavens are of great importance to Origen. Two types of speculations come into prominence in this era and figure strongly in Origen's speculations on the importance of the stars. First, the idea begins to be formulated that the human soul has a 'vehicle' which is made of an astral substance. Second, associated with this idea is the view (which has its origins in astrology and in the pessimistic interpretation of Plato) that the stars are malevolent and harm the soul before or after death. The part concludes with Clement of Alexandria's cautious appraisal of the stars' place in Christian eschatology, since this anticipates some interesting aspects of Origen's work.

The final part will investigate Origen's own background in astronomy and astrology, and the ambitious use he made of the concept of living heavenly bodies in his theology. Specifically, attention will be given to the importance of the stars in understanding Origen's cosmology, theodicy, doctrine of the Fall, and eschatology.

PART I

1

FROM THE PRE-SOCRATICS TO PLATO
AND HIS SCHOOL

In contrast to many other pre-industrial societies, a formal cult of
the stars was almost unknown in ancient Greece.[1] Aristophanes,
Plato, and Aristotle regarded their worship as either an archaic or
foreign practice,[2] but the veneration of heavenly bodies, particularly the sun and moon, was not unusual in popular piety.
Common practices always affect intellectual life, and Greece was
no exception: even in the Parthenon, the very symbol of classical
Athens, the sun and moon appear as gods.[3] We see reflections of
this feeling in Sophocles, who knows of a view which makes the
sun the parent of the gods and father of all things[4] and says that
everyone worships the circuit of the sun.[5] The same may also
have been true of Socrates: Xenophon reports that though
Socrates had little interest in astronomy (which he regarded as
impractical), he argued that stars have soul and intellect.[6] Plato
goes even further and represents Socrates as worshipping at the
rising of the sun,[7] and has him say in his *Apology* that, far from
being an atheist, he believes the stars are gods 'like everyone
else'.[8]

The best-known philosophers to take this view were the

See Martin P. Nilsson, *Geschichte der griechischen Religion* (HAW 5. 2; 2nd edn.,
Munich: Beck, 1955), 1.34. 839 f. For some exceptions see Jacob Bernays, 'Die
unter Philons Werken stehende Schrift Über die Unzerstörbarkeit des Weltalls'
AAB (1883), 44, and *FrGrHist* 2a. 168. 3–7.
[2] Aristoph. *Pax* 406; Plato *Crat.* 397c8–d2; Arist. *Metaph.* 1074ª39–ᵇ8, cf. *De
Caelo* 284ª11–13.
[3] See Jula Kerschensteiner, *Platon und der Orient* (Stuttgart: W. Kohlhammer,
1945), 186.
[4] Frag. 1017 Nauck (752 Pearson), cited by Pierre Boyancé, *Études sur le Songe
de Scipion* (Paris: A. Bontemps, 1936), 94.
[5] Frag. 672 Nauck (738 Pearson), cf. *Oed. Rex* 660; Euripides frag. 781 Nauck.
[6] Little interest: *Mem.* 4. 7. 5 f.; soul and intellect: 1. 4. 8.
[7] *Symp.* 220d3–5; cf. Plutarch *Vita Pomp.* 14 (3. 2. 262. 4–7 Ziegler).
[8] 26d1–3. cf. *Laws* 887e2–7; Arist. *De Caelo* 270ᵇ5–9.

4 The Pre-Socratics to Plato

Pythagoreans in Magna Graecia. They seem to have taken a special interest in the stars, believing that they are gods[9] and that the human soul comes from heaven and returns there at death.[10] Alcmaeon of Croton (*c.*500 BC), the best attested of the Pythagorean sources on this topic, apparently affirmed the divinity of the stars,[11] and proposed that both the human soul and the heavenly bodies are in continuous motion,[12] reflecting the fundamental relationship which existed between human life and the life of the heavens.

And yet this common supposition that the heavens were alive was increasingly examined, questioned, and even rejected as Greek astronomy began its scientific development on the other side of the Greek-speaking world among the Ionians. As a result, belief in the divinity of the stars is conspicuously rare in Greek philosophy between Alcmaeon and Plato.[13] When the Ionian philosophers speculated about the heavens, they looked upward, not in reverence, but in a spirit of enquiry. Their naturalistic explanations should not be mistaken for the scepticism of modern materialists,[14] but, as Friedrich Solmsen put it, 'Men do not "explain" what they do not question',[15] and it is significant that the Ionians began to explain the nature of the stars. Aëtius, probably following Theophrastus, has this report:

Thales thinks that the stars are made of earth and fire. Empedocles, that they are fiery bodies from the fiery nature which the air, containing it within itself, squeezed out in the first separation. Anaxagoras, that the surrounding ether is a fiery substance which, by the momentum of its revolution, tore stones from the earth, ignited them, and made them stars. Democritus, that they are rocks. Diogenes [of Apollonia] thinks the stars are like pumice stones, that they are the exhalations of the world,

---

[9] D/K 58 B 1 (449. 16 f.); Epicharmus DK 23 B 8.
[10] See Louis Rougier, *L'Origine astronomique de la croyance pythagoricienne en l'immortalité céleste des âmes* (Cairo: Institut français d'archéologie orientale, 1933), *passim*, esp. 80–2. Cf. Aristoph. *Pax* 832–4.
[11] D/K 24 A 12.
[12] D/K 24 A 1 and 12.
[13] As J. B. Skemp notes, *The Theory of Motion in Plato's Later Dialogues* (Amsterdam: Adolf M. Hakkert, 1967), 44.
[14] As Charles H. Kahn notes, citing Aristoph. *Nub.* 140 ff., 247 ff., and 367 ff., *Anaximander and the Origins of Greek Cosmology* (New York: Columbia University Press, 1960), 107. See also Gregory Vlastos, *Plato's Universe* (Seattle: University of Washington, 1975), 22.
[15] *Plato's Theology*, CSCP 27 (Ithaca, NY: Cornell University Press, 1942), 34.

and that they are fiery. Archelaos said the stars are red hot stones set on fire. Anaximander, that they are circular, compacted air, full of fire, periodically emitting flames from their mouths. Parmenides and Heraclitus think the stars are compacted of fire.[16]

Anaximander likened the sun to a wheel filled with fire, while Xenophanes of Colophon said it consisted of compacted bodies of fire arising from moist exhalations, or that it was a fiery cloud.[17] Anaximenes is reported to have believed that earth, moon, and stars were borne along on air currents, and that stars are kindled mists arising from the earth.[18] Anaxagoras (who taught at Athens in the age of Pericles) said that sun, moon, and stars were fiery stones,[19] and that shooting stars were sparks caused by the circular movement of heaven.[20] This naturalism readily combined with a scepticism about the traditional gods which is not only evident in the open critique of Xenophanes,[21] but in the silence on religious matters of a Thucydides (who is said to have been a student of Anaxagoras).[22] The precise religious beliefs of the Ionian naturalists or of those who accepted their teachings on the heavens is not clear,[23] but they were perceived as denying the gods, as Aristophanes' play *The Clouds* makes clear.[24] And indeed, scepticism about the sanctity of heaven, combined with a loss of faith in the traditional gods, caused a crisis in fifth- and fourth-century BC Greek religion which is frequently referred to in the literature of the period.[25]

The popular reaction to this was to dismiss those who studied

[16] *DDG* 341 f.
[17] Aëtius *DDG* 348. 3–7; D/K 21 A 32. For stars as derived from moist exhalations see also the report on Thales, *DDG* 276. 20–3.
[18] Anaximenes: D/K 13 A 7; cf. ps.-Plutarch *DDG* 580. 3–5.
[19] Hippolytus *DDG* 562. 14 f.; D/K 59 A 12, cf. 59 A 1.
[20] Hippolytus *DDG* 563. 1 f.
[21] D/K 21 B 14–16.
[22] Marcellinus Rhetor *Vita Thucy.* 22 (10 f. Jones), following Antyllus. This may be a standard charge against those suspected of irreverence since the same claim is made for Euripides, D/K 59 A 7.
[23] One story makes Anaxagoras' interest in astronomy a reflection of his piety, DL 2. 7 (59. 23–5 Long).
[24] See A. B. Drachmann, *Atheism in Pagan Antiquity* (London: Gyldendal, 1922), 58.
[25] See Protagoras D/K 80 B 4; Thrasymachus of Chalcedon DK 85 B 8; Critias D/K 88 B 25; Aeschylus *Agam.* 369; Euripides *Bacchae* 1348, *Cycl.* 316 ff., and frag. 286 (Nauck); Xenophon *Mem.* 1. 4. 11, etc.

the heavens as fools or worse.[26] Plutarch indicates the unpopu-
larity of this naturalism with respect to the heavens, referring
here to the teachings of Anaxagoras:

It was still not talked about and spread only among a few, who received
it with some caution rather than giving it much credence. They could not
bear the natural philosophers and what were then called the 'star-
gazers', because they frittered away divinity into irrational causes,
unforeseen forces, and necessary occurrences.[27]

In time of war and political disaster in Athens, this fear and
intolerance hardened: Anaxagoras was put on trial for his offence
against piety,[28] and near the beginning of the Peloponnesian War
a decree was passed equating meteorological speculation with
Anaxagoras' atheism.[29] This charge was included in the attack on
Socrates, who was accused of atheism, of denying the divinity of
the sun and moon,[30] and of introducing new gods.[31]

    And yet despite this repugnance, scepticism about traditional
views of the gods in general, and about belief in the divinity of
the heavenly bodies in particular, was widespread in fifth- and
fourth-century BC Athens.[32] In what is probably his last work, the
Laws, Plato confirms that the popular view of astronomy is that it
leads to atheism,[33] and this sentiment is echoed in a dialogue
attributed (probably wrongly) to Plato, the *Epinomis*.[34] This
combined attack on traditional religion and on the older view of
the heavenly bodies is carried on into the third century by
Epicurus (who called himself Democritean). Epicurus, whose
religious views were notorious in antiquity, said that the sun
was made of a porous earthy material filled with fire, and he
denied that any of the stars or planets moved themselves[35] or

[26] E. R. Dodds, *The Greeks and the Irrational* (Berkeley: University of California
Press, 1951), 201 n. 64, and Plato *Phaedr.* 270a3–8.
[27] Plutarch *Nicias* 23 (1. 2. 117. 13–17 Ziegler), with Dodds loc. cit.
[28] D/K 59 A 1.
[29] D/K 59 A 17.
[30] Plato *Apol.* 26c5–d9. The charge is false (26e7–9, and Xenophon *Mem.* 4. 7).
[31] *Apol.* 24c1; Xenophon *Mem.* 1. 1; DL 2. 40 (73. 19–22 Long).
[32] Though controversial, Anaxagoras' writings were available in the market-
place for 'at most a drachma', *Apol.* 26d6–e4.
[33] 967a1–5.
[34] 982d3–7.
[35] Democritean: Plutarch *Mor.* 1108 E (6. 2. 175. 21 f. Pohlenz/Westman); sun:
Aëtius *DDG* 350. 21–351. 2; move themselves: DL 10. 77 (530. 9–17 Long);
Lucretius 5. 76–9, 5. 114–16.

were gods.[36] They had come into being 'by chance' (ἀπὸ τοῦ αὐτομάτου).[37]

Socrates knew Anaxagoras' teachings but had little interest in them.[38] His student Plato (d. 347) had a very different attitude, and took seriously the theories of the Ionian astronomers. Plato is sympathetic to astronomical research, and apparently eager to take account of new discoveries: the existence of celestial poles and Anaxagoras' discovery that the moon takes its light from the sun are treated as recent findings in the *Cratylus*,[39] and in the *Laws* the same is true of the discovery that the word 'planet' is a misnomer since the planets really do not 'wander' (πλανάω) but follow a consistent path.[40] Plato includes in his myth at the end of the *Phaedo* Anaxagoras' view that the earth is a sphere[41] which is kept in place by universal homogeneity,[42] and the *Theaetetus* knows that its size is vast.[43] The myth of Er at the end of the *Republic* presents a model of planetary motion,[44] which we shall see was a continuing interest to Plato. The *Timaeus* is the chief example (albeit mythological) of Plato's willingness to incorporate cosmological speculation in philosophy, and this example proved to be of great importance for Hellenistic thought.

And yet Plato follows Socrates in dismissing the importance of Anaxagoras and the other Ionians for philosophy. Plato's low opinion of Anaxagoras is not a rejection of astronomy, but is based on the conviction that Anaxagoras is philosophically

[36] Robert Philippson, 'Nachträgliches zur epikureischen Götterlehre', *Hermes* 53 (1918), 359; Georgios Manolidis, *Die Rolle der Physiologie in der Philosophie Epikurs*, MPF 241 (Frankfurt-on-Main: Athenäum, 1987), 82.

[37] Epicurus Test. 383 (Usener), cited by Jean Pépin, *Théologie cosmique et théologie chrétienne* (Paris: Presses universitaires de France, 1964), 69.

[38] He is said to have known Anaxagoras' work through Anaxagoras' student Archelaus, Cicero *Tusc.* 5. 4. 10 (408. 27 f. Pohlenz), cf. D/K 59 A 7; little interest: see above n. 6, below n. 60.

[39] Poles: 405c9; moon: 409a7–b1. Plato incorporates the latter idea into his myth of Er, *Rep.* 616e9–617a1. Recent: as D. R. Dicks notes, *Early Greek Astronomy to Aristotle* (Bristol: Western Printing, 1970), 52.

[40] 821b5–822c5. This becomes a commonplace, see W. and H. Gundel, 'Planeten bei Griechen und Römern', *PW* 20. 2 (1950), 2021.

[41] 108e5; as associated with Anaxagoras: 97d8–e1. For the newness of this see Erich Frank, *Plato und die sogenannten Pythagoreer* (Halle: Max Niemeyer, 1923), 184 f. That Plato believed this is contested, see *CQ* 50 (1956) 193, *Phron.* 3 (1958) 121–5, 4 (1959) 71 f., 101–19, but also Dicks *Astronomy* 98.

[42] With Anaximander, D/K 12 A 26.

[43] 174e2–5.

[44] 616c4–617b7; cf. *Tim.* 38e3–39b2.

mistaken since he explains causation materially rather than teleologically.[45] Plato is less concerned with how things happen than with why they happen, and for this reason he regards astronomy as only of secondary importance. Though Plato does associate wisdom and purity with gazing upon heaven,[46] his ideal is not the astronomer but the philosopher. Like geometry,[47] astronomy is a discipline in which knowledge of what is eternally true can be available, but such knowledge is of no use unless it is first subordinated to philosophy. Plato has little interest in observational astronomy: true astronomy is not concerned merely with what is seen in heaven[48] but with the understanding of what lies behind what is seen.[49] Even if the *Greater Hippias* is not a genuine Platonic work, it is faithful to Plato in depicting the learned, pompous, and intellectually shallow Hippias as particularly expert in astronomy.[50] The destiny of the soul is not to look upon the sensible heaven but upon the 'superheavenly place', which is not possible for physical eyes but only for the soul.[51] The stars, inasmuch as they are visible, do not embody exact knowledge, which can only be grasped by the mind and thought.[52] For Plato, as also for the Pythagoreans,[53] astronomy was useful chiefly as a means of understanding what was purely rational. To the mind which understood properly, there was true harmony in heaven[54] even if this was not possible for the material bodies of heaven, even as there is exactness in geometry though it is not part of any merely visible diagram. This is the understanding of sun, moon, and stars enjoyed by the inhabitants of the 'true earth' in the *Phaedo*.[55] Thus geometry and astronomy

[45] *Phaedo* 97b1–99c6.
[46] *Crat.* 396b7–c3, *Rep.* 586a1–b4.
[47] *Rep.* 527b7 f.
[48] 529a6–c3.
[49] 530b6–c1. There is a long-standing debate among scholars whether Plato flatly condemns all observational astronomy or whether he means only that one should study real rather than apparent motions. Ivor Bulmer-Thomas, 'Plato's Astronomy', *CQ* 78 (1984), 107, gives sources on both sides of this question. The latter position is dominant in the most recent scholarship, see Erkka Maula, *Studies in Eudoxus' Homocentric Spheres*, CHLSSF 50 (Helsinki: Societas Scientiarum Fennica, 1974), 4, and Dicks, *Astronomy*, 104–6.
[50] 285b8–c1.
[51] *Phaedr.* 247c3–d5.
[52] *Rep.* 529d1–5.
[53] See Geminus *Elem.* 1. 19–21 (5 Aujac).
[54] Cf. the myth of Er in *Rep.* 617b6 f.
[55] 111c1–2.

are part of the necessary training for insight into what was immutable and eternal.[56]

Just as Plato accepts elements of the latest astronomical research but not the philosophical and religious implications it was sometimes thought to have, so too before his later writings he can accept the popular veneration of the heavens without taking it altogether seriously. In the *Republic*, Plato does say that the craftsman of heaven, like Daedalus, fashioned the courses of the stars with the greatest beauty possible,[57] and at one point Plato even goes so far as to refer casually to 'the gods in heaven', one of which is the sun,[58] and yet he also openly doubts that the visible stars are eternal and immutable.[59] Even in his 'middle period' Plato shows little interest in the visible stars and planets and with observational astronomy. In this again he was similar to Socrates, who by all accounts avoided the investigation of the heavens and concerned himself mainly with ethical questions.[60]

It is a fundamental conviction of Plato that the presence of intelligence is *ipso facto* the presence of soul, that mind ($\nu o \hat{\upsilon} \varsigma$) must exist in soul ($\dot{\varepsilon} \nu \ \psi \upsilon \chi \hat{\eta}$).[61] When the mature Plato turned from the Socratic problem of the nature of virtue to the problem of the beauty and intelligibility of the physical world, he therefore assumed that the universe itself was alive and ensouled since mind was present in it.[62] Moreover, it is the nature of soul in the universe to point beyond itself to its origin in that which is divine and eternal, and increasingly Plato wrote as if the direction to which the soul pointed was upward. Thus in the *Phaedrus* myth we are told that the soul had its origin above, and the Olympian gods are now described in the language of astrology.[63] One should not interpret this language too literally: in the *Phaedrus* the Olympians are described as invisible (and therefore as not

[56] *Theaet.* 173e3–174a2. For Plato's interest in geometry in tradition and legend, see Alice Swift Riginos, *Platonica*, CSCT 3 (Leiden: E. J. Brill, 1976), anecdotes 31 and 98–101.

[57] *Rep.* 530a4–6, cf. 529c8–d1.

[58] Ibid. 508a4–7.

[59] *Ibid.* 530a7–b3. See also his attitude toward the worship of the stars in the *Cratylus* in n. 2 above.

[60] Arist. *Metaph.* 987[b]1–4; Cicero *Tusc.* 5. 4. 10 (409. 1–4 Pohlenz), *Acad.* 1. 4. 15 (7. 1–9 Plasberg); ps.-Galen *DDG* 597 f.

[61] *Soph.* 249a4, *Phil.* 30c9 f., *Tim.* 30b2, 46d4–6.

[62] *Phil.* 30a5–8, *Tim.* 36d8–e5.

[63] See Karl Kerényi, 'Astrologia Platonica', *ARW* 22 (1924), 245–56, with Kerschensteiner, *Platon*, 98 f.

simply identical with heavenly bodies), and the highest God is explicitly said to be beyond heaven,[64] but it is nevertheless important that Plato renews the ancient compact between the heavens and religion.

This is evident in the *Statesman*, one of the later dialogues.[65] Here Plato comes to grips with a fundamental problem in naked eye astronomy, namely the observation that the circuits of the planets (i.e. the sun, moon, and five planets visible to the naked eye) have a motion opposite to the direction of the circuits of the stars. The main interlocutor, who is simply called 'the stranger', explains to the young Socrates that in the first era of history God imparts his own motion to the universe, but that there is another era in which the universe begins to move in the opposite direction under its own power, since its Maker has made it both living and rational.[66] Thus for the first time (if the usual chronologies of Plato's works can be trusted), Plato suggests that an independent rational power is at work in at least some of the heavenly bodies (i.e. the planets), and that this accounts for an observable phenomenon. As is so often the case in Plato the distinction between myth and reality is not clear, but it is an important step in the history of Platonism that an account of God is combined with an explanation of heavenly movement.

Plato expands upon this attempt mythically to understand God and the world in a work which was of fundamental importance for all subsequent Hellenistic philosophy, the *Timaeus*. The dialogue is named after the chief interlocutor, who is chosen to describe the generation of the world and the human race since he is the most learned in their group in matters of astronomy and the nature of the universe.[67] He claims that the supreme beauty of the world and the goodness of its craftsman (the 'demiurge') shows that it has been fashioned after the pattern of the eternal forms, which are the source and perfection of all beauty and intelligibility in the world of becoming.[68] The craftsman made the

[64] 246c7–d1, 247c2–7.
[65] Skemp suggests it was written between 366 and 362, about the same time as (probably just before) the *Timaeus*, see *Plato's Statesman* (London: Routledge & Kegan Paul, 1952), 17. Most authorities agree that both the *Statesman* and the *Timaeus* are relatively late, see Sir David Ross, 'The Order of the Dialogues', *Plato's Theory of Ideas* (Oxford: Clarendon, 1951), 2 and 10.
[66] 269c4–270a8.
[67] *Tim.* 27a3–8.
[68] 28c5–29a6, 53b4–7; cf. Arist. *Metaph.* 991^{a}20–3.

best world possible, and since that which lives is superior to that which does not, the world itself is alive,[69] and is in fact a god.[70] As the body of heaven is supreme among that which is visible, so its invisible soul constitutes the best thing in all that has been made.[71] Since heaven, visible or invisible, is the best part of the world, Plato can use the word 'heaven' (οὐρανός) as a synonym for 'world' (κόσμος).[72]

This soul which permeates the cosmos ('World Soul') is divine, but only in a derived and secondary way since it is not eternal but has come into being. It is conceived as intermediate between that which is corporeal and the eternal forms.[73] The body of heaven is, like the body of the world, compacted out of the four elements,[74] but particularly of fire, which is by its structure the most mobile element.[75] As in the *Statesman*, the question of heavenly motion is linked to a discussion of heavenly souls. Stars have two types of movement: the first is called the 'revolution of the Same', referring to the daily uniform East–West circuit of the fixed stars. As we have already seen in the *Statesman*, this is a motion imparted to the star by God rather than one which has its source in the star's own immanent soul. Thus Plato says the stars are made to follow the intelligent motion of World Soul ('the Supreme'), meaning that the motion of each is 'controlled by the circuit of the Same and Uniform'.[76] This motion is not conceived as the self-moved motion of an ensouled body, but a motion which is imparted to the heavenly bodies by the demiurge,[77] in which the heavenly body is carried along on a revolving circuit.[78] The other motion of the stars is their rotation, which is the circular motion proper to World Soul.[79] This is again originally an assigned motion,[80] but is also explicitly linked to their intelligence: 'each one always thinks in the same way about the same

[69] 30b4–31a1, 32d1, 36e2–5, 69c1–3, 92c6–7.

[70] 34a8–b9, 68e1–4.

[71] 36e5–37a2.

[72] 31b3, 92c7–9.

[73] The mythological expression of this is that soul is composed of both the same and the different, and both the divisible and the indivisible, *Tim.* 35a1–8.

[74] 32b3–c2.

[75] Mostly fire: 40a2, cf. *Epin.* 981d7–e1; mobile: *Tim.* 56a2 f.

[76] 40a2–b2.

[77] 36c2–4.

[78] See A. E. Taylor, *A Commentary on Plato's Timaeus* (Oxford: Clarendon, 1928), 147 f.

[79] 34a1–4.   [80] 34a1, 4.

things.'[81] The presence of this second motion is a sign of their status as divine and everlasting living beings, and it is this motion which is due to the star's soul.[82]

The planets are governed by the motion of the Same and by an additional motion which is also imparted by the demiurge, the motion of the Different. The combination of these movements causes the planets to move in a spiral.[83] Thus in contrast to his view in the *Statesman*, Plato now states that the specific West–East motion of the planets, which distinguishes them from the stars, is due to a force imparted by the demiurge rather than one arising from the planet itself. The planets are also said to have an additional motion which either reinforces or counters the motion of the Different, and this motion accounts for variations in planetary speed.[84] Several ancient commentators assume that this third motion must have its source in the planet's own soul.[85] Since Plato does say that the planets, like the stars, are alive,[86] which is also implicit in the tradition, begun by Plato and customary thereafter, to refer to the planets, not simply as Hermes or Cronos, but as belonging to such a god (ὁ τοῦ Ἑρμοῦ, etc.),[87] this interpretation has the advantage of allotting a function to the planetary soul. This is especially necessary as it does not appear that he believes that the planets rotate.[88] If this is correct, soul here is still a source of planetary motion, but only in a new and restricted sense.

The living stars and planets play an important role in the creation of human souls. Souls are made by the demiurge in numbers equal to the stars.[89] Within its assigned star the soul is taught that it is subject to passions but that the soul which is able

---

[81] 40a8–b1.

[82] Divine: 40b5; soul: as Atticus notes, frag. 6 (58 f., 21–31 des Places).

[83] 39a5–b2.

[84] 36d5–7, 38c7–d6, see Francis MacDonald Cornford, *Plato's Cosmology* (New York: Harcourt, Brace & Co., 1937), 107 n. 3. For a different opinion see Gregory Vlastos, *Universe*, Appendix K, 109 f.

[85] See Cornford, *Cosmology*, 107 n. 3.

[86] 38e5 f.

[87] For sources see W. H. Roscher, 'Planeten', *Lexikon der griech. und röm. Mythologie* 3. 2 (1902–9), 2525, and W. and H. Gundel, 'Planeten', 2113. The implication presumably is that an invisible god is the source of the visible motion.

[88] See Dicks, *Astronomy*, 131 (with Taylor *Timaeus* 226, to 40b6), against Cornford, *Cosmology*, 119.

[89] 41d8.

to overcome them is able to return to its native star.[90] After the demiurge made the rational part of the human soul and sowed human souls in the earth and planets,[91] the 'young gods' (who include both the stars and planets)[92] fashioned human bodies, and also made the two lower, mortal parts of the human soul, will ($\theta\nu\mu\delta\varsigma$) and passion ($\dot\epsilon\pi\iota\theta\nu\mu\iota\alpha$), which they set in the trunk.[93] Time came into being with heaven, and its markers are the sun, moon, and the other five planets.[94] The succession of days, nights, months, and years which we see in the movements of the heavenly bodies has then given us not only our understanding of time but our concept of number and the ability to enquire about nature, which has in turn brought about the greatest gift of heaven, philosophy.[95] Sight was invented so that we might observe the circuits of heaven and so be improved in our minds, which are akin to the stars and also rotate, though much less perfectly.[96] Indeed, human souls fall well short of the souls in heaven; from the very start human souls are made of a less pure mixture of World Soul.[97] Furthermore, if they live ill and inharmoniously this myth suggests they might become women in their next incorporation, and if they persisted in evil they could fall into the ignorant condition of the lowest creatures, becoming the souls of birds, animals, and fishes.[98]

Plato believes the soul and God are invisible, and he also stresses that God cannot be spatially located;[99] to say that God is beyond heaven is not to set him in a particularly remote place, but to say that he cannot be thought of in terms of time and space which have themselves come into being. In light of this, it is surprising how physically located higher religious realities are: the higher one goes physically, the nearer (it would seem) one is to God. We have already seen that though heaven is not the ultimate deity, it contains a type of life which is higher and better

---

[90] 41e1–42b5; cf. ps.-Galen *DDG* 614. 8–10.

[91] 42d2–5.

[92] 41a3 f. They are 'young' since they are subsequent to the demiurge.

[93] 42d5–e1, 69c3–72d8.

[94] Time: 37e1–3, 38b6 f.; markers: 38c3–6.

[95] 47a1–b2.

[96] 47b5–c4.

[97] 41d6–7, cf. *Phaedr.* 248c5–8, *Phil..* 29c1–3.

[98] 42c1–4, 90e6–92c3. For transformation into a woman as a punishment see also *Laws* 944d5–e2.

[99] *Symp.* 211a9–b1, cf. *Parm.* 138a1–b6.

than the life below. In contrast to earth, there is no disharmony in heaven.[100] We on earth are hemmed in by our air, which is thick and turbid, but just above it is the ether (which Plato identifies with the visible heaven),[101] a region of particularly bright and clear air.[102] The heavenly bodies in this higher and purer region perform, at least mythically, a variety of functions in the formation of the human soul, and are said to be the the soul's ultimate goal. And yet despite the fact that the stars are gods (even if 'young gods') Plato does not define the proper place of the heavenly bodies in religion until his final work, the *Laws*.

The first word in the *Laws* is 'god' ($\theta\epsilon\acute{o}\varsigma$), and the first question that is settled in this dialogue is that gods have instituted the laws of Athens and Sparta. Humanity is meant to be ruled by the gods much as it in turn rules over the animals, and Plato conceives of law as a means by which the divine in us can control our inherent capacity for evil.[103] He believes that true law is a divine institution, and thus can speak of 'law' and 'god' as almost synonymous.[104] The authority and maintenance of religion in an ideal state is a major theme of the *Laws*, and the results are quite chilling. Atheism (which especially includes Ionian astronomy) is now not only foolish but illegal, and a menace to the state since proper religious belief strengthens respect for law and authority.[105] The elderly Athenian, who has the leading part in this dialogue, says that one must first try to convince atheists by argument, though he admits the difficulty of mastering his own annoyance in the face of such wickedness.[106] But argument is not the only weapon of this ideal state. Those who cannot be persuaded of their error are to be put in solitary confinement and, if they persist in their errors, to be put to death.[107] Those who engage in cultic practices outside of the one public cult are also liable to the death penalty.[108] Agnostics, necromancers, and

---

[100] *Theaet.* 176a5–7.
[101] *Phaedo* 109b7–c1.
[102] *Tim.* 55d1–3.
[103] *Laws* 713c5–714b1.
[104] As Eugene Dönt notes, *Platons Spätphilosophie und die Akademie*, Oesterr. Akad. Wiss., philos.-hist. Kl. 251. 3 (Vienna: Hermann Böhlaus, 1967), 20, citing 741d3–4.
[105] *Laws* 885b4–9.
[106] 887c7–888a7.
[107] 909a5–8.
[108] 910b8–e1.

other religious eccentrics are subject to life imprisonment; at
death their bodies are to be taken outside the city where it is
forbidden for any to bury their polluted bodies.[109] It is just as well
that Socrates is not one of the interlocutors in the *Laws*, since he
clearly would have had no place in Plato's utopian society.

And whereas Socrates is credited with bringing philosophy
down from heaven, the *Laws* very definitely puts philosophy back
in heaven.[110] In this state in which religion is tightly controlled, it
is said to be excellent and profitable for the good man 'to make
sacrifices and always to commune with the gods by prayers,
offerings, and every service of the gods'.[111] We are also told that
heaven hears prayers, and provides blessings and curses in
response.[112] The Athenian argues for the existence of the gods *e
consensu gentium*, noting with approval that both Greek and non-
Greek offer prayers and prostrate themselves at the rising and
setting of the sun and moon.[113] At one point he makes an off-
hand reference to 'the sun and the other gods',[114] and elsewhere
he contrasts the 'visible gods' (the heavenly bodies) to man-made
images of the gods.[115] The planets, the moon, and the span of
years are gods[116] (since time and the heavenly bodies are
identical), and one important body of judges (the εὔθυνοι) are
simultaneously priests of Apollo, who is identified with the
sun.[117] Citizens are to be provided with a more exact knowledge
of the movements of the sun, moon, and other planets in order
that the city may celebrate its religious festival correctly[118] and
that its people may understand the true nature of planetary
movements,[119] namely that they are supremely intelligible,
which is another way of saying that they are supremely holy.

The most important religious function of the heavenly bodies is
connected to the *Laws'* strong emphasis on the priority of soul in

[109] 909a8–c6.
[110] Cicero, *Tusc.* 5. 4. 10 (409. 1–4 Pohlenz), as Willy Theiler notes, *Forschungen
zum Neuplatonismus*, QSGP 10 (Berlin: Walter de Gruyter, 1966), 143.
[111] 716d6–e1.
[112] 931c1–d1.
[113] 887e2–7.
[114] 950d3.
[115] 930e7–931a4.
[116] 899b1–8, *Phil.* 62a7–9.
[117] 945c4–946a1, 946b5–c2, 947a5–6.
[118] 809c6–d7.
[119] 817e8–818a2.

shaping our world—a familiar Platonic theme in a book that is in many ways unfamiliar. The Ionian philosophers based their views which were so damaging to religion on the assumption that the world had come into being not by mind, God, or skill, but by nature and chance.[120] Atheism had been the result,[121] but in Plato's view it was of the utmost importance to realize that this was not a correct inference. The fundamental principle of the cosmos is soul, which is older than body, self-moving, and controlling all physical things.[122] The universe did not come into being as a result of the nature of certain elements, nor by some accidental series of events, but by the activity of mind (νοῦς) working through the medium of soul (ψυχή), and the perfectly ordered movement of the stars proves the existence of the supreme soul which directs them.[123] The elderly Athenian argues that if the heavenly bodies lacked soul and intelligence, they would never move in such an altogether precise manner.[124] Plato had long believed that the movements of heaven corresponded to mathematical law, and he now believes that the fact that mind controls the motion of heaven, together with the general acknowledgement that soul must be older than any being with an unself-moved motion, constitutes the best proof of the existence of God.[125] The activity of mind in bringing order to the world is evident everywhere, but especially in the skies above: no one but a fool could look upon heaven and remain an atheist.[126]

A problem which Plato acknowledges at this point is that there are different ways that soul can be operative in heaven. This was evident in the *Statesman* where he said the older motion was from God but the more recent motion came from immanent souls; the same is also true in the *Timaeus*, where now there were two motions which stemmed from God (i.e. the motions of the Same and the Different) and again other motions which were (presumably) immanent (i.e. stellar rotation and specific planetary movements). Taking the case of the sun as an example, the

---

[120] 889b1–c6.
[121] See above nn. 33 f.
[122] Older: 896c1–3, 966d9–e2; self-moving: 895e10–896b1; control: 896e8–9.
[123] 897c4–9, cf. 886a2–4.
[124] 967b2–4, cf. *Epin.* 982b1–2.
[125] 966d9–e4; cf. Arist. *De Phil.* frag. 13 (Ross).
[126] 966e4–6; cf. Cicero *De Har. Resp.* 9. 19 (98. 22–99. 5 Maslowski).

Athenian in the *Laws* says there are three possible ways in which soul determines her course:

Either it exists within this visible spherical body and conveys it in every way, just as our soul carries us about in every way; or, as some teach, from someplace outside it furnishes itself a body of fire or of some air and pushes the body by a bodily force; third, being apart from body but having some other surpassingly wonderful powers, it acts as a guide.[127]

The astral soul is either immanent or transcendent; if it is immanent it acts directly on the body, if transcendent, it acts either through the intermediary of a special material body which it provides itself, or through some unknown agency. Plato does not make clear at this point the number of souls in heaven: his usual assumption is that each heavenly body has its own soul and is a god, but if in heaven soul transcends its body there might be only one heavenly soul.[128] It is also not clear in the *Laws* (as it was in the *Timaeus*) if stars are gods as well as planets: the *Laws* only explicitly refers to the divinity of the planets (which is the view found in the *Statesman*).

One thing which is clear is that the astral soul itself is invisible:[129] we do not look upon the soul, we only calculate its movements mathematically. As Plato had said earlier in the *Republic*, it is not what is seen in heaven which is important, but what is intelligible. Thus, strictly speaking, one would expect Plato to assert that the heavenly bodies are not gods, but are merely controlled by gods in some way. More specifically, one might expect him to say that the visible star or planet is a body joined eternally to a soul, which is how he says he imagines the gods in the *Phaedrus* myth.[130] But Plato is very elusive in matters of religion,[131] and in the end his real opinion is never clear. What is clear is that he has no objection to calling the planets (and sometimes the stars) gods and worshipping them, just as he includes devotion to images in the religion of the state, though he

---

[127] 898e8–899a4.

[128] *Laws* 898c1–5 suggests this possibility (cf. 967e1; also Xenocrates frag. 17 Heinze), a view which Leo Elders accepts as Plato's, *Aristotle's Cosmology* (Assen: van Gorcum & Co., 1966), 180, but note Plato's ambiguity in 898c7 f.

[129] 898d9–e3.

[130] 246c6–d2.

[131] This is intentional, see V. Goldschmidt, *La Religion de Platon*, repr. in *Platonisme et pensée contemporaine* (Aubier: Montaigne, 1976) 13, and *Crat.* 400d7 f.

is well aware that the image is only a lifeless representation of a living god.[132] Perhaps dispensing with the stars, like dispensing with the Olympians, for whom he had little regard and yet whom he often included in myth and even worship,[133] was too drastic a step. For Plato saw himself as upholding the religious traditions of his ancestors,[134] providing a bulwark against the threat posed by the social radicals symbolized by Callicles in the *Gorgias* and Thrasymachus in the *Republic*. He recognized the possibility that his pursuit of the truth might be labelled a retreat into popular conventions,[135] but in the turmoil of fourth-century BC Athens the affirmation of tradition had its own appeal. With regard to the stars and religion, it appears that his later efforts to incorporate both astronomical advances and the popular veneration of heaven into an attempt to rule mankind by philosophy (since Plato by this point had come to the conclusion that rulers were incapable of becoming philosophers) affirmed certain aspects of the popular tradition which would have been hard to defend in philosophical terms. The irony is that his emphasis on the worship of the stars was so much stronger than almost anything in previous Greek religion that it was now not Socrates but Plato who was 'introducing new gods'.

One gauge of the importance of these speculations on the relation between religion and the visible heavens for Plato's thought is the amount of interest in them among his students and associates after his death. Unfortunately, aside from the *Epinomis* and Aristotle's extant ('acroamatic') works, we only know of these speculations in a very fragmentary form.

Simplicius, who is following a lost work by Sosigenes, who in turn is using a lost work by Aristotle's pupil Eudemus of Rhodes, says that Plato set before those interested in astronomy the problem of explaining planetary movement in a uniform way which presumed their circular movement, and that this challenge was accepted by Eudoxus of Cnidus.[136] Eudoxus' pursuit of

---

[132] *Laws* 931a1–4.
[133] Myth: *Phaedr.* 246e4 ff.; worship: *Laws* 717a6–7, 848d5–7. Plato complained about the 'poetic' depiction of the Olympians (*Rep.* 377d4–378a6), but this was of course the only important existing account of them.
[134] *Laws* 887d2–e2.
[135] *Gorgias* 482e2–5.
[136] *In De Caelo* (488. 18–24 and 492. 31–493. 5 Heiberg). Some have doubted this report, but in a similar way Philodemus says that Plato suggested problems to mathematicians, *Index Herculanensis* (15 f. Mekler).

astronomy[137] was joined by many other members of the Academy. Philipp of Opus wrote a variety of treatises on celestial matters,[138] and Xenocrates of Chalcedon also did six books on this subject, discussing planetary motion, the difference between stars and planets, and the shape of stars.[139] Heraclides Ponticus proposed the axial rotation of the earth, and thought that Mercury and Venus revolved around the sun.[140] The discovery of the great size of all the heavenly bodies and of the vast distance between earth and the stars was apparently quite new,[141] and there was much debate in the Academy about Eudoxus' theories of concentric spheres, which helped explain planetary motions but could not account for differences in planetary brightness.[142]

The Academy also followed Plato's lead in speculating on the religious importance of the heavens. Like the early Aristotle, Xenocrates thought that the supreme God is mind ($νοῦς$),[143] but he also said that the stars and planets are gods,[144] and elsewhere wrote that heaven was a god and the stars were Olympians.[145] Heraclides Ponticus also believed that heaven and the planets were gods,[146] and his speculations on the origin and nature of the soul were probably of great historical importance. He apparently took seriously the Pythagorean view,[147] repeated in mythic form in the *Timaeus*, that the soul has descended from above. In one passage an opponent accuses him of teaching that the human race has fallen into life from the moon,[148] and this may not be so very far off target: we are told elsewhere that he regarded the

[137] See also DL 8. 89 (435. 8–10 Long), and F. Lasserre, *Eudoxos von Knidos*, D 6–17.

[138] See Hans Joachim Krämer, 'Die ältere Akademie', in Hellmut Flashar (ed.), *Die Philosophie der Antike* (Basle/Stuttgart: Schwabe, 1983), 3. 104.

[139] See frag. 71 (Heinze), and Krämer, 'Akademie', 57.

[140] Axial: frag. 104–8; Venus/Mercury: frag. 109 f. (Wehrli).

[141] Size: the subject of a treatise by Philipp of Opus, also *Epin.* 983a1–6, and Arist. *Meteor.* 339^{b}34–6; distance: Arist. *Meteor.* 345^{b}1–4, *De Caelo* 298^{a}18–20.

[142] See Thomas L. Heath, *Aristarchus of Samos* (Oxford: Clarendon, 1913), 261.

[143] Frag. 15 (Heinze); cf. Plato *Phil.* 28c6–8; Arist. *Peri Euchés* frag. 1 and *Protreptikos* frag. 10^c (Ross).

[144] Frag. 17 (Heinze).

[145] Frag. 15 (Heinze).

[146] Frag. 111 (Wehrli). For Origen's knowledge of Heraclides see frag. 78 (Wehrli).

[147] See above n. 10. Heraclides was very much interested in Pythagoras, DL 5. 88 (245. 11 Long). This was common in the Academy, see Frank *Plato*.

[148] Frag. 115 (Wehrli).

heavenly bodies as habitable like the earth,[149] and that he thought the soul has descended from the Milky Way.[150] Most important, Heraclides Ponticus seems to have discussed this old concept in physical terms, suggesting that the soul's substance was ether or light.[151] This coupling of light with ether is also evident in his theory that the infinite medium in which the stars are set is ethereal.[152] Heraclides' idea that the human soul was identical to this heavenly substance marks a significant addition to Plato's view. Plato had suggested that there was some type of kinship between the human soul and the divine but had not precisely identified it.[153] Even the share of the upper part of the soul in World Soul in the *Timaeus* is obscured by the remark that the human soul is only composed of World Soul in an impure manner.[154] But Heraclides Ponticus believes there is simply an identity between the essence of heaven above and of the soul within, an idea which would be systematically pursued by the Stoics.

Emphasis on the importance of the heavens is carried to its furthest extreme in the *Epinomis*, which is intended (as its title indicates) as a sequel to Plato's *Laws*. The *Epinomis* has many parallels in the Platonic corpus (especially the *Laws*), and stylistically is so close to Plato, even in minute points,[155] that many have regarded it as an authentic work.[156] However, differences in style, vocabulary, and content do exist, and on the whole it is easier to explain its similarities as imitations than to argue that its differences are peculiarities.[157] An examination of its concept of an astral cult shows that it has not only imitated Plato but put forward new ideas of its own.

The author of this work (probably Philipp of Opus)[158] tells us

[149]   Frag. 113 f. (Wehrli).
[150]   Frag. 97 (Wehrli).
[151]   Ether: frag. 99; light: frag. 98, cf. 100 (Wehrli), and also *SVF* 2. 788. See Paul Moraux, 'Quinta Essentia', *PW* 24 (1963), 1193 f.
[152]   Frag. 113ac (Wehrli).
[153]   *Rep.* 611e2 f., *Statesman* 309c1–3, *Critias* 120e1–3.
[154]   See n. 97 above.
[155]   See É. des Places, 'Sur l'authenticité de l'Epinomis', *Études platoniciennes 1929–1979*, EPRO 90 (Leiden: E. J. Brill, 1981), 105–19.
[156]   H. Raeder, F. Novotny, O. Specchia, J. Burnet, A. E. Taylor, J. Harward, É. des Places, A. J. Festugière, Ch. Mugler, D. R. Dicks.
[157]   So U. v. Wilamowitz, C. Ritter, W. Jaeger, J. Pavlu, H. Friedrich, W. Theiler, F. Müller, H. Cherniss, L. Billig, B. Einarson, H. Lier, and L. Tarán.
[158]   DL 3. 37 (137. 17–19 Long); see Krämer, 'Akademie', 104.

as Plato did that most people regard the stars as lifeless because of their uniform motion, but that this is in fact a clear sign of their intelligence.[159] The planets do not 'wander', and youths should learn enough astronomy to avoid such an error.[160] Mathematical training is combined with astronomical theory, for number is a divine gift which has been granted to humanity to be learned through the observation of heavenly revolution, and is a prerequisite of wisdom.[161] Their precise movement is a proof of universal divine providence and of the priority of soul to body, as it was also in the *Laws*.[162] The divinity of the stars and of the seven planets is both presumed and stated throughout the dialogue, as it is in much of the Platonic corpus.

And yet the religious and philosophical importance of the stars now goes far beyond anything in Plato. Plato regarded mathematics as a preliminary training for dialectic, and included astronomy as a branch of applied mathematics.[163] He claimed that the circular movement of the heavens can be a guide to us in the exercise of mind ($\nu o\hat{v}\varsigma$),[164] and he provided a mythic rationale for the importance of heaven by suggesting that the soul moved in a circular fashion in the process of making correct judgements and in knowing.[165] But this did not mean the movement of mind occurred in space.[166] Though Plato believed the heavenly bodies were ensouled, he at times attributed their motions to other sources besides an immanent soul, and still had an open mind at the end of his life on the question of the origin of heavenly motion.[167] The stars are honoured as gods, but Plato retains some ambiguities about their divinity,[168] and this is evident in his provisions for the public cult, which acknowledges Olympians, national gods, daemons, and heroes—but not the astral gods.[169]

---

[159] *Epin.* 982c5–e4.
[160] 990c1–5, cf. n. 119 above.
[161] 977b1–d4, cf. n. 95 above.
[162] 991c6–d5, cf. 980d1–3; *Laws*: cf. nn. 122 f. above, and 900c—903a; antiquity of soul: *Tim.* 34c4 f., *Laws* 896c1–3.
[163] Propaedeutic: *Rep.* 536d5–8; astronomy: see above n. 55.
[164] See above n. 96.
[165] *Tim.* 37a2–c3.
[166] Skemp, *Motion*, 85.
[167] See above nn. 66, 76 f., 83, and especially 127.
[168] See above n. 59.
[169] Goldschmidt, *Platonisme*, 106. In classical usage the Greek words δαίμων refers to a divine or semi-divine being who may be either good or evil. In later usage the same word comes to refer exclusively to an evil spirit. I use the word 'daemon' to describe the former, and 'demon' to describe the latter.

In contrast, the *Epinomis* declares the wise man to be, not the philosopher, but the astronomer.[170] Like Aristotle, the *Epinomis* erroneously interprets Plato's circular movement of soul in spatial terms, and proceeds to identify mind with celestial revolution, interpreting Plato's metaphor in literal terms.[171] At different points it repeats Plato's hesitation about whether the astral soul is immanent, briefly questions whether the stars are after all divine and immortal, and also considers the possibility that the stars are not so much gods as divine images made by the gods themselves.[172] And yet the hesitation is only momentary, and in view of the larger themes of the dialogue is scarcely noticeable. More important for future speculations on the stars are its claims that mind is the immanent cause of astral motions and that the stars are each self-moving gods.[173] In addition, the *Epinomis* declares that the stars oversee all things (more than just a metaphor since in Platonic terms vision is due to the emission of a beam of light from the eye),[174] so that the light of the stars is a sign of their life and providence. Openly indifferent about the Olympians, this dialogue names the stars together with whatever is perceived along with them (i.e. their visible nature) as the greatest of the gods.[175] The view of Plato and of other members of the Academy that the Supreme God is above the heavens, or is mind or even beyond mind,[176] is replaced by a religion of the heavenly bodies.

Cultic language is used throughout the *Epinomis* as part of a protreptic to this astral religion. It speaks of honouring the stars, hymning them, and of praying to and magnifying heaven.[177] The *Epinomis* attacks those who would allow the heavenly bodies to be denied the festivals, sacrifices, and religious holidays which

[170] 989a6–b2 and 990a2–b2, with Leonardo Tarán, *Academica*, MAPS 107 (Philadelphia: MAPS, 1975), 26; cf. 991b5–c1.

[171] Tarán, *Academica*, 59 f.

[172] 983c2, 981e6–982a3, 983e5–984a1. Probably an incorrect interpretation of *Tim.* 37c6 f., Tarán, *Academica*, 86.

[173] 982e1–4, 986e6.

[174] 985e3, cf. 984d6; Platonic theory of vision: *Tim.* 45b2–d3.

[175] Olympians: 984d3–5; greatest gods: 984d5–8; contrast *Rep.* 526e2–4, 532c3–d1.

[176] *Rep.* 509b6–10, *Phaedr.* 247c2, *Tim.* 51e5 f.; Xenocrates frag. 15 (Heinze); Arist. *Protr.* frag. 10ᶜ, *Peri Euchés* frag. 1 (Ross).

[177] 984a4, 983e6, 977a2–6, with Jean Pépin, 'Über das Gebet' in P. Moraux (ed.), *Frühschriften des Aristoteles*, WdF 224 (Darmstadt: Wissenschaftliche Buchgesellschaft, 1975), 343.

make up Greek public veneration.[178] As A. J. Festugière notes, it gives names to the stars and planets in part because this would enable one to pray to them, and it considers the stars to be images of the gods in part because an active Greek cult could not imagine imageless worship.[179] And thus the most powerful voice urging Greeks to worship the stars in the fourth century BC was not that of popular religion, but of a philosopher and astronomer. Moreover, the author of the *Epinomis* is so skilful in (literally) attaching this treatise to Plato's *Laws* that he not only convinced many modern scholars that his work was genuine, but he led even some of the sceptical to consider the *Epinomis* as the logical conclusion to Plato's thought or the nearest equivalent to a Platonic work.[180] By assuming the authority of Plato, the *Epinomis* did much to increase the importance of the astral soul and astral religion in Hellenistic philosophy.

[178] 985d1–986a3.
[179] Naming: 987b2–c7 (the author is aware that this is an innovation, c7–d2); images: 983e5–984a1; A. J. Festugière, *La Révélation d'Hermès Trismégiste* (Paris: Librairie Lecoffre, 1954), 2. 205.
[180] So Wilhelm and Hans Georg Gundel, *Astrologumena*, Sudhoffs Arch. 6 (Wiesbaden: Franz Steiner, 1966), 86, Kurt von Fritz, 'Philippos von Opus' *PW* 19. 2 (1938), 2366, and Daniel Babut, *La Religion des philosophes grecs*, SUP 4 (Paris: Universitaires de France, 1974), 88. A. J. Festugière writes, 'si l'*Epinomis* n'est pas de Platon mais d'un faussaire—mettons Philippe d'Oponte—ce faussaire est un très grand homme, un penseur digne de Platon', *Les Trois 'Protreptiques' de Platon: Euthydème, Phédon, Epinomis* (Paris: Librairie philosophique J. Vrin 1973), 102.

2

ARISTOTLE

Aristotle's view of the nature and religious function of the stars is a complex problem and a challenge to his interpreters. At different points in his career, Aristotle at least appears to talk about the motion of the stars in three different ways. Cicero gives the following report which is taken from one of Aristotle's early popular ('exoteric') works, now no longer extant:

Aristotle, indeed, is entitled to praise for having laid down that everything which moves does so either by nature, necessity, or choice. Moreover, the sun, moon, and all the stars move, but things which move by nature are carried either downwards by their weight or upwards by their lightness, neither of which happens to the stars, since their course is directed around in a circle. And it certainly cannot be said that it is some greater force which makes the stars move in a way contrary to nature, for what greater force can there be? It remains, therefore, to conclude that the movement of the stars is voluntary, and the person who should look upon them would be acting impiously as well as foolishly, if he denied the existence of the gods.[1]

It would seem that Aristotle has another, very different explanation in the *De Caelo*. Following the views of Eudoxus, Aristotle believes that a series of concentric spheres are responsible for heavenly movement.[2] These spheres were mathematical concepts for Eudoxus, but Aristotle believed each one was a body (σῶμα).[3] Aristotle refers to this substance as 'the first body', or

---

[1] *De Philosophia* frag. 21b (= Cicero *DND* 2. 16. 44, trans. Francis Brooks (adapted)). The original is as follows: Nec vero Aristoteles non laundandus in eo quod omnia quae moventur aut natura moveri censuit aut vi aut voluntate, moveri autem solem et lunam et sidera omnia: quae autem natura moverentur, haec aut pondere deorsum aut levitate in sublime ferri, quorum neutrum astris contingeret, propterea quod eorum motus in orbem circumque ferretur. nec vero dici potest vi quadam maiore fieri ut contra naturam astra moveantur. quae enim potest maior esse? restat igitur ut motus astrorum sit voluntarius. quae qui videat, non indocte solum verum etiam impie faciat, si deos esse neget.

[2] *De Caelo* 2. 8.

[3] 293ª7; cf. Heath, *Aristarchus*, 217.

'the first element', or 'ether',[4] and thinks that both the spheres
and the stars within them are composed of it.[5] Stars are fixed in
their ethereal sphere and move not by themselves but only as a
result of the heavenly motion,[6] while planetary motion is
considered to be the result of a complex series of spherical
movements.[7] The stars are not allowed self-movement, for if they
moved themselves, as spheres they would either rotate or roll,
but Aristotle brings forward reasons why neither of these is
possible.[8] The power of immanent individual movement was also
denied to the heavenly bodies in Plato's concept of the circuit of
the Same and the Different, but now Aristotle further denies that
the heavenly bodies rotate, and special planetary movements are
explained by the interaction of various spheres. Thus in contrast
to Plato he believes that heavenly motion is not due to the
activity of soul.[9] Indeed, Aristotle remarks that the life of a soul
subject to such eternal compulsion would not be blessed.[10]

The natural motion of this first body or ether is circular and
eternal.[11] The latter is evident from the very etymology of the
word, for ether (αἰθήρ) is derived from ἀεὶ θεῖν, 'always run-
ning'.[12] Aristotle would appear to have here an explanation of
movement based entirely on natural properties: as it is natural for
the four sublunary elements to move in straight lines up and
down, so one would think that Aristotle now implies that the
movement in heaven of the first element in a circle is also
natural.

There also appears to be a third, different explanation of the

---

[4] The terms are equivalent, see *De Caelo* 270^{b}10–25, *Meteor.* 339^{b}16–19.

[5] *De Caelo* 289^{a}11–15, *Meteor.* 340^{b}6–10 (cf. Aëtius *DDG* 343 B 1 f.; Arius
Didymus *DDG* 450, 16 f.; Simplicius *In De Caelo* (435, 21 f. Heiberg)). By claiming
that stars are made of this one substance, Aristotle opposes Plato (who thought
the stars were composed of four elements, see ch. 1 n. 74) and Xenocrates (who
thought they were composed of two elements, frag. 56 Heinze).

[6] Fixed: 289^{b}33; not by themselves: 291^{a}27 f.; heavenly motion: 290^{b}8 f.

[7] *Metaph.* 1074^{a}10–12 puts the number of spheres at 55.

[8] 290^{a}7–29, with Harold Cherniss, *Aristotle's Criticism of Plato and the Academy*,
(Baltimore: Johns Hopkins, 1944), 543.

[9] *De Caelo* 291^{a}22–8.

[10] 284^{a}14–35; Cherniss, *Criticism*, 540. Epicurus agreed, Cicero *DND* 1. 20. 52
(331. 3 Pease, see his note).

[11] 269^{a}2–7, cf. *Phy.* 230^{b}12 f. Circular motion as eternal: *De Caelo* 1. 2 f., *Phy.*
265^{a}13–28.

[12] 270^{b}20–4, cf. *Meteor.* 339^{b}25–7; Plato *Crat.* 410b6–8. This becomes a
commonplace: ps.-Arist. *De Mundo* 392^{a}5; Achilles *Isag.* (50. 20–7 Maass); etc.

source of heavenly motion in Aristotle's theory of the existence of a mover outside of the heavens. The possibility of a transcendent mover appears to be excluded in one passage in the *De Caelo*,[13] but four other passages in this same work presuppose the possibility of such a mover.[14] The idea is worked out at greater length in the *Physics* and the *Metaphysics* where it is argued that the eternal motion of the heavenly bodies is attracted by a prime mover which is itself unmoved; this mover must be located in the periphery since this is where motion is swiftest.[15] But Aristotle does not say how such a theory would be combined with an explanation of movement based on the activity of immanent soul (as we saw in *De Philosophia*) and on the physical nature of heavenly bodies (as we saw in *De Caelo*). Thus it seems that at different times Aristotle explains heavenly movement by all three of the possibilities mentioned by Cicero in *De Philosophia* fragment 21b.

A different kind of problem is raised by a number of passages which Ross has collected as *De Philosophia* fragment 27. The most important sections are again preserved by Cicero, who claims that Aristotle believes that the 'fifth nature'[16] (which is presumably identical to what the *De Caelo* calls the first body, the first element, or ether), is the element of both the star and the human mind (*animus*). There is no passage in the acroamatic corpus which unambiguously teaches this, but in the *De Generatione Animalium* Aristotle suggests that within the *pneuma* in human sperm there is a psychic material which is more divine than the elements and analogous to the substance of the stars.[17] This is sometimes taken as a later, more cautious version of the identification of soul with ether in fragment 27 of *De Philosophia*. The difficulty here is that this claim of a material basis of human psychology (since ether is a body) is contradicted by numerous

---

[13] 279ᵃ33–ᵇ3.

[14] 277ᵇ9–12, 288ᵃ27–ᵇ7, 288ᵇ22–30, 311ᵃ9–12.

[15] *Metaph.* 1072ᵇ1–14, *Phy.* 256ᵃ33–257ᵇ13, 267ᵇ16 f., *De Caelo* 277ᵇ6–9.

[16] Moraux ('Quinta' 1172) says against Jaeger (*Aristotle*, 144 n. 2, see n. 22 below) that there is no evidence that Aristotle ever called ether the fifth element; Jean Pépin disagrees with Moraux, *Idées grecques sur l'homme et sur Dieu* (Paris: Les Belles Lettres, 1971), 351.

[17] 736ᵇ33–737ᵃ7. The literature on this passage is considerable: see Paul Moraux, *Aristote: Du Ciel* (Paris: Les Belles Lettres, 1965) xl n. 2.

passages in the Aristotelian corpus which claim that the soul is immaterial.[18]

There are three basic ways of accounting for these apparent contradictions. We must assume one of the following: (1) that there is something wrong with the text of Aristotle (either the acroamatic corpus, the fragments, or both), (2) that the difficulties represent different stages of Aristotle's career, in which he changed his mind at various times, or (3) that Aristotle is at times unclear and confusing, but not self-contradictory. The first alternative was chosen in its most extreme form by Valentine Rose, who made what is still the most complete collection of Aristotle's fragments. Rose cut the Gordian knot and argued that all of the so-called exoteric works were pseudepigraphic, precisely on the basis of the difference between the fragments of these works and the acroamatic corpus.[19] This argument has recently been reversed by a few scholars who accept many of the exoteric fragments as genuine but think the acroamatic corpus in fact reflects the early Peripatetic school rather than Aristotle himself.[20] Most scholars who reject these views consider the problem of the Aristotelian text in one of two ways: (1) those who support a developmental hypothesis believe that the apparent contradictions between different works show the existence of stages in Aristotle's thought, and contradictions within the extant works are evidence of interpolations by the later Aristotle onto his earlier writings;[21] (2) those who think Aristotle's work is not always clear but has not significantly changed attack the accuracy of some of the reports of the exoteric works, which are seen as sometimes unauthentic or as transmitted in misleading ways, and

[18] Even in the early, exoteric works: *Eudemus* frag. 5. 8, *Protrepticus* frag. 5 f. (Ross); cf. K. Reinhardt, 'Posidonius von Apameia' *PW* 22.1 (1953), 585; G. Verbeke, *L'Évolution de la doctrine du pneuma du stoïcisme à S. Augustin* (Paris: Desclée de Brouwer, 1945), 60 n. 157.

[19] Valentine Rose, *Aristoteles Pseudepigraphus* (Leipzig: Teubner, 1863), already Alexander of Aphrodisias, see R. W. Sharples, 'Alexander of Aphrodisias', *ANRW* 2. 36. 2 (1987), 1180 n. 24.

[20] J. Zürcher, *Aristoteles' Werk und Geist* (Paderborn: F. Schöningh, 1952); cf. also Anton-Hermann Chroust, *Aristotle* (London: Routledge & Kegan Paul, 1973), 2. 227.

[21] Even those who doubt this hypothesis agree that marginal notes made by Aristotle himself have been incorporated into the text, see Ingemar Düring, 'Aristoteles' *PW* Suppl. 11 (1968) 192.

explain apparent contradictions in the extant works as the result of incorrect interpretation.

The developmental hypothesis dominated scholarship for some time after the publication of Werner Jaeger's brilliant and provocative book, *Aristoteles*.[22] Though disagreeing with Jaeger in various details, many scholars accepted the principle that Aristotle's thought underwent serious changes in his own lifetime, and that the stages of these transitions from different periods can be traced across the fragments and the corpus. A number of theories about the stages of Aristotle's thought were subsequently put forward, and these led to the publication of several different editions of the fragments.[23]

And yet the attempt to understand difficulties in Aristotle's thought by the assumption that his views changed and developed has fallen on hard times in recent years, in part because this approach has been criticized for being methodologically flawed,[24] and also because it has been found to be unsatisfactory in exegetical detail. Aristotle's concept of heavenly movement, the astral soul, and astral religion have been among the subjects explained developmentally, but in each case Aristotle's position can be accounted for without recourse to theories of a fundamental change in viewpoint.

Turning first to the question of heavenly movement, the suggestion that the early Aristotle believed that stars move because of the voluntary action of self-moving souls (which, as we have seen, is the position of the *Epinomis*) is problematic. The source for this is Cicero, and this fragment is usually said to have been derived from the *De Philosophia*. However, Cicero also refers to ether (whose existence is the basis of a supposedly different explanation) in what are thought to be fragments of the same dialogue.[25] Moreover, in fragment 26 (which is explicitly from the *De Philosophia*) Aristotle is said to refer to ether as a god,

---

[22] *Aristoteles, Grundlegung einer Geschichte seiner Entwicklung* (Berlin: Weidmann, 1923), 2nd edn., *Aristotle: Fundamentals of the History of his Development*, trans. Richard Robinson (Oxford: Clarendon, 1934).

[23] W. D. Ross, *Fragmenta Selecta* (Oxford: Clarendon, 1955); R. Walzer, *Dialogorum Fragmenta in Usum Scholarum* (Florence: Sansoni, 1934), M. Untersteiner, *Aristotele Della Filosofia* (Rome: Edizioni di storia e letteratura, 1963).

[24] See Düring 'Aristoteles', 319, and Hellmut Flashar, 'Aristoteles', in id. (ed.), *Die Philosophie der Antike*, (Basle/Stuttgart: Schwabe, 1983), 3. 177–85.

[25] Frag. 21, 26 f. (Ross).

which is in keeping with his discussion of ether in the *De Caelo*.[26] The *De Caelo* explains the circular movement of heaven as the result of the natural motion of ether,[27] and if this were true as well in the *De Philosophia* then the circular movement of the star would not be due to an act of self-moved soul but would be the result of the natural tendency of ether. Jaeger and Solmsen conclude that at the time of *De Philosophia* ether must have had a different meaning so that circular movement at this point could still be regarded as voluntary.[28] They believe that a new understanding of ether is put forward in the *De Caelo*, which represents a later stage in Aristotle's thought, and that the theory of transcendent movers represents a still further stage. This view is possible, but it posits major shifts in Aristotle's thought.

Against Jaeger, a number of scholars (led especially by Paul Moraux) have come up with an easier explanation for these difficulties. They suggest that there is something wrong with the way Aristotle's text (particularly in Cicero) has been transmitted. Both fragments 21a and b of the *De Philosophia* are in the form of a Stoic proof for the existence of God,[29] and there is nothing in either section which could not have been affirmed by a Stoic philosopher. Indeed, fragment 21a clearly shows signs of Stoic redaction since it presupposes only four elements while *De Philosophia* knows five.[30] It also speaks of stars as coming into being (*in aethere astra gignantur*), which is understandable in Stoic terms but is impossible to reconcile either with *De Philosophia* fragment 18, which clearly states that sun, moon, planets, and stars are ungenerated and incorruptible, or with the *De Caelo*. Likewise it is possible that fragment 21b represents not so much Aristotle as a Stoic misunderstanding of Aristotle.[31]

---

[26] See especially $270^{b}1$–24.

[27] *De Caelo* $269^{a}2$–7.

[28] Jaeger, *Aristotle*, 154; Friedrich Solmsen, *Aristotle's System of the Physical World*, CSCP 33 (Ithaca, NY: Cornell University Press, 1960) 301, 287 n. 1, and 451.

[29] See Andreas Gräser, 'Zu Aristoteles *Peri Philosophias* (Cicero, *Nat. deor.* II 16, 44)', *MH* 27 (1970), 17.

[30] For a different opinion see David E. Hahm, 'The Fifth Element in Aristotle's *De Philosophia*: A Critical Re-examination', in John P. Anton and Anthony Preuss (eds.), *Essays in Ancient Greek Philosophy* (Albany, N Y: SUNY, 1983), 2. 404–28.

[31] See Moraux, 'Quinta', 1223, and Bernd Effe, *Studien zur Kosmologie und Theologie der aristotelischen Schrift 'Über die Philosophie'*, Zet. 50 (Munich: Beck, 1970), 131.

This misunderstanding becomes all the more explicable in light of the subtlety of the Aristotelian position. First, as has been noted by commentators on Aristotle both ancient and modern, the fact that soul does not compel motion and that ether moves naturally in a circle does not exclude the possibility that stars have souls: as Alexander of Aphrodisias says, the motion is not enforced but is in accordance with the heavenly body's own will.[32] Since Aristotle rejected the idea which he (wrongly) attributed to Plato that mind (νοῦς) moves spatially in a circle,[33] it is not surprising that he attempted to explain the movement of heaven by another means, i.e. by positing a substance existing in heaven with a natural circular motion. That Aristotle did not thereby mean to imply that heaven was lifeless is evident from passages from throughout the acroamatic corpus. He writes in the *Physics*,

There are also some who allege that this world and all the spheres exist by chance . . . This is really quite astonishing. For they say that animals and plants neither exist nor come into being accidentally, but that their cause is either nature or mind or some such thing . . . and yet that heaven and the most divine of what is visible have come to be by chance, and that there is no such cause for them as there is for animals and plants . . . In addition to the inherent strangeness of this claim, it is even more strange that they should say it even when they see nothing happening in heaven by chance, but much occurring accidentally in those things they claim are not accidental, even though of course it should be the other way around.[34]

Though he clearly distinguished between the motion of animals and that of lifeless elemental forces,[35] Aristotle says again and again that stars and heaven (which he often does not differentiate) were living and ensouled.[36] Passages which appear

---

[32] Ap. Simplicius *In De Caelo* (472. 8–20 Heiberg). See Moraux, 'Quinta', 1199, and also Harry Austryn Wolfson, 'The Problem of the Souls of the Spheres from the Byzantine Commentaries on Aristotle through the Arabs and St Thomas to Kepler', in Isadore Twersky and George H. Williams (eds.), *Studies in the History of Philosophy and Religion* (Cambridge, Mass.: Harvard University, 1973), 1. 22–59.

[33] *De Anima* 406^{b}26 ff.; Jaeger, *Aristotle*, 153 n. 2.

[34] 196^{a}24–^{b}5, see also *Part. Anim.* 641^{b}20–3; cf. Plato *Soph.* 265c1–10.

[35] *Phy.* 254^{b}33–255^{a}7.

[36] Stars: *De Caelo* 292^{a}18–21, 292^{b}1 f.; heaven: 279^{a}30–b3, 285^{a}27–30; cf. *Part. Anim.* 641^{b}18–20. This was recognized by the doxographers, see *DDG* 305. 8–13, 330. 7–10, 432. 4–8 (Aëtius), 450. 12–20 (Arius Didymus).

to imply that stars do not have souls (such as *De Caelo* 291ᵃ22–4)
need not be interpreted in this sense.³⁷ Since the motion of the
stars is eternal and immutable, it was natural for Aristotle even to
refer to heaven, the stars, and ether as divine (θεῖος) or the divine
(τὸ θεῖον).³⁸ Though this was an impersonal observation (in
contrast to Stoic feelings about the heavens at a later date), it is a
sign of the great esteem which Aristotle had for the heavens and
their movement. Aristotle is thus never inclined to a completely
mechanistic understanding of the nature of the cosmos.

If there is an astral soul, what is its relation to the heavenly
ether, and what is its purpose? Scholars ancient and modern have
suggested that ether should be understood as the body in which
the soul operates.³⁹ There is a perfect adaptation of the souls of
stars and planets to their ethereal bodies. If this is what Aristotle
has in mind, then the astral soul and ether would act in the
manner of soul and body, not forming a union, but co-operating
(as Aristotle puts it) like a well-ordered state.⁴⁰

The purpose of the soul of the star (or of its sphere—Aristotle is
again imprecise about the *locus* of heavenly soul) is to be attracted
to the transcendent mover. This other way Aristotle has of
discussing heavenly motion may seem like a new and super-
fluous addition, but in fact Aristotle believes that all motion
ultimately depends on an external source which brings it into
activity. Developmental interpreters sometimes think this is a
relatively late addition to Aristotelian thought. This position,
defended in the past by Jaeger and Solmsen, has recently been
supported by Pépin, who argues that such a mover cannot be
present in the *De Philosophia* since fragment 21b asks what power
can be greater than the natural force of the star, obviously
expecting a negative answer.⁴¹ Such a conclusion, however, is
unnecessary, for the Stoic nature of this rhetorical question is
evident in that the source of this fragment, Cicero, uses a similar
question to prove the Stoic view that the pervasive heat which

---

³⁷ See Cherniss, *Criticism*, 544 f.
³⁸ Eternal: *Metaph.* 1073ᵃ34 f. (stars); divine: *De Caelo* 292ᵇ28–293ᵃ2 (stars),
286ᵃ10 f. (heaven), 269ᵃ30–2 (ether), *Phy.* 196ᵃ33 f. (heaven), *Eth. Nic.* 1141ᵃ34–
ᵇ2 (heaven); the divine: *Metaph.* 1026ᵃ16–18 (stars), *De Caelo* 286ᵃ9–12 (heaven).
Cf. *De Anima* 405ᵃ32, *De Caelo* 270ᵇ5–7, *Meteor.* 339ᵇ25 f., *De Part. Anim.* 644ᵇ24 f.
³⁹ Simplicius *In De Caelo* (116. 27–117. 2 Heiberg), Cherniss, *Criticism*, 602.
⁴⁰ *Mot. Anim.* 703ᵃ29–ᵇ2, cited by Verbeke, *Pneuma*, 26.
⁴¹ Pépin, *Idées*, 341.

holds all things together is self-moving.[42] Furthermore, Cherniss and Ross have argued that a transcendent mover was present even in such early works as *De Philosophia* and *De Caelo*.[43] Such a mover is necessary since in Aristotelian terms the motion of the heavens requires an unmoved being who is not part of the heavens.[44] In the *Metaphysics* we see that this being moves only as the object of desire, and if this is so then the heavenly body (or sphere) must possess a soul which is actualized by this mover.[45] The *Physics* states that it is necessary for this mover to be either at the centre of the world or its circumference,[46] and since speed is proportional to proximity to the mover, it must be in the circumference.[47] Thus the three options of heavenly movement which Plato brought forward in the *Laws*—the action of immanent soul, of soul acting in co-ordination with body, or of some transcendent incorporeal activity—are not seen as three separate options but as three aspects of a single problem.[48] However, due to the complexity of Aristotle's solution and the compactness of his presentation, it was almost inevitable that later interpreters in antiquity would misunderstand him.

In the same manner, the alleged Aristotelian identification of star and soul with the element ether may have arisen from a misunderstanding. It must be said at the outset that identification of mind or soul with ether was already an old theory by Aristotle's day. Diogenes of Apollonia (a contemporary of

---

[42] *DND* 2. 11. 31 (619. 1–3 Pease; this is Posidonius frag. 357 Theiler), with David E. Hahm, *The Origins of Stoic Cosmology* (Columbus: Ohio State University, 1977), 273.

[43] For *De Phil.* see Cherniss, *Criticism*, 595, and *Selected Papers*, ed. Leonardo Tarán (Leiden: E. J. Brill, 1977), 463, with *Metaph.* 1072^{b}2 f., and also Gräser, 'Peri Philosophias', 16. This would mean that frag. 21b (see above n. 1) could not be Aristotle's after *circumque ferretur*, as Effe notes, *Studien*, 131. For *De Caelo* see W. D. Ross, *Aristotle's Metaphysics* (Oxford: Clarendon 1924), 1. cxxxiv.

[44] *Mot. Anim.* 699^{b}32 ff.

[45] *Metaph.* 1072^{b}3–14.

[46] 267^{b}7, with W. D. Ross's commentary, *Aristotle's Physics* (Oxford: Clarendon, 1936), 727 f.

[47] 267^{b}6–9, cf. *Metaph.* 1074^{b}3, *De Caelo* 284^{a}5–8, ps.-Arist. *De Mundo* 397^{b}24 ff. This poses something of a problem since *Metaph.* 1072^{b}3–14 supposes that the mover is not spatially located (cf. also *Peri Euchés* frag. 1, and Sextus' report in *SVF* 2. 1037), but it will be argued below that the problem does not reflect a change of heart in Aristotle but is an example of the deference he sometimes shows to tradition.

[48] The parallel is not exact since the transcendent source of motion is a self-mover in the *Laws*: Skemp, *Motion*, 86 f., and Cherniss, *Criticism*, 591.

Anaxagoras) believed that ether was the substance of mind,[49] and a variety of Pythagorean sources claim that soul is a portion of ether.[50] In addition, Leucippus and Democritus said that star and mind or soul were both composed of smooth round atoms, identifiable with some kind of fire or heat.[51] It was a common idea, even if not an Aristotelian one.

Most important, this tendency was later strengthened by Stoic psychology, so that the coupling of star and soul becomes routine in the Hellenistic period. Thus when it is stated in fragment 27 of the *De Philosophia* that the 'fifth nature' (presumably identical to what *De Caelo* refers to as the first nature or ether) is the substance of both star and soul—in other words, when soul is said to be a certain type of body—we may suspect that Aristotle is again being confused with the Stoics. The justification for this assumption is, as we have seen, that this materialist psychology contradicts numerous discussions of the soul (in both the exoteric and acroamatic works) in which Aristotle assumes that it is immaterial, while on the other hand the view that soul is material is of course compatible with Stoicism.[52] Furthermore, Karl Reinhardt notes that when fragment 27b is put in its context, Aristotle is discussed together with other philosophers who believe that the soul is immaterial,[53] so that Cicero's text even as it stands shows signs of the immaterialist Aristotelian psychology.

That a Stoic philosopher (such as one of Cicero's teachers)[54] could have misunderstood Aristotle's teaching on the soul is in this case understandable not only because of the difficulty of his teaching but because Aristotle is in some ways close to the Stoic position. Aristotle believes that the activities of soul are put into effect by heat. This 'vital heat' is an agent of growth in living

[49] See Solmsen, *Theology*, 51 f.
[50] See Erwin Pfeiffer, *Studien zum antiken Sternglauben*, Stoicheia 2 (Leipzig: Teubner, 1916), 114.
[51] D/K 67 A 28; cf. DL 9. 44 (459. 15–18 Long), D/K 22 B 36.
[52] See Moraux, 'Quinta', 1225, Verbeke *Pneuma*, 60 n. 157. Moraux also notes how close frag. 27 is to the Stoic view that each soul is a portion of World Soul, *Der Aristotelismus bei den Griechen* (Berlin: Walter de Gruyter, 1984), 2. 29.
[53] 'Poseidonios' 576; cf. H. J. Easterling, 'Quinta Natura', *MH* 21 (1964), 77.
[54] Georg Luck suggests Antiochus of Ascalon: *Der Akademiker Antiochus* (Bern: P. Haupt, 1953), 37–40; so also independently John M. Rist, *The Use of Stoic Terminology in Philo's Quod Deus* (Berkeley: Center for Hermeneutical Studies, 1976), 8.

beings,[55] and the higher animals have more of this heat.[56] The heart is the source of heat, and the size of the human brain is directly linked to the purity of the heat in the region around the heart.[57] Aristotle is vague about the nature of this heat, saying that it is the finest (λεπτότατον) of the elemental bodies, and that it should not be confused with the flame of terrestrial fire, which is an impure and mixed type of fire.[58] Moreover, he is inconsistent in his use of the word 'ether': he only adopts it somewhat hesitantly to refer to the first body in the *De Caelo*, and uses it in its older sense of fire in one passage in the *Physics*.[59] A Stoic interpreter might come across the Aristotelian view that the soul has an important relationship to vital heat, see that Aristotle can both refer to ether as fire and say that the soul material in the *pneuma* of sperm is analogous to the astral substance, which is very close to the Stoic view, and assume that Aristotle simply identifies soul, vital heat, and ether.[60]

That this would be the wrong inference is clear since in the *De Caelo* and the *Meteorologia*, where Aristotle asserts that the element specific to heaven is ether, he says that ether lacks all qualities, including heat (which leads him to conclude that the heat produced by heavenly bodies is caused by friction rather than by radiation).[61] However, Aristotle's language about star, soul, fire, and ether lends itself readily to an incorrect Stoic reading.

It appears then that both fragments 21 and 27 represent not so much Aristotle as a Stoic reading of Aristotle. With regard to

---

[55] See Friedrich Solmsen, 'Cleanthes or Posidonius? The Basis of Stoic Physics', *MNAW* 24. 9 (1961), 275 f.

[56] *Respir.* 477[a]17. See Friedrich Solmsen, 'The Vital Heat, the Inborn Pneuma and the Aether', *JHS* 77 (1957), 119–23. Aristotle links the inferiority of women (which he takes for granted) to a natural shortage of this heat, *Gen. Anim.* 775[a]14–16, *Probl. Phys.* 879[a]33–6.

[57] Source: *Part. Anim.* 670[a]24 f.; brain: *Gen. Anim.* 744[a]26–9, Franz Rüsche, *Blut, Leben und Seele*, SGKA. E 5 (Paderborn: Ferdinand Schöningh, 1930), 197 n. 3. Cf. Origen *In Is.* Hom. 6. 5 (8. 276. 11–14 B.).

[58] Finest: *De Caelo* 303[b]13–21; flame: *Meteor.* 355[a]9–15; mixed: *Gen. Anim.* 761[b]18–21, Rüsche, *Blut*, 230.

[59] 212[b]20–2; cf. Dicks, *Astronomy*, 261 n. 386.

[60] See *SVF* 1. 126, Moraux, 'Quinta', 1205 f., 1223 f., and Solmsen, 'Vital', 123. For a different way in which a Stoic might have misunderstood Aristotle's position see Hahm, 'Fifth Element', 423 n. 27.

[61] *De Caelo* 289[a]19–35, *Meteor.* 341[a]17–36 (cf. Xenophon *Mem.* 4. 7. 7; Moraux, *Aristotelismus*, 574).

heavenly motion, Aristotle did believe that stars were ensouled and that they were made of ether; he did distinguish between heavenly and sublunary motion, and denied heavenly motion was automatic or mechanical, or that it was compelled contrary to the nature of the star. The assumption that heavenly motion was due to an unmoved ethereal soul acting under its own impulse was easy to make, but probably not Aristotle's meaning.[62] In fragment 27, the identification of the substance of soul with that of the star was again easy to make because Aristotle does use language which would suggest such an interpretation, particularly to a Stoic listener. But it is a misunderstanding of Aristotle which attributed to him such a view of the astral soul's activity and its relation to the human soul.

Aristotle has also been represented as believing the whole starry heaven was as it were a temple, but this again is probably the result of a misunderstanding.[63] Aristotle's assessment of astronomy is more modest than that of the author of the *Epinomis*. Like Plato, he regards it as a branch of mathematics,[64] and though its subject matter makes it the closest of the mathematical disciplines to philosophy, it still only examines what is perceptible.[65] It is true that Aristotle praises Anaxagoras for reportedly saying that he was born so that he might look upon heaven, but Aristotle does not applaud Anaxagoras' interest in astronomy so much as his choice to live in order to seek knowledge.[66] In Aristotle's view, the end of human life was not specifically the study of the heavens, but knowledge of all aspects

---

[62] In this context it should be noted that frag. 24 (Ross) of *De Phil.* which asserts that stars are able to see and hear but lack the other senses, is traceable to neo-Platonic interpretation of Aristotle and not to a lost Aristotelian work, see Effe, *Studien*, 128 f. n. 6., and Wolfson 'Spheres' 34–40.

[63] Frag. 14a of the *De Philosophia* (Ross, from Seneca *QN* 7. 30) is as follows: 'Egregie Aristoteles ait numquam nos verecundiores esse debere quam cum de diis agitur. si intramus templa compositi, si ad sacrificium accessuri vultum submittimus, <si> togam adducimus, si in omne argumentum modestiae fingimur, quanto hoc magis facere debemus, cum de sideribus de stellis de deorum natura disputamus, ne quid impudenter aut ignorantes affirmemus aut scientes mentiamur?' Ross assumes this whole text is from the *De Philosophia*, but Effe notes there is no reason to assume that the words after 'de diis agitur' stem from Aristotle, *Studien* 98.

[64] *Phy.* 194ª7 f., *Metaph.* 1026ª27.

[65] *Metaph.* 1073ᵇ3–6; cf. Theophrastus *Metaph.* 10 ª 5–9.

[66] *Eth. Eud.* 1216ª11–16, *Protrep.* frag. 11 (Ross).

of the cosmos and of human life, a goal which is faithfully pursued throughout the acroamatic corpus.

Aristotle's views on the relation of the stars to religion are difficult to judge since his religion is almost as elusive as Plato's. Aristotle did not even regard piety as a matter open to discussion: people who question whether the gods ought be honoured should be punished rather than debated.[67] And yet there can be little doubt that the heavens had a significant place in Aristotle's own piety, as they did in the lives of most of his contemporaries. Some scholars have gone too far in limiting the importance of *De Philosophia* fragment 12, where Aristotle says that religious belief has its foundation in primitive man's observance of the movement of sun and stars. They have suggested that this is meant in a strictly historical and anthropological sense and is not Aristotle's own opinion.[68] This, however, does not explain the close parallel this passage has with an argument of Plato (whom Aristotle probably is following) and with Cleanthes (who in turn is probably following Aristotle), for whom this argument is valid in its own terms.[69] Nor does it take into account either Aristotle's deep respect for the divine order evident in heaven,[70] or the fact that Aristotle regards arguments based solely on antiquity and tradition as persuasive. Aristotle thought that tradition was directly linked to nature, and so had great respect for common or ancient opinion and for religious custom.[71] As Verdenius notes, this respect for 'natural' opinion is sometimes at odds with his own exercise of reason.[72] Thus as we have seen Aristotle can at times speak as if the prime mover were physically located at the periphery of the world, which is a traditional way of speaking about God but is not in keeping with his own emphasis on the

[67] *Top.* 105ᵃ2–9.
[68] Cherniss, *Papers*, 403, Effe, *Studien*, 74 n. 10, Tarán, *Academica*, 148. Lucretius is an example of someone who accepts this as true in a merely historical sense, 5. 1183–93.
[69] Plato *Laws* 966ᵈ9–967ᵉ1; Cleanthes, *SVF* 1. 528.
[70] *Part. Anim.* 641ᵇ18 f. He regards heaven as the best part of the cosmos, ibid. 656ᵃ13.
[71] Nature: see W. J. Verdenius, 'Traditional and Personal Elements in Aristotle's Religion', *Phron.* 5 (1960), 57, see also Plato *Phil.* 16c7 f.; opinion: Verdenius, 'Traditional', *passim*, also Elders, *Cosmology*, 94; custom: *Eudemus* frag. 3 (Ross).
[72] 'Traditional' 59.

mover's transcendence.[73] Aristotle's respect for the past contrib-
utes to a sense of the religious importance of heaven even when
such a view may be in conflict with his own philosophy.
Therefore, particularly in light of Aristotle's own language about
the stars and heaven, there is no reason to doubt that Aristotle
not only accepted the historical validity of the traditional view
that religion had its beginning in the experience of heaven, but
considered this way of thinking to be quite proper.

Finally, there is reason to believe that the heavens were
religiously important to Aristotle since he believed that they did
play an important role in the regulation of sublunary life. The
sun's role in terrestrial generation is an obvious example,[74] but
not the only one since the motions of heaven cause the
movement of elemental bodies.[75] It would appear then that astral
souls in Aristotle have the role of daemons, acting as intermediate
divine beings who are more divine than humans (since they are
eternal and immutable) but who are still not regarded as the
highest deity. Aristotle never actually makes such an identification, and in fact the question of the ontological relationship
between the astral gods and the prime mover is never discussed.
Nor is the precise religious status of the heavens ever made clear;
both questions were of much greater interest to a later age than
they were to Aristotle himself.

Aristotle's theories on heavenly motion leave many questions
unresolved. Moraux asks, if star and sphere are made of ether,
which does not admit of change, what is the difference between
them? If stars are indeed ethereal, why do they not move
themselves rather than as part of a sphere?[76] Is the star ensouled
or only its sphere? How does a body like ether, which lacks all
qualities, emit light? In the late second century AD Aristotle's

[73] Sextus Empiricus noted this contradiction, *Adv. Math.* 10. 33 (310. 6–18
Mutschmann). Ross calls this 'an incautious expression which should not be
stressed', *Metaphysics* 1. cxxxiv. This would make Aristotle more consistent, but
Aristotle speaks in this way several times, once even within a few pages of the
more consistent view (see above n. 47); it is also not uncommon for later writers
to put Aristotle's mover in the fixed sphere, see Willy Theiler, 'Ein vergessenes
Aristoteleszeugnis', *Untersuchungen zur antiken Literatur* (Berlin: Walter de
Gruyter, 1970), 309–17.
[74] *De Gen. et Corr.* 336^{b}17–19, *Phy.* 194^{b}13; cf. Plato *Rep.* 509b2–4.
[75] *Meteor.* 339^{a}27–32, *De Gen. An.* 716^{a}15–17.
[76] Moraux, *Du Ciel*, xlv–xlvi, cii.

critic Atticus raised other objections: by positing ether Aristotle created the self-contradictory concept of a body which had no qualities.[77] If ether were neither heavy nor light, and if it were in its proper place (i.e. on high), one would then think that ether would be motionless rather than moving in a circle.[78] Finally, since bodies whose source of motion is internal are alive and those whose source of motion is external are lifeless, Aristotle's concept of heavenly motion deprives the stars of life.[79] In strict Aristotelian terms this last objection may not be true, but it must be said that the way that Aristotle understands the stars to have life is so subtle and appears at least on the surface to be so self-contradictory that not only have some of his interpreters misunderstood the sense in which this was true, but some have also erred in the other direction and denied that the stars have life at all: Alexander of Aphrodisias says the heavens cannot be called living 'except in an equivocal sense',[80] and several other ancient scholars of Aristotle deny that he believed the stars were alive at all.[81] The same is true of the interpretation of *De Philosophia* fragment 27, where even some Peripatetics understood Aristotle as the Stoics would and taught that star and soul were made of the 'fifth substance' or ether.[82] For a later era which was even more interested in the religious importance of the heavens than the Academy, Aristotle was an important source for the understanding of the nature of the astral soul, of ether, and of a religion of the cosmos. Ironically, it was the way that he was misunderstood which was his most important contribution to the way that the astral soul was discussed by the age of Philo and Origen.

[77] Frag. 5 (55 f. 15–32 des Places).

[78] Frag. 6 (60. 55–70 des Places).

[79] Source of motion: frag. 6 (59. 38–40); not alive: frag. 6 (58 f., 21–31 des Places).

[80] Ap. Simplicius *In De Caelo* (463. 3–6 Heiberg), quoted and translated by Wolfson, 'Spheres', 35.

[81] Eudemus ap. Theon of Smyrna (201. 23–202. 2 Hiller). See further A. S. Pease *Ciceronis De Natura Deorum* (Cambridge, Mass.: Harvard University 1955), 639.

[82] See Tertullian *De An.* 5. 2 (6. 9 f. Waszink); Macrobius *In Somn. Scip.* 1. 14. 20 (59. 7 f. Willis); Aëtius *DDG* 303. 6 f., Verbeke, *Pneuma*, 92.

3

THE OLD STOICS

Zeno founded the Stoic school in 301, and was succeeded in turn by Cleanthes and Chrysippus. Their careers span almost all of the third century BC, and though none of their writings survives intact, the enormous impact of their teachings is evident in the mass of fragments which have been preserved by later writers.[1] Though the opinions of the first Stoics were not uniform (Chrysippus in particular seems to have been innovative), the differences between them have been obscured during the transmission of their teachings, and so the resulting philosophy will appear to be more of a unified system than it actually was.[2]

The Stoics differed from both Plato and Aristotle in denying that spiritual activity could account for the maintenance of the world. The two principles which are responsible for all things are causal and material,[3] but even the causal principle (λόγος, mind, or God) acts corporeally, since whatever acts or is acted upon must be a body.[4] Thus God is equated with a corporeal substance,[5] but this material was not passive like Peripatetic or neo-Platonic matter. It was instead a dynamic and productive fire, τεχνικὸν πῦρ,[6] which according to Cleanthes 'is life-promoting and healthful, preserves and nourishes and increases and sustains all things, and endows them with sensation'.[7] This fire (also called ether)[8] extends throughout matter (or the material cause) like honey through a honeycomb or heat through iron,

---

[1] Collected by J. von Arnim, *Stoicorum Veterum Fragmenta* (Leipzig: Teubner, 1905).
[2] See Max Pohlenz, *Die Stoa* (Göttingen: Vandenhoeck & Ruprecht, 1959), 1. 32.
[3] *SVF* 2. 303; Seneca *Ep.* 65. 2 (175. 26 f. Reynolds); see Hahm, *Origins*, 29.
[4] *SVF* 1. 89 f., 1. 98, 2. 336, 2. 363, 2. 387.
[5] See *SVF* vol. 2 section 2. 7. 4 'Deum esse corpus'.
[6] *SVF* 1. 120, 1. 157, 1. 171, 2. 774.
[7] *SVF* 1. 504 (Cicero *DND*, trans. Francis Brooks), cf. 1. 120, 1. 87.
[8] *SVF* 1. 134, 1. 532, 2. 580.

making God the immanent cause of order and growth in plants and animals.[9] As in Aristotle, pure fire is separated from terrestrial fire, but whereas for Aristotle ether, the 'divine body', existed only in heaven, for the Stoics it is immanent in the world.[10] Though in a mixed state below, it is present in a pure state at the periphery; here where it is diffuse it forms heaven, and where it is compacted it forms the heavenly bodies.[11]

Plato believed that the world was a living creature, and suggested (at least mythically) that it had come to be.[12] So also the Stoics believed that it was a living and rational animal, one which came to be and (in contrast to Plato) even passed away, and which was animated by God.[13] Any absolute distinction between living and lifeless is false, for all things partake of the divine life, their passive matter being quickened by the causal principle. This is the meaning of the Stoic assertion that the world is God.[14]

The way that this immanent activity proceeds is understood in different ways by the Stoics. Zeno thought that reason and intelligence arise from pure fire, while soul is made of *pneuma*, a mixture of air and fire, and so is called a 'fiery breath'.[15] World Soul is pure fire, and whereas mind is a direct result of divine activity, soul for Zeno (as for Plato in the *Timaeus*) is only a less pure form of World Soul. World Soul exists in an unadulterated form in heaven, and thus Zeno can refer to God both as World Soul and as ether.[16] Cleanthes follows Zeno in distinguishing between soul which is *pneuma* and World Soul which is pure fire.[17] Again, God is identical with the latter,[18] and Cleanthes adds that since the sun is the largest and most important body in

[9] *SVF* 1. 155, 2. 477, 2. 1027, 2. 1047.

[10] Separated: *SVF* 1. 120; immanent: Achilles *Isag.* 5 (36. 3 f. Maass).

[11] Periphery: *SVF* 1. 115; compacted: 2. 668; pure: 2. 684; Zeno says the stars are made of productive fire, 1. 120.

[12] Living: *Phil.* 30a5–8, *Tim.* 30b7. For the question of whether Plato believed in creation in time see E. Zeller, *Die Philosophie der Griechen* (5th edn., Leipzig: O. R. Reisland, 1922), 2.1. 791–6.

[13] See Pohlenz, *Stoa*, 1. 43, Boethus frag. 6 (*SVF* 3, p. 265), Posidonius frag. 304 (Theiler), Varro frag. 226 (Cardauns), etc.

[14] For sources see Pease, *De Natura.* 1. 77 f., 257.

[15] Reason: *SVF* 1. 134; soul: *SVF* 1. 135 f., 1. 140.

[16] World Soul: 1. 157; ether: 1. 154. God's power extends to the ether, Zeno ap. *SVF* 2. 1021 (p. 305, 21 f.).

[17] *Pneuma*: 1. 484, 1. 521; fire: 1. 513.

[18] *SVF* 1. 530, 1. 532, 1. 534.

heaven, the governing part (ἡλεμονικόν) of World Soul is the sun.[19] Zeno and Cleanthes thus distinguish between the substance of heaven (creative fire) and the substance of soul (fire and air).

Chrysippus approached this problem of the unity and internal coherence of the world in another way. Zeno's explanation was that there was a natural tendency to the centre, and that order was preserved by a natural flux of the four elements; these factors kept the elements from flying off into the void which surrounded the cosmos.[20] Like Plato, Chrysippus and many subsequent Stoic philosophers assert that the world is an animal, and like an animal it has a soul; this soul (made of *pneuma*) has the same nature as the soul of earthly creatures: the microcosm and the macrocosm correspond.[21] Chrysippus makes this *pneuma* (rather than creative fire or mind) the active principle or immanent divine power.[22] *Pneuma* is still seen as a mixture of fire and air, and now it is this *pneuma* which permeates the cosmos and binds together the bodies through which it moves.[23] The human soul is again composed of *pneuma*,[24] but it has a wider sense, for *pneuma* is also operative in things without soul, such as plants and stones.[25] While Plato had explained variation in matter on the basis of a distinction in transcendent form, Chrysippus explained it on the basis of a difference in concentration of the immanent *pneuma*.[26] The human soul is a particularly hot and dry form of *pneuma*,[27] and differences in

[19] *SVF* 1. 499; cf. Zeno *SVF* 1. 124. The key astronomical position of the sun had long been recognized: see W. Capelle, 'Meteorologie', *PW* Suppl. 6 (1935), 343.

[20] Centre: *SVF* 1. 99; flux: Cicero *DND* 2. 33. 84 (758. 4–759. 2 Pease, see his note); void: *SVF* 1. 95, 2. 524, etc.

[21] Joseph Moreau, L'Âme du Monde de Platon aux stoïciens (Paris: Les Belles Lettres, 1965), 164 n. 7; Festugière, *Révélation*, 1. 92–4.

[22] It may be that this approach in fact goes back to Cleanthes: see Verbeke, *Pneuma*, 55 and Hahm, *Origins*, 159. For an emphasis on Chrysippus' role in this see Michael Lapidge, 'Stoic Cosmology', in John M. Rist (ed.), *The Stoics* (Berkeley: University of California, 1978), 170, 179.

[23] Mixture: *SVF* 2. 144–6, 310, 841; permeates: *SVF* 2. 441 (p. 145,17), 2. 473 (p. 154,8), 2. 1027; binds: *SVF* 2. 439 f., 2. 441 (p. 145, 15–17 and 31–4), 2. 442 (p. 146, 9). The Stoic concept of 'tension' also has an important function here, see *SVF* vol. 2, section 2. 1. 10.

[24] *SVF* 2. 885 (p. 238, 32 f.), 2. 774, 2. 777, etc.

[25] *SVF* 2. 715 f.

[26] *SVF* 2. 634, cf. 2. 443.

[27] *SVF* 2. 715, 2. 787.

intelligence and character are explicable by the quality of *pneuma* present in soul. Thus (in contrast to Zeno) the human soul can be said to be a portion of the one World Soul.[28]

Like Zeno, Chrysippus believes that all the elements had their beginning in pure fire/ether, and that this fire is the ruling principle (ἡγεμονικόν) of the world, identifiable with Zeus.[29] The difference is that now ether (as with Aristotle) is strictly located in heaven.[30] This, however, led to confusion in later writers, because to say that the human soul consists of hot and dry *pneuma* is to bring it close to fire (which is also hot and dry), and seems to downplay the importance of air in soul (since air is hot and wet).[31] Furthermore, *pneuma*, by being the active principle and the source of intelligence, has taken on many of the characteristics of pure fire, and even within Chrysippus' own system *pneuma* and pure fire/ether are sometimes described in similar ways.[32] Inevitably, the two come to be treated as synonymous,[33] even though one consists of a single element and the other is a mixture of two elements.

This confusion about the World Soul and the individual soul's relation to it is reflected in language about humanity's relationship to the stars. One tendency in Stoic thought which is nearer to Zeno and Cleanthes says that the human mind is the same nature as heaven; another tendency closer to Chrysippus and his followers says the human soul is similar to heaven. This distinction (as subtle as ether itself) naturally was lost in many later writers, who speak of the identity of the soul with the star, or of the similarity of mind to star, or for whom there is no real distinction between mind and soul and each is in some way

[28] *SVF* 2. 633.

[29] Beginning: *SVF* 2. 579; ruling: 2. 644, cf. 2. 601; Zeus: 2. 1077; Zeno: *SVF* 1. 102, 1. 169.

[30] Chrysippus: *SVF* 2. 527 (p. 168, 29 f.), 2. 579 f., 2. 642; later ps.-Heraclitus *Hom. Probl.* 23. 5 (28 Buffière), cf. Plato above ch. 1 n. 101. The question of whether ether and heaven were simply identical was a matter of debate in Stoic circles, *SVF* 2. 555 (p. 175, 23); cf. Posidonius frag. 334 (Theiler).

[31] For the qualities of each element see Aristotle *De Gen. et Corr.* 331^{a}1–6, *SVF* 2. 580, Philo *Her.* 135, Hermetic *Definitions* 2. 1 (2. 363 Mahé), etc.

[32] In addition to the dryness of *pneuma* in the human soul, both ether and *pneuma* are described as subtle: ether, *SVF* 2. 688, 2. 579; *pneuma*, 2. 473 (p. 155, 33 f.).

[33] *SVF* 2. 471, ps.-Galen *DDG* 618. 22.

related to the stars or heaven (which are also not distinguished).[34]

Though there are some problems in the Stoic discussion of the
nature of the soul which are not quite worked out, their
approach was able to explain in physical terms the descent and
ascent of the soul which Plato had described mythologically. Both
fire and air are hot by nature, but since air is also moist it is
proximate to water, which is cool by nature, and the coolness of
water makes it in turn proximate to earth, so that elemental
movement occurs naturally. Our world comes into being as a
result of this unfolding of the elements,[35] location in the world
for any given thing being determined by the mixture of their
qualities. Again as in Aristotle, elements in their pure state form
spheres with fire at the top of the cosmos, then air, water, and
finally earth.[36] Soul becomes attached to creatures in the world
by a process of chilling[37] in which its wetness (from air) attaches
it to water and its dryness (from fire) attaches it to earth. Thus
von Arnim judges Origen's derivation of the word 'soul' ($\psi v \chi \acute{\eta}$)
from the word 'cooling' ($\psi \widehat{v} \xi \iota \varsigma$) as Stoic.[38] All Stoics believe that
soul is hot, even when it is within a terrestrial body[39] (for fire and
air are both hot), so its place in the body is inherently unstable.
The soul accordingly ascends at death, for when it has been
separated from the body its nature is to be borne upward like any
heat.[40] The old Stoics agreed that this state was not permanent,[41]
and furthermore thought that the soul only rose as far as the

[34] Identity of soul and star: Hipparchus ap. Pliny *NH* 2. 24. 95 (2. 41 Beaujeu);
soul and ether: DL 8. 28 (404. 9 Long); mind and star: Cicero *De Repub.* 6. 15. 15
(129. 22–5 Ziegler), Cicero in Arist. frag. 27 *De Philosophia* (Ross); mind and ether:
ps.-Apuleius *Asclep.* (303. 7 f. N/F); kinship of mind and star: *SVF* 2. 1151; of soul
and heaven: Achilles *Isag.* (30. 15–18 Maass), Cicero *Tusc.* 1. 19. 43 (239. 21–9
Pohlenz). Identification of the soul or mind with ether was an old idea in Greek
philosophy, see ch. 2 nn. 49–51, and the idea that the two are at least related is a
commonplace by this point.
[35] *SVF* 1. 102, 2. 579–81, 2. 590; cf. Arist. *Part. Anim.* 648ᵇ2 ff.
[36] Arist. *Meteor.* 354ᵇ23–6; ps.-Arist. *De Mundo* 392ᵇ35–393ᵃ3; Manilius 1.
149–70; *SVF* 2. 527.
[37] *SVF* 2. 806.
[38] *SVF* 2. 808. For the history of this etymology and the controversy about
Origen's use of it see J. H. Waszink, *Tertulliani De Anima* (Amsterdam: J. M.
Meulenhoff, 1947), 330.
[39] *SVF* 1. 135, 3. 305, cf. *SVF* 2. 779, etc.
[40] *SVF* 2. 821; Posidonius frag. 400 bd (Theiler).
[41] *SVF* 1. 146; see *SVF* 2 section 2. 5. 5, 'Anima non immortalis, sed morti
superstes'.

circuit of the moon[42]—thus the view that while the ether of the stars is swift and rarefied, the ether of the moon is dense and slow since it is mixed with air,[43] for soul (which is fire and air) rises to the place where ether is in contact with air and is (like the soul) a mixture. The Stoics thought of air as dense and dark, and regarded the thicker air nearer the earth as Hades,[44] while better souls had a destiny nearer the circuit of the moon. The soul abides for a time in the upper regions of the air and circulates about the earth until its eventual dissolution.[45] So once again the soul is related to the stars and has a destiny above, but once again the exact relationship between star and soul is not clear, and moreover now physical speculation has taken the place of specifically astronomical speculation: the soul's origin is not the star but the mixture of air and fire, and since the soul is not a pure substance its destiny cannot quite be heaven. However, as Stoicism was combined with Platonism, later Stoics came to the conclusion that the soul had its seat in heaven (or the stars) and would rise there again.[46]

In addition to its lack of clarity about the relationship of the human soul both to World Soul and to the stars, Stoicism (like Aristotle) does not make plain what the relationship is between the stars and the heavenly ether. As in the *Timaeus*, the Stoics explain the perfectly synchronized movement of the stars by one movement while that of the planets is explained by another.[47] As in Aristotle's *De Caelo*, ether has a circular motion; the stars are fixed in this ether and revolve with it.[48] The stars have come into

---

[42] *SVF* 2. 812, 814.

[43] Dense: *SVF* 2. 668, cf. Plutarch *De Fac.* 935b (5. 3. 64. 20–5 Hubert/Pohlenz) and SVF 2. 674; mixed: *SVF* 2. 671, Posidonius frag. 262, 281, 398 (Theiler). Zeno had a different view, *SVF* 1. 120.

[44] Dark: *SVF* 2. 429 f., Philo *Op.* 29; Hades: SVF 2. 430, 2. 1076, Cornutus 5 (4. 16–18 Lang), ps.-Apul. *Asclep.* 28 (2. 334 f. N/F), *Acta Philippi* 144 (86. 2 f. Bonnet), ps.-Heraclitus *Hom. Probl.* 23. 9 (29 Buffière).

[45] Dwelling in the air: for sources see Josef Kroll, *Die Lehren des Hermes Trismegistos*, BGPhMA 12 (Münster: Aschendorff, 1914), 295 n. 5. Circulating: *SVF* 2. 817 'in modum siderum vagari in aere', also Posidonius frag. 373a (Theiler), Cicero *De Repub.* 6. 26. 29 (136. 7–17 Ziegler), Marcus Aurelius 4. 21 (28. 19–29. 1 Dalfen).

[46] Heaven: *SVF* 2. 813 (224. 16), Achilles *Isag.* 1 (30. 15–18 Maass), Seneca *Ep.* 92. 30 (359. 2–4 Reynolds); stars: Seneca *De Otio* 5. 5 (202. 19–22 Reynolds).

[47] *SVF* 2. 580, 2. 650; later Posidonius frag. 280 (Theiler).

[48] Circular: SVF 1. 101; fixed: *SVF* 2. 527, 2. 642, 2. 650, ps.-Heraclitus *Hom. Probl.* 36. 6 (43 Buffière), Scholia *In Aratum* (512 f. Maass).

being in the ether,[49] and are made of the divine and creative fire.[50] But if the stars are composed of a substance which is eternal,[51] how can they be said to have come into being? Or again, an important problem which neither Aristotle nor the Stoics answered was why, if the stars were made of ether, they should only move within ethereal spheres and not move themselves.

This last question is especially puzzling since the Stoics clearly regarded the stars as ensouled. Zeno said that the stars were intellectual and sensible,[52] and they are often presumed to be living beings by all three of the oldest Stoics.[53] Achilles reports that while the Epicureans believe the stars are inanimate, Chrysippus specifically affirmed that they were alive in his book *On Providence and the Gods*.[54] Elsewhere we are told that those who deny this are guilty of nothing less than impiety,[55] for it is a universal Stoic view that the stars are gods or are divine.[56]

But the Stoics are not clear about what the astral soul does. One explanation was (following Plato's *Timaeus*) that heavenly motion was due to World Soul.[57] Another was that since the stars are composed of ether, which is the source of self-motion, heavenly movement is accordingly voluntary.[58] But when the movement of heavenly bodies was understood on the analogy of self-moving souls choosing their own motion,[59] it was inevitable

[49] Coming to be: *SVF* 2. 580, 2. 1049; cf. Achilles *Isag.* 35. 3 ff. (Maass), Cicero *DND* 2. 15. 42 (639. 5 Pease, see his note).
[50] *SVF* 1. 120, 1. 504, 2. 593, 2. 682.
[51] *SVF* 2. 682.
[52] *SVF* 1. 120 f.
[53] *SVF* 1. 501, 1. 504, 2. 579, 2. 685, 2. 687, 2. 788.
[54] *SVF* 2. 687.
[55] *SVF* 2. 788; note the similarity to Aristotle *De Philosophia* frag. 21b—another sign of Stoic influence in its transmission.
[56] See Zeller, *Philosophie*, 3. 1. 194, and also *SVF* 1. 51, 1. 165, 1. 510, 1. 530, 2. 527 (168. 29 f.), 2. 613, 2. 1009, 2. 1027, 2. 1049. For later Stoics see Posidonius frag. 271abc (Theiler); Cicero *De Repub.* 6. 15. 15 (129. 22–5 Ziegler); Varro frag. 24 and 226 f. (Cardauns); Seneca *De Benef.* 4. 23. 4 (106. 1–6 Hosius); Sextus Empiricus *Adv. Math.* 9. 87 (2. 234. 8–10 Mutschmann); Marcus Aurelius 12. 28 (120, 19–21 Dalfen).
[57] Cleanthes in *SVF* 1. 528.
[58] Cicero *DND* 2. 16. 43 (643. 2 f. Pease); Geminus *Elem.* 12. 23 (67 Aujac); cf. *SVF* 1. 172.
[59] Posidonius frag. 280, ps.-Plutarch *Vita Hom.* 105 (7. 386. 3–8 Bernardakis), Cleomedes 2. 1 (150. 25 Ziegler); soul as self-moving: *SVF* 2. 803, Cicero *De Senectute* 78 (39. 17–26 Simbeck), cf. Plato *Phaedr.* 245c5–9.

that some Stoics would deny that stars move in spheres at all.[60] If they were alive, each individual heavenly body must be responsible for its own motion, and stars must be individual self-moved movers. This of course flatly contradicts their view that the planets move with the seven spheres while the stars are fixed in the eighth and outermost sphere,[61] but there is no way out of this contradiction until the problem of the relationship between the stars and their spheres is settled.

Along these same lines, since ether was eternal and stars were made of ether, the Stoics could speak at times as if the stars were eternal.[62] However, since stars were also thought to have come into being, and Aristotle's *De Caelo* had shown that what is generated is also destructible, the stars as part of the world were presumably destructible and would return to fire at the universal conflagration.[63] Plutarch asks Cleanthes how we can treat the stars seriously in religious terms if they perish with the rest of the world.[64] On the other hand, in purely physical terms, it is difficult to understand how stars would be affected by a conflagration since they are already a dense and pure type of fire.

Another source of confusion to later writers was the Stoic use of the word 'God', since they employed this word to refer to ether in general, to notable concentrations of ether such as the stars or heaven, to the world (since ether or *pneuma* was here generally active), and to the wise man (since ether or *pneuma* was here not only present but especially active). Origen cites the following passage from Herophilus' *Stoic Definitions*:

. . . they say that God is called an immortal, rational, excellent living being, so that every good soul is a God, even if it is contained in a human being. But then in another way they say that God is called an immortal, excellent being living self-existently, so that souls contained in wise human beings are not Gods. And in still another way they say that God is an immortal, excellent living being who has an authority over the administration of the world which is comparable to that of the sun and moon. But in another way he [*sic*] calls God the first administrator of the

---

[60] Cicero *DND* 2. 21. 54–6 (678–83 Pease).

[61] *SVF* 2. 527.

[62] *SVF* 2. 688, 2. 1009 (p. 300, 20).

[63] Destructible: see *SVF* 2 section 2. 2. 9 'Mundum esse interiturum'; into fire: *SVF* 1. 511, 2. 596, Philo *Aet.* 107.

[64] *SVF* 1. 510.

world. In addition to all these they say that God is an incorruptible and unbegotten living being and the first ruler, whom the whole universe has as its place.[65]

Within the framework of Stoic philosophy one can see how all these definitions could be true at the same time. The Stoic position is that God is always physically present in anything throughout the entire cosmos since all of it has unfolded from the same primeval divine substance, but the divine is present in greater or lesser states of purity. To call something divine is therefore to denote the presence of World Soul. The stars are particularly important gods for the simple reason that the divine substance happens to be present in its pure form here. Therefore, even more than Plato, the Academy, or Aristotle, it was the Stoics who gave philosophical support to the popular idea that the stars or the highest heaven was divine.[66] And yet the Stoic presentation of the internal relationship between physics and theology was so full of difficulties (both real and apparent) that later writers often complained about 'Stoic self-contradictions'.

Stoic veneration of heaven was particularly earnest because of their denial of any incorporeal causal principles. While the fundamental religious interest of Plato and Aristotle was fixed on a transcendent God, the world above had a direct and immediate importance for the Stoics. They had a direct sense of the divine presence, and an appreciation of heaven which was not dampened (as it was for Platonism) by the sense that the true God was somehow even higher. There is a religious appreciation of the heavens in Plato and Aristotle, but more than these this was Stoicism's legacy to Hellenistic religion.

Though the old Stoics (like Aristotle) were very much interested in older religious beliefs (even allegorizing archaic myths to fit their cosmology), they were not sympathetic to traditional images and temples, which they believed were

---

[65] *Selecta in Psalmos* (PG 12. 1053b—1056a); cf. Pépin, *Théologie*, 130, Arist. *De Philosophia* frag. 26 (Ross).

[66] Thus the Stoic Boethus of Sidon (second century BC) suggests that it was not the whole world which was divine, but strictly the ether or the fixed sphere, presumably since here the causal or active principle was not mixed with the material principle, frag. 2 f., 6 (*SVF* 3 p. 265, 5–7, 18 f.). Despite its unorthodoxy this way of thinking would continue in many of the later Stoics, see J. Stobaeus *Ecl.* (1. 38. 1–3 Wachsmuth), Cicero *De Repub.* 6. 17. 17 (130. 19–22 Ziegler), Cornutus *Theol. Graec.* 18 (33. 12 f. Lang).

unworthy of the gods.[67] Since the world was a god, vitalized as it
was by an immanent divine power, the whole world was a
temple.[68] The stars were citizens of the city which is our
universe,[69] and they are the gods which unite all humanity in a
common worship.[70] Following the *Epinomis* and Aristotle's *De
Philosophia*, the Stoics argued that religion had its origins in
primitive man's experience of heaven,[71] and according to
Cleanthes the regularity of astral motion which was the source of
religious feeling was also the most important proof of the
existence of the gods.[72] For the Stoics it was also a proof of the
specific divinity of the stars,[73] and of divine providence for the
world.[74] That the human soul was able to track the complex
array of heavenly movements was seen as evidence that it is a
portion of the divine.[75] Thus observation of the stars could show
that there were gods, that the stars were gods, that the gods (or
God) cared for life on earth and were preserving it, and that the
soul was divine. Since the Stoic God was not located only in
heaven but was immanent in the world, the stars were not
supreme deities, and they play only a small role in the piety of
some of the greatest Stoic philosophers, such as Epictetus and
Marcus Aurelius. And yet the Stoics are important in the
propagation of astral religion, first because they carry on Plato
and Aristotle's emphasis on the religious importance of the
heavens, and second because their physical theories lend credence to beliefs that previously had been based either on
tradition or myth.

Plato's interest in the life and divinity of the stars, which was only
part of a deeper and more serious religious interest, lived on in
different philosophical guises in the Academy, Aristotle, and the
old Stoics. None of them quite succeeds in providing a convincing

[67] *SVF* 1. 146, 1. 264, 2. 1076. See Festugière, *Révélation*, 2. 272.
[68] See Festugière, *Révélation*, 2. 233–8, Pépin, *Théologie*, 289.
[69] *SVF* 2. 645, 2. 528 (169. 25–8).
[70] See Nilsson, *Geschichte*, 2. 295 f.
[71] *SVF* 1. 528, 2. 1009.
[72] *SVF* 1. 528.
[73] Cicero *DND* 2. 16. 43, 2. 21. 54 (643. 2 and 678. 2 Pease).
[74] Cicero *Pro Milone* 83 (73. 14–74. 2 Clark); Seneca *De Prov.* 1. 2 (1. 8–2. 3 Reynolds); cf. *SVF* 2. 527 (p. 168, 31), 2. 1147, 2. 1150.
[75] Ps.-Plato *Axiochus* 370b2–c6, with the note in Jackson P. Hershbell's edn. (Chico, Calif.: Scholars, 1981), 18, and also Philo *Det.* 87–90.

argument for the stars' divinity: the Platonists cannot say how such divinities can be corporeal; the Peripatetic explanation of astral motion makes it difficult to see how the stars are alive at all, and both they and the Stoics leave the interrelation of ether, spheres, and the heavenly medium in a muddled state. As a result of classical philosophy's speculations, the stars are firmly linked to piety in the Hellenistic era, but this relationship is also problematic. The second part will consider how the specific insights of these philosophers and their specific difficulties are understood by sources which Origen is known to have used, and by writers whose positions exemplify views with which Origen shows himself to be familiar.

PART II

4

THE HELLENISTIC SCHOOLROOM

Unlike Clement, Origen is reluctant to display his interest in classical and contemporary learning, and it is only by comparing widely scattered allusions in Origen's bulky corpus that we come to understand the breadth of his knowledge. It is hard to judge silence, and Origen is usually silent about what (besides scripture) he has read. We have two reports about Origen's philosophical background from later (not always reliable) sources. The philosopher Porphyry, who disapproved of Christianity in general and Origen in particular, reports that Origen

was continually studying Plato, and he busied himself with the writings of Numenius and Cronius, Apollophanes, Longinus, Moderatus, and Nicomachus, and those famous among the Pythagoreans. And he used the books of Chaeremon the Stoic, and of Cornutus.[1]

A century later Jerome tells us that

Origen wrote ten books of *Stromateis*, in which he compares together the opinions held respectively by Christians and by philosophers, and confirms all the teachings of our religion by quotations from Plato and Aristotle, from Numenius and Cornutus.[2]

There can be no doubt that some of these pagan writers listed by Porphyry and Jerome influenced Origen's teachings on the nature of the heavens. Origen cites Chaeremon the Stoic's treatise on comets,[3] and he seems to have read a good deal of Numenius,[4] who was very interested in the relationship of

---

[1] Ap. Eusebius *HE* 6. 19. 8, trans. NPNF (2. 115 Bardy).
[2] *Ep.* 70. 4 (1. 705. 19–706. 3 Hilberg), trans. NPNF (slightly adapted). Jerome's friend Theophilus of Alexandria claims that Origen juxtaposed Stoic teachings and scripture (Jerome *Ep.* 96 = *SVF* 2. 631).
[3] *CCel.* 1. 59 (1. 110. 6–9 K.) = Chaeremon frag. 3 (van der Horst). For Chaeremon's interest in astrology see below in this chap. n. 19.
[4] See below, ch. 6 n. 51.

astronomy to philosophical teachings on the soul.[5] The fragmentary nature of the remains of these writers makes their
influence very difficult to trace. Furthermore, in addition to
direct access to Plato, Aristotle, and the great Stoic philosophers
(especially Chrysippus), Origen no doubt read many other
middle-Platonic or middle-Stoic treatises which are no longer
extant. The discussion of Origen's philosophical background is
therefore largely not a matter of detecting specific influences, but
of exploring views which are comparable to Origen's and
represent a way of thinking that must have been familiar to him
in some form.

The classic work on Origen's philosophical inheritance is Hal
Koch's *Pronoia und Paideusis*,[6] and in a similar manner this
chapter on the 'Hellenistic schoolroom' attempts to understand
Origen's debt to contemporary philosophical discussion, focusing
specifically on his understanding of the life in heaven and its
importance for life on earth. Chapter 5 will contain a study of
Philo's speculations on this question, since he is not only a good
source for middle-Platonic views, but a writer who has had a
significant and direct influence on Origen.

It must be said, however, that while studies of Origen's
philosophical background have been valuable, such approaches
in the past have tended to be methodologically flawed. Origen is
such an eclectic philosopher that concentration on a single body
of evidence, such as the extant middle-Platonic corpus, will be
too one-sided to be a genuine account of his intellectual setting.
Origen had a strong interest in Jewish apocalyptic and his works
contain many references to this literature. Furthermore, growing
up and spending the early part of his career in Alexandria, Origen
was exposed to various gnostic speculations which were an
important part of early Egyptian Christianity. He combated the
Valentinian Heracleon in an early commentary, publicly debated
another Valentinian named Candidus, and also knew the
teachings of Dositheus, Simon, the Cainites, and the Ophites.[7]

[5] Frag. 35 (des Places) = test. 42 (100–2 Leemans).
[6] See also Berchman, *From Philo*. For the influence of middle-Platonism on
Clement of Alexandria see S. R. C. Lilla, *Clement of Alexandria* (London: Oxford
University, 1971).
[7] Candidus: see Jerome *Apol. Contra Ruf.* 2. 19 (55. 7–22 Lardet). Cf. Adolf von
Harnack, *Der kirchengeschichtliche Ertrag der exegetischen Arbeiten des Origenes*, TU 42.
3 (Leipzig: J. C. Hinrich, 1918), part 2, 72–6. Origen also converted a certain

These opponents left their mark (as opponents always do), and so apocalyptic and gnostic speculations on the heavens will be considered in the sixth chapter. The second part of this book will conclude with a study of Clement of Alexandria, a man of even wider learning (but less insight) than Origen, and one who again has strongly influenced the way Origen thought about the stars.

Great strides were made in astronomy during the Hellenistic age, and in the philosophical schoolrooms there was a broad consensus on the nature of the cosmos. The earth is a sphere, remaining motionless at the centre of the universe, and all the other heavenly bodies were likewise spheres.[8] Surrounding the earth are the seven planets (which include sun and moon), each moving in its own sphere,[9] and these in turn are enclosed by an eighth sphere containing the fixed stars.[10] This general picture of the universe was very common, and worked its way into popular philosophy so that calling the cosmos 'the whole eight' became an adage ($\pi\alpha\rho o\iota\mu\iota\alpha$).[11]

Aside from the Epicureans, all the major philosophical schools in the Hellenistic era believed in the divinity of the stars.[12] Even the notorious atheist Euhemerus (fl. 300 BC) acknowledged that they (at least) were gods.[13] And yet such an identification was not without its difficulties.

A problem particularly vexing for Platonists[14] was the visibility of the stars (since divinity was thought to be perceptible to the mind only and not to the senses), and this was a frequent topic of

Ambrose from Valentinianism according to Eusebius *HE* 6. 18. 1 (2. 112 Bardy, see his note). Dositheus: see *Prin.* 4. 3. 2, 60–4; Cainites: *CCel.* 3. 13 (1. 213. 9 f. K.). For the Ophites see ch. 6 n. 127.

[8] Cleomedes 1. 8 f. (72–90 Ziegler); Ptolemy *Math. Synt.* 1. 3 (72–6 Heiberg).

[9] Theon of Smyrna. (148. 6 f. Hiller), etc.

[10] Alcinous (*once* Albinus) *Did.* 14 (170. 36–171. 11 Hermann); Apuleius *De Platone* 1. 11 (94. 9–16 Thomas). Already in Chrysippus, *SVF* 2. 527.

[11] Ps.-Iamblichus *Theologoumena* (75. 5 f. de Falco, for sources see his note); also J. Bidez and Franz Cumont, *Les Mages hellénisés* (Paris: Les Belles Lettres, 1938), 1. 173 n. 3.

[12] See above ch. 3, n. 56, and also Georg Mau, *Die Religionsphilosophie Kaiser Julians* (Leipzig: Teubner, 1906), 42.

[13] See Drachmann, *Atheism*, 111.

[14] I will include neo-Pythagoreanism under Platonism since the two in this era are closely joined, a result of the fascination with Pythagoras in the early Academy. See further John Whittaker, 'Platonic Philosophy in the Early Centuries of the Empire', *ANRW* 2. 36. 1 (1987), 117–21.

56   *The Hellenistic Schoolroom*

discussion in Platonic circles. Unfortunately, the fullest extant
treatments of this topic are in philosophers who are later than
Origen, namely Plotinus (who is about twenty years younger),
Plotinus' student Porphyry, and Iamblichus (who is born about
the time of Origen's death). Because of the fragmentary nature of
our evidence from the era prior to them, it is difficult to see how
new their work on this problem was. Much of it, however,
probably represents longstanding school debate,[15] and so can
help us understand ways of thinking which Origen had known.
The same can be said of the early fifth-century Platonist Hierocles
of Alexandria, who has many affinities with earlier middle-
Platonism in general and with Origen in particular.[16] There are
always difficulties and risks in arguing from later materials, but
their use to explicate the state of previous philosophical discussion on astral souls is defensible on two grounds: (1) these
materials have close parallels in earlier Platonism, and (2) there
are also parallels among later figures (especially Hierocles) which
represent separate developments in Platonism with a common
source in an earlier period. They therefore may be helpful in
telling us about the state of philosophical debate on the nature of
astral souls in Origen's day.

In his *Epistula ad Anebonem* Porphyry puts a number of
questions to an Egyptian priest. Among the questions he asks are:
'By your account how will sun and moon and the luminaries of
heaven be gods if gods are only incorporeal?',[17] and again, 'what
is it which joins those gods which have a body in heaven with
incorporeal gods?'[18] This letter is particularly interesting for
students of Origen because one of Porphyry's major sources for
Egyptology is a Stoicizing interpretation of Egyptian religion by
Chaeremon,[19] whom we know has influenced Origen. If one

[15] This is particularly true of Porphyry, see Waszink, 'Bemerkungen', 130 n. 3,
and Dörrie, 'Die Schultradition im Mittelplatonismus und Porphyrios', *Platonica* 9.
[16] Middle-Platonism: Karl   Praechter,   'Christliche-neuplatonische
Beziehungen', *Kleine Schriften*, ed. Heinrich Dörrie (Hildesheim: Georg Olms,
1973), 141 f., also Koch, *Pronoia*, 291, and Theo Kobusch, *Studien zur Philosophie
des Hierokles von Alexandrien*, Epimeleia 27 (Munich: Johannes Berchmans, 1976);
Origen: Koch *Pronoia* 291–301. All three think Origen has influenced Hierocles,
but see Ilsetraut Hadot, *Le Problème du Néoplatonisme Alexandrin Hiéroclès et
Simplicius* (Paris: Études augustiniennes, 1978).
[17] 1. 3 (6. 11 f. ed. Sodano); cf. Augustine *De Civ. Dei* 10. 11, 13. 17, 13. 19 (284.
10–17, 398. 19–21, 402. 39–55 Dombart/Kalb).
[18] 1. 3 (7. 3 f. Sodano).
[19] 2. 12 (23. 7–25. 7 Sodano) = Chaeremon frag. 5 (van der Horst). Like

supposes, as later Platonism usually did, that stars were composed of soul and body,[20] of sensible and intelligible,[21] of superior and inferior, of ruling and ruled,[22] one would think that only the soul of the star would be divine and not its body. One response was to say that in the case of the stars, soul was perfectly adapted to body[23] and the lower and visible part to a higher intelligible part.[24] The 'secondary' gods exist through the higher invisible gods, depending on them as the star's radiance depends on the star.[25] In the star the divine soul exercises a perfect supremacy.[26]

Chaeremon does not seem particularly interested in any other gods besides the visible ones,[27] but such a view was unusual in philosophers of the period, for if the supreme God is altogether simple and is in no way made of ruler and ruled,[28] it is difficult to understand how any visible (and therefore material) body could be truly divine. Recognizing this, Alexandrian astronomers began to refer to the planets by their appearance rather than using the

Porphyry, he seems to have been both attracted by such lore (Chaeremon is said to be an Egyptian priest (frag. 4 van der Horst), while Porphyry shows some interest in hieroglyphics, see J. Bidez, *Eos* (Brussels: L'Académie royale de Belgique, 1945), 91), and yet also repelled, composing works against astrology, which was often associated with Egypt, *Ad Aneb.* 2. 15 (26. 23–27. 2 Sodano) = Chaeremon frag. 8 (van der Horst; associated with Egypt: Porphyry ap. Stobalus 2. 169. 24–170. 3 Wachsmith). Porphyry's *Ad Aneb.* supposedly addresses issues of Egyptian lore, but the discussion has been heavily coloured by philosophical speculations. As often in Hellenistic philosophy, the discussion of 'foreign' wisdom in fact shows the state of a particular Greek philosophical debate.

[20] Plutarch *Defect. Or.* 433de (3. 111. 16–25 Sieveking); Plotinus 2. 1. 2. 16–21; Porphyry *De Abst.* 2. 37 (103 Bouffartique/Patillon); ps.-Apuleius *Asclep.* 19 (318 N/F); Augustine *De Civ. Dei* 10. 29 (306. 70–5 Dombart/Kalb).
[21] Apuleius *De Deo Socr.* 4 (11. 13–16 Thomas); Arius Didymus ap. J. Stobaeus *Ecl.* (2. 49. 16–18 Wachsmuth); *CH* frag. 21 (3. 91 N/F); H. Hepding, *AthMitt* 32 (1907) 356–60; cf. Boethus Sidonius fr. 8 (*SVF* 3 p. 267, 3–5).
[22] Hierocles *In Aur. Pyth. Carm.* 26. 1 (111. 3–9 Köhler); cf. Alcinous *Did.* 7 (161. 30–2 Hermann) and Plutarch's remark that God is either the sun or the lord of the sun, *Def. Or.* 413c (3. 67. 10 f. Sieveking).
[23] Plotinus 4. 4. 42. 24–30; Hierocles *In Aur. Pyth. Carm.* 26. 1 (110. 22–111. 9 Köhler).
[24] See E. R. Dodds, *Proclus: The Elements of Theology* (2nd edn., Oxford: Clarendon, 1963), 283.
[25] Plotinus 3. 5. 6. 19–24, Iamblichus *De Myst.* 1. 17 (50–2 des Places); invisible: Plotinus 5. 1. 4. 4 f., cf. Julian *Contra Galil.* 65b (3. 336 Wright).
[26] Iamblichus *De Myst.* 1. 17 (51. 4–6 des Places).
[27] Porphyry *Ad Aneb.* 2. 12 (23. 7–24. 6 Sodano) = Chaeremon frag. 5 (van der Horst).
[28] Alcinous *Did.* 10 (165. 30 Hermann); Maximus of Tyre 27. 8 (330. 5–8 Hobein); Numenius frag. 11 (des Places) = frag. 20 (137. 28–30 Leemans); Origen *In Jo.* 1. 20. 119 (4. 24. 23 P.); etc.

names of gods, since the mythological associations of the older practice were plain to them.[29] If the stars are divine in so far as they are subordinate to the higher divinity, then they are divine in the same sense that the human soul is divine. But if it is only relation to divinity which makes the star divine, one would then conclude that it is only the ontologically superior invisible god, the soul of the star, who is worthy of worship. If this were so, that which is visible in heaven would seem to be a matter of indifference—the view of Plato in the *Republic*. In other words the problem remains unsolved, and the Jewish and Christian criticism of the philosophers that one should only worship God and not one of his dependants in fact touches on a weak spot in the Platonic devotion to the heavenly bodies.

The usual counter-argument of the later Platonists was that they were carrying on both popular and philosophical traditions. The Jewish and Christian refusal to worship the stars was met with scorn by Platonists such as Celsus,[30] who took such worship for granted. And yet since Plato and Aristotle seemed to recognize a deity above the stars, their worship had to be modest or reserved. Philosophers of this period devised a wide variety of ways of referring to the astral gods which emphasized their intermediate divine nature which was superior to the human condition but inferior to the supremely divine.

Most of these ways of talking about the heavenly bodies stemmed from Plato and from the *Epinomis*. Plato's practice of saying that the planets belonged to a particular god was very common in the philosophical schools.[31] Already the *Epinomis* raised the possibility that the stars were images of the divine, and this was followed by many later authors.[32] The metaphor of the

[29] Franz Cumont, 'Les Noms de planètes et l'astrolatrie chez les Grecs', *AnCl* 4 (1935), 5–43, especially 32. The practice did not catch on, but see ch. 8 n. 29.

[30] Celsus ap. Origen *CCel.* 5. 6 (2. 5. 25–6. 8 K.). While Plato regarded the worship of heaven as a foreign practice (above ch. 1. n. 2), in the fifth century the neo-Platonist Proclus said that only foreigners (i.e. Christians) denied this worship: *In Crat.* 125 (74. 5–15 Pasquali); cf. also Apuleius *De Deo Socr.* 3 (8. 20–9. 3 Thomas).

[31] See above ch. 1. n. 87. For later sources see A. Bouché-Leclercq, *L'Astrologie grecque* (Paris: Ernest Leroux, 1899), 68, and also Plutarch *De Gen. Socr.* 591c (3. 496. 2 Sieveking).

[32] See above ch. 1. n. 172; Plutarch *De E* 393d (3. 22. 13–23 Sieveking); Iamblichus *De Myst.* 1. 19 (57. 16–58. 5 des Places); Hierocles *In Aur. Pyth. Carm.* 27. 7 f. (120. 27–121. 9 Köhler), Julian *Contra Galil.* 65b (3. 336 Wright), *Frag. Ep.* (2. 1. 89. 16–20 Bidez); Proclus *In Tim.* (1. 11. 14 f. Diehl).

stars as a chorus dancing harmoniously around heaven is at least
as old as the classic tragedians, is made philosophically respect-
able by Plato and the *Epinomis*, and becomes a commonplace.[33]
Plato compared the relation of the young gods to the demiurge as
that of children to their father, and again following him later
Hellenistic philosophers refer to the heavenly bodies as God's
offspring or as younger than God.[34] Other metaphors of Plato
which became popular are the comparison of God to a king with
his subjects or to a commander (στρατηγός) with his troops, and
this is later applied to the relation of God to the stars.[35] So
although Plato never clearly stated that the stars were intermediate divine beings, his philosophy suggested it and his
language seemed to imply it, and this came to be a standard
feature of Hellenistic ontology.

Such an interpretation caused some confusion since there
already existed an intermediate divine being, the daemon, who
was described in Plato's *Symposium* and *Cratylus*, and in the
Epinomis.[36] Again in the *Epistula ad Anebonem* Porphyry asks,
'what is it which distinguishes the daemons from the visible and
invisible gods, since the visible gods are united with the
invisible?',[37] a question which becomes clearer considering that
Porphyry (following Plotinus) believes that daemons (like the
stars) are fiery,[38] and also regards the heavenly God as made of
light and dwelling in the ether.[39] If the heavenly bodies are
joined with higher, invisible essences so that they are gods, why

[33] Euripides *El.* 467; Plato *Phaedr.* 247a7, *Tim.* 40c3, *Epin.* 982e4 f. For an
extensive discussion of this theme see James Miller, *Measures of Wisdom* (Toronto:
University of Toronto, 1986).
[34] *Tim.* 42e6 f.; Achilles *Isag.* 5 (35. 7 Maass); Plutarch *Def. Or.* 433e (3. 111.
20–2 Sieveking); Maximus of Tyre 2. 10 (28. 8–10 Hobein).
[35] King: Plato *Ep.* 2. 312e1–3, *Laws* 904a6, *Rep.* 597e2; applied to stars: ps.-
Aristotle *De Mundo* 398ª10 ff., Celsus ap. *CCel.* 8. 35 (2. 250. 16–21 K.);
commander: Plato *Phaedr.* 246e6, later sources see Zeller *Philosophie* 3. 2. 221 n. 4,
Moraux, *Aristotelismus*, 2. 68, Erik Peterson, *Der Monotheismus als politisches Problem*
(Leipzig: Jakob Hegner, 1935), 48 f., and *The Book of Thomas the Contender* (NH 2.
142. 32).
[36] *Symp.* 202d 11–203a4, *Crat.* 397d8–e1, *Epin.* 984e1–3. For later sources on
the intermediate position of daemons see Willy Theiler, *Untersuchungen*, 486.
[37] 1. 3 (7. 5–7 Sodano). Iamblichus attempts to answer Porphyry by
subordinating daemons to both species of gods in *Myst.* 1. 20 (61–4). Cf. further
Augustine *De Civ. Dei* 9. 1 (249. 3–16 Dombart/Kalb).
[38] Porphyry *In Tim.* frag. 57 (43. 1–4 Sodano); cf. *De Regressu Animae* (32*. 21–5
and 34*. 10 f. Bidez), Plotinus 2. 1. 6. 54.
[39] *De Simul.* 2 (2*. 1–7 Bidez).

cannot the same be said of fiery daemons? And in fact in the early centuries of the common era the older philosophical distinction was often simply ignored: daemons are a species of gods,[40] and heavenly bodies are simply a species of daemons. Nicomachus of Gerasa (who again was an author familiar to Origen) knows the identification of planets with angels, who at this time are often equated with daemons,[41] and one of the magic papyri identifies stars and angels.[42] In the generation after Origen, two of Plotinus' students, Amelius and Porphyry, also associate daemons with heavenly bodies.[43] The lines between stars and daemons had never been clear, and the situation later grew even worse under the influence of the independent Jewish association of divine epiphanies both with fire and with angelic intermediaries.

Because the *Epinomis*, however, definitely subordinates daemons to stars, identification of astral and daemonic soul is only sporadic in Hellenistic literature. Usually daemons are seen as ontologic- ally superior to the human race but inferior to the heavenly bodies.[44] Beginning with the *Epinomis* they are creatures of the air much as the stars are creatures of heaven, and this is the most common philosophical understanding of them throughout the schools.[45]

Plato had laid down the principle that God did not mingle directly with terrestrial affairs, and this became orthodox among Platonists and Peripatetics.[46] The function of both daemons and

---

[40] Porphyry asks Anebo why it was theurgic practice to invoke terrestrial and subterranean beings in the same way as celestial gods, *Ep. ad Aneb.* 1. 2 (4. 1 f. Sodano); cf. his *De Phil. ex Orac.* (111 Wolff).

[41] Ap. ps.-Iamblichus *Theologoumena* (57. 6–9 de Falco), see Wilhelm Bousset, 'Zur Daemonologie der späteren Antike', *ARW* 18 (1915), 170–2, and also Nechepso/Petosiris frag. 33 (Riess). Familiar to Origen: see n. 1 above.

[42] *PGM* 1. 74–6. The idea of this piece that the divine stars can take human shape is an old one; see the prologue of Plautus' *Rudens*.

[43] Amelius identifies daemons with planets, ap. Proclus *Ad Alcib.* (70. 10–15 Westerink); Porphyry identifies them with stars, *De Regressu Anim.* (34*. 10–12 Bidez).

[44] Hierocles *In Aur. Pyth. Carm.* (121. 2 ff. Köhler), and ap. Photius *Bib.* 251 (462 A 10–15 Henri); Apuleius *De Platone* 1. 11 (95. 8–15 Thomas); cf. below ps.- Plutarch *De Fato* 9 in n. 52 below.

[45] *Epin.* 984e4 f.; *SVF* 2. 1014; Varro frag. 226 (Cardauns); Philo *Gig.* 8 f.; Apuleius *De Deo Socr.* 6 (13. 18–20 Thomas).

[46] *Symp.* 203a1 f.; Apuleius *De Deo Socr.* 4. 18 (11. 10 ff. Thomas); ps.-Aristotle *De Mundo* 398ᵃ 4 ff. In contrast, the Stoics identified Providence with nature and fate, *SVF* 1. 176.

the astral gods was to serve as agents or assistants of God.[47] As we have seen, they were the satraps of the great king, or the lieutenants of the supreme commander. Plato had already included the stars in the creation of the human race, and had closely identified time and the heavenly bodies.[48] Aristotle believed that the heavenly bodies preserved all generation beneath the moon, and Posidonius and others taught that the motions of the stars are the causes of that which occurs in the natural world.[49] As a result, belief that the heavenly bodies affected terrestrial life was common but ill-defined.

One view which was frequent in Stoic and Platonic circles was that as the stars were intermediate and subordinate gods, so they regulated an intermediate and subordinate providence. The idea as we have seen is implicit in Plato, Aristotle, and the Academy and, despite the ambiguity of the stars' relation to ether or God in Stoicism, it was taken over by Chrysippus, who believed that stars govern the world in accordance with providence.[50] Because the relationship between the stars and the heavens is not worked out, Posidonius transmits another form of this teaching in which heaven's circular motion saves and preserves the world.[51] A common later expression of this is that there are different grades of providence, namely primary and secondary, and in some writers tertiary. Primary providence (that of the supreme God) sees to the beneficial arrangement of universals, while secondary providence operating through the stars sees to the generation and arrangement of that which is mortal and particular beneath the moon, and a tertiary providence is sometimes assigned to the daemons.[52]

This concept of the stars' activity is in part shaped by older ideas on the place of heaven in controlling generation and daily occurrences such as the weather, and was strengthened by the growth in importance of astrology in the Hellenistic period. Much of what was said in older philosophy helped pave the way for

[47] Despite the occasional protest that God would not need outside help, see Moraux, *Aristotelismus*, 2. 67.
[48] Above ch. 1. n. 94. For later sources see Pease *De Natura* 1. 188–90.
[49] Arist. *De Gen. et Corr.* 2. 10; Posidonius frag. 255 (Theiler).
[50] *SVF* 2. 527 (p. 168, 31).
[51] Frag. 280 (Theiler).
[52] Ps.-Plutarch *De Fato* 9 (3. 455. 18–24 Sieveking); Apuleius *De Plat.* 1. 12 (96. 2–12 Thomas); Nemesius 43 (125. 21–126. 6 Morani).

astrology,[53] and, despite some vigorous protests,[54] both Stoicism and Platonism were thought by many of their later representatives to be compatible with this discipline. The combination of philosophy with astrology reaches its height in the fourth and fifth centuries AD, but it is already present in philosophy before Origen in the view that the stars mediate divine oracles,[55] and particularly in the view that the stars exercise control over destiny (εἱμαρμένη). Thus a variety of factors were at work causing the stars to be ascribed with important functions concerning terrestrial life. This in turn increased the pressure on philosophers to give some account of their religious importance.

[53] With regard to Plato, Franz Boll writes, 'Ein Astrolog ist Platon nicht, aber er bahnt doch den Weg, der hernach zur Übernahme astrologischer Anschauungen durch die Griechen führt', 'Der Sternglaube in seiner historischen Entwicklung', *Kleine Schriften* (Leipzig: Köhler & Amelang, 1950), 383. For Aristotle cf. above ch. 2, nn. 74–5. The Stoic doctrines of sympathy and fate also readily combined with astrology; for Stoic interest in astrology see Moreau, *L'Âme*, 169.

[54] By Eudoxus ap. Cicero *De Div.* 2. 87, Panaetius ap. 2. 91–7 (496 f. and 503–16 Pease), and especially by Carneades, see Paul Wendland, *Die hellenistisch-römische Kultur*, HNT 1. 2 (Tübingen: J. C. B. Mohr, 1912), 109.

[55] Alcinous *Did.* 15 (171. 20–4 Hermann); ps.-Apuleius *Asclep.* 38 (2. 349. 9–15 N/F); Diodorus Siculus 2. 30. 4 (1. 219. 23–220. 2 Vogel); cf. Porphyry *De Phil. ex Orac.* (138 and 166 Wolff).

5

PHILO

One philosopher who struggles with this problem in a way particularly important for Origen is Philo of Alexandria. Many gaps in our understanding of the Hellenistic philosophical concept of the stars are filled by him because of his strong interest in this problem, and because there is a large corpus of his writings extant. Philo had virtually no impact on Jewish thought, but he was read with great interest by early Christians who were concerned with the relationship between scripture and pagan philosophy.

Until recently Philo has been dismissed by scholars as an unoriginal compiler of schoolroom commonplaces—Festugière frequently uses the word 'banalité' in his important discussion of Philo's cosmology.[1] This, however, is not altogether just: those who take part in relatively new undertakings (in Philo's case, showing that the best of Greek philosophy is already implicit in Jewish scripture)[2] will inevitably be unoriginal in some other respects. Philo's interpretation of Judaism in new terms was a great achievement which stands as a landmark in the history of theology, and recent scholars have been right in thinking that scholars of the past (even giants like Festugière and Dodds) have been unfair to him.

And yet there is a danger that Philo might be praised more than he deserves. Like many other philosophers of his day he is often content to transmit doxographic commonplaces with a minimum of reflection, and indeed with more than a little confusion. He is 'Philo Judaeus', but he is also 'Philo of Alexandria', and so reflects the rather sorry state of philosophy in his era. Both aspects of

[1] *Révélation* 2. 521–85.
[2] Philo did have predecessors in this project, see Burton L. Mack, 'Philo and Exegetical Traditions in Alexandria', *ANRW* 2. 21. 1 (1984), 242 f., and David M. Hay, 'Philo's References to Other Allegorists', *SPh* 6 (1979/80), 42 f. Origen read one of these writers, namely Aristobulus, *CCel*. 4. 51 (1. 324. 13 K.).

Philo's thought are helpful to students of Origen's cosmology, since Philo's wooden use of his philosophical sources enables us to see the outlines of pagan teachings on the stars, and his fundamental respect for Jewish scripture shows us the extent to which Origen is indebted to Philo in labouring to reconcile this body of knowledge with biblical traditions.

Philo is a key source for our understanding of Hellenistic cosmology in the early empire period, telling us much about what must have been taught about the nature of the heavens in Alexandrian classrooms. In Philo once again we are told that the earth is the centre of the cosmos and that there are seven planets enclosed by the star-filled fixed sphere.[3] In a couple of passages Philo speaks of the existence of nine spheres, but this is only because he counts the earth along with the seven planets and the stars.[4] As in Plato's *Phaedrus*, the fixed sphere of the stars marks the boundary between the cosmos and the purely intelligible world of divinity.[5] Following the Peripatetics, Philo distinguishes between terrestrial and heavenly fire,[6] and says that the stars receive their light from the substance of heaven, ether.[7] The revolution of the stars is (as in Aristotle's *De Caelo*) traced to the movement of ether.[8] Planetary motions are explained as in Plato's *Timaeus* as a combination of the movements of the Same and the Different, and yet also as in the *Statesman* the movement of the stars was considered the result of an involuntary force while the retrograde motion of the planets was said to be due to a voluntary (ἐθελούσιος) one.[9] The stars were made to give light, to serve as signs of future events (though not to cause them), and to be the source of time and number.[10] As usual in Hellenistic

----

[3] Earth: *Mos.* 1. 12 (abbreviations follow usage in the LCL edition), *Conf.* 5; planets: *Cher.* 22.

[4] *Congr.* 103–5, *QG* 4. 110. Not an uncommon practice, see Cicero *De Rep.* 6. 17. 17 (131. 10–13 Ziegler), and later Julian *Or.* 11 (4), 146c (2. 2. 122 Lacombrade). In all of these one counts from the top so that the earth is the ninth sphere.

[5] See Marguerite Harl, *Philo d'Alexandrie: Quis rerum divinarum heres sit* (Paris: du Cerf, 1966), 98 n. 2.

[6] *Her.* 136, *Mos.* 2. 148, *Abr.* 157.

[7] Receive: *QE* 2. 80; heaven: *QE* 2. 73. Philo at one point suggests that the sun is condensed ether, comparable to the Stoic view, *Deus* 78, cf. ch. 3 n. 11.

[8] *QG* 1. 57; it is thus also called the revolution of ether: *Plant.* 3, *Her.* 283, *Somn.* 1. 21.

[9] *Cher.* 22 f. The more complex propositions of the *Timaeus* on specific planetary motions were ignored.

[10] *Mos.* 2. 148, *Op.* 55–60; not causes: *Spec.* 1. 13.

astronomy, the sun was thought to be the leader of the other planets.[11] The moon marked the boundary between the air and the ether, and, following the Stoic view, was said to be a mixture of 'ether-like and air-like substance'.[12]

Philo agrees with the view common to Platonic, Peripatetic, and Stoic schools alike that below the moon there is imperfection but above it only perfection,[13] though he avoids the dictum (always attributed to the Peripatetics) that there is no providence below the moon.[14] According to Philo, the four elements below the moon do not exist in a state of purity since they are always mixed with one another here, but this is not true of heaven which is accordingly separate, pure, immutable, and lacking all evil.[15] God is viewed (as usual in later Platonic and Peripatetic circles) as the great but distant king, far removed from the impurity of earth by the vast expanse of the pure heaven,[16] ruling through the heavenly bodies and through his own divine powers which are superior to heaven.[17]

Though there was some common ground among the philosophers on these issues, Philo recognized that cosmology by his day was an exceedingly difficult topic. After listing a number of the standard schoolroom disagreements on the nature of the stars and planets, Philo adds,

all these and suchlike points pertaining to heaven, that fourth and best cosmic substance, are obscure and beyond our apprehension, based on guess-work and conjecture, not on the solid reasoning of truth; so much so that one may confidently take one's oath that the day will never come when any mortal shall be competent to arrive at a clear solution to any of

[11] *Op.* 56 f., *Her.* 223. See Franz Cumont, 'La Théologie solaire du paganisme romain', *MAIBL. E* 12. 2 (1913), 447–80.
[12] *Somn.* 1. 145 (= *SVF* 2. 674), see above ch. 3, n. 43. Air as below the moon: *Mos.* 2. 118, *Abr.* 205.
[13] For sources see Wilhelm Bousset, *Jüdisch-christlicher Schulbetrieb in Alexandria und Rom* (Göttingen: Vandenhoeck & Ruprecht, 1915), 29 n. 3, and J. Kroll, *Lehren*, 175.
[14] The idea (not in Aristotle's acroamatic works) is a *topos* in doxography; to consider only Alexandrian sources see Basilides ap. Hippolytus *Ref.* 7. 19. 2 (284. 5–10 Marcovich), Clement of Alexandria *Protrep.* 5. 66 (51. 2 f. St.), *Strom.* 5. 90 (385. 19–21 St.); Origen *CCel.* 3. 75 (1. 266. 24–8 K.), Hom. 14. 3 *In Gen.* (6. 124. 6–7 B.), *In Rom.* 3. 1 (*PG* 14, 927b); Cyril of Alexandria (*PG* 69. 917b).
[15] Mixed: *QG* 3. 6; separate and pure: ibid. and 1. 64, *QE* 2. 73; immutable: *QE* 4. 8; no evil: *Op.* 73, 168, *QG* 4. 157.
[16] *Decal.* 61, *QG* 3. 34, *Prov.* 2. 102.
[17] *Leg.* 6.

these problems. This is why the fourth and waterless well was named 'Oath', being the endless and altogether baffling guest of the fourth cosmic region, heaven.[18]

And yet despite this recognition of the difficulties which faced the investigator of heaven, it is a subject to which Philo keeps returning. The fascinating but by now confused philosophical assessment of heaven is a tar-baby to which Philo often becomes stuck. One example is the question of whether heaven is made up of one of the four elements (i.e. fire) or a fifth element (i.e. ether). Philo chooses the former in the passage just quoted, and it is evident also in his acceptance of the Stoic view that the elements are arranged by their weight in the order (from top to bottom) of fire, air, water, and earth.[19] This formulation equates heaven with fire, and such a view in fact is very common in Philo.[20] But this obviously clashes with Philo's acceptance of the Peripatetic view that ether, the heavenly substance, is a separate fifth element.[21]

Philo's understanding of humanity's relation to heaven is also confused. We saw earlier that Plato's view of this relationship was couched in myth, that Aristotle's language was suggestive and misleading, and that the Stoic position was ultimately unclear, and the situation does not improve with Philo. He agrees with the standard view that the best part of a human being is not the body which is made up of the four terrestrial elements but comes from heaven, the true home of the true part of a human being.[22] The precise relationship of the essence of a human being to heaven is a question which he addresses frequently but not successfully. Philo writes that the reasoning part of man comes from the fixed stars,[23] and he says that soul is made of ether, the substance of the stars.[24] Elsewhere Philo says the lower soul is blood (since the Bible says that blood is life), while the reasoning part of the soul is

[18] *Somn.* 1. 23 f., trans. LCL.
[19] *Aet.* 33. 115; see ch. 3 n. 36.
[20] *Conf.* 157, *QG* 1. 57, *Aet.* 107, etc.
[21] *Her.* 282, *QG* 3. 6, 4. 8 (280 Marcus), *QE* 2. 73, 85, cf. Bousset *Schulbetrieb* 17. This confusion of fire and ether also occurs in Apuleius, see Stephen Gersh, *Middle Platonism and Neoplatonism: The Latin Tradition* (Notre Dame, Ind.: University of Notre Dame, 1986), 1. 305.
[22] *Her.* 267, 274, *Conf.* 78, *Agr.* 65, *QG* 4. 74, cf. *Her.* 280, 283. Cf. Bousset, *Schulbetrieb* 11 ff.
[23] *Det.* 84 f.
[24] *L A.* 3. 161, *Det.* 46, *Her.* 283; cf. Josephus *BJ* 2. 154.

made of *pneuma*.[25] Not surprisingly he also combines these views, saying that the soul is made of ethereal *pneuma* (or perhaps something better), or that mind is hot and fiery *pneuma*.[26] Passing over the loose way soul is sometimes used when mind (*νοῦς*) is meant, this would mean that Philo at times follows those later Stoic interpreters who identify ether and *pneuma* and make them the source of intelligence.[27] To say, however, that mind is material is impossible for Philo for two different reasons: first it is incompatible with a Platonic or Aristotelian psychology, which has also influenced Philo, and second it contradicts his own identification of the human *pneuma* with the incorporeal breath (*pneuma*) which God breathed into man at creation (Genesis 2: 7).[28] Thus on the one hand he denies that mind is *pneuma* since it must be completely incorporeal,[29] and on the other hand he also denies that it is a fragment of the ether since it is made of no created thing but stems directly from that great *Pneuma* who is God.[30] As in the *Timaeus* myth, mind does not come from the stars, but from the demiurge (or rather the Creator).[31] We are thus left with a flat contradiction: the best part of man both is and is not the substance of the stars. Philo uses the language of heaven to describe the nature and origin of the soul, but in the end is unable to give a satisfactory philosophical exposition of their interrelationship. Due to the complex state of the question in his day, it would have been difficult to do so in any case, but this problem becomes even more confused in Philo's writings.

Philo is more successful in explaining how the soul got from heaven to earth, doing much to harmonize two different Platonic myths. Plato says in the *Timaeus* that the soul comes into existence together with all generation as a result of the goodness and lack of jealousy of the demiurge, and yet also says in the *Phaedrus* that not all souls fall, and that the souls who fall do so in different degrees according to their merits.[32] Philo interprets the

[25] *Det.* 80–3, *Spec.* 4. 123.
[26] Ethereal *pneuma* or better: *Spec.* 4. 123; mind is fiery *pneuma*: *Fug.* 133f.
[27] See ch. 3, n. 34. Loose: also *LA.* 1. 91.
[28] *Op.* 135, *Plant.* 19, *Her.* 56, *Det.* 86.
[29] *Somn.* 1. 30.
[30] *Plant.* 18.
[31] *Det.* 82, *Op.* 135.
[32] *Tim.* 29e1–3, *Phaedr.* 248c3–249 c4; cf. E. R. Dodds, *Pagan and Christian in an Age of Anxiety* (Cambridge: Cambridge University, 1965), 22 f.

Genesis account in terms of both these myths so that the creation of the world is good and the result of divine plan (as in the *Timaeus*), but the story of Adam symbolizes the soul's fall because of sin (as in the *Phaedrus*). According to Philo, originally the soul existed without corruption in heaven,[33] but it turned away from God and so fell to earth[34] (which the *Phaedrus* myth calls the loss of the soul's wings). The story of Adam and Eve is transformed into an account of the pre-existent soul and of its sin in heaven. Philo, however, does not pursue this image, and indeed in a number of passages he discusses the soul's descent in completely natural terms. In Stoic fashion Philo derives the word 'soul' from 'cooling', and here he does not say that the soul's descent is the result of sin but instead he follows his Stoic source in saying that it is the result of the soul's mixture with air.[35] Likewise he has a completely naturalistic explanation of the rise and fall of the elements (including the fiery soul) in *De Aeternitate Mundi*.[36]

Moreover, Philo leaves some ideas about the fall of the soul undeveloped: as in Plato's *Phaedrus*, Philo says that some souls have not descended into bodies,[37] but (again like Plato) he does not say that the heavenly bodies are those souls who have not sinned. He does come close to such a view, saying that the pure heavenly mind of a star differs from a human mind in that the former is incapable of any vice or evil, with the result that it eternally rejoices.[38] They are 'naturally liable to correction' but 'in virtue of their excellence never destined to undergo it'.[39] And yet he never fits together these speculations on the stars and includes them in a coherent cosmological myth of the soul's fall. This he leaves to Origen.

The flight of the soul through heaven is a common theme of Philo's day,[40] and strongly influenced his cosmology. For Philo, as for so many Hellenistic philosophers, the imagery of this

[33] *QG* 3. 11, *Her.* 240.

[34] See Henry Chadwick, *Early Christian Thought and the Classical Tradition* (Oxford: Clarendon, 1966), 84 with n. 34, *Abr.* 134 f.

[35] *Somn.* 1. 31.

[36] *Aet.* 109–11; cf. *SVF* 2. 555.

[37] *Gig.* 12; Plato *Phaedr.* 248c3–5.

[38] *Op.* 73; eternally: *QG* 4. 188.

[39] *Spec.* 1. 19, trans. LCL.

[40] Festugière, *Révélation*, 2. 531. The classic study is Franz Cumont's 'Le Mysticisme astral dans l'antiquité', *BCLAB* (1909) 256–86, though his theory that this theme originated in Chaldaean practices has not won acceptance.

discussion of the soul's return to heaven is again taken from Plato's *Phaedrus*. The soul which turned away from the disorder of this world and was devoted to eternal truths would soar through heaven like the winged soul in the *Phaedrus*, contemplating both the heavens and even the supercelestial reality.[41] Since in Platonic terms vision implies a union between the observer and what is seen,[42] the soul which looks upon the heavens with understanding is physically joined to the stars which are seen. The philosophical observer of the stars becomes one with this higher reality.

Heaven then is the best thing in the world for one to contemplate. Philo believes that heaven is the greatest of the created things, and a place of absolute tranquility.[43] Knowledge of heaven is the queen of the sciences, and was Abram's chief occupation before he was set apart by God.[44] Following the tradition of the *Epinomis*, once again we are told that number and philosophy arise from observation of the stars' movements, and as in the *Laws* that these astral movements prove the existence of God.[45] The manna which God gives to the people in the wilderness (Exodus 16: 4) is wisdom from heaven.[46] As with the Stoics, we are repeatedly told that the cosmos and especially heaven are God's temple[47]—a surprising claim for a Jew to make at a time when the second Temple was at the height of its glory.

Like all the philosophers of his day (except the Epicureans), Philo believes that Anaxagoras' theory that stars consist of fiery metal is an impiety.[48] The stars are not collections of lifeless

[41] See Runia, *Philo*, 278, and P. Courcelle, 'Flügel (Flug) der Seele', *RAC* 8 (1972), 33 f.
[42] See below ch. 6 n.8.
[43] *De Ios.* 145, *Conf.* 177.
[44] Knowledge: *Congr.* 50, *Spec.* 3. 202; Abram: *Cher.* 4. *Abr.* 70 says he was a converted Chaldaean! A number of sources (both Jewish and pagan) say that Abram invented astrology, see Bouché-Leclercq, *L'Astrologie*, 578 n. 1. There is an ancient astrologer who called himself Abram extant ap. Vettius Valens 2. 29 f. (92 f. Pingree), and referred to several times by Firmicus Maternus (see the index of the Kroll/Skutsch/Ziegler edn., s.v. Abram). The names of biblical characters were often borrowed for works of this sort, see e.g. the astrological and magical works attributed to Solomon listed by Heeg in *CCAG* 8. 2 (1911), 139.
[45] *Epin.*: see ch. 1 n. 161; philosophy: *Op.* 54, 60, *Abr.* 164, *Spec.* 1. 322; existence of God: above ch. 1. n. 123, Philo *Spec.* 1. 34.
[46] *Mut.* 259 f.
[47] See Festugière, *Révélation*, 2. 538, 568 f., *Op.* 55.
[48] *Somn.* 1. 22, *Aet.* 47.

matter but are living beings. Philo assumes as a matter of course
both that our mind consists of a heavenly element and that the
stars are each mind.[49] He passes on the Stoic commonplace that
each region of the cosmos—earth, sea, air, and heaven—has a
life-form that is peculiar to it: animals to earth, fish to the sea,
birds to the air, and the stars to heaven.[50] As with the Stoics, the
stars are depicted as citizens of the world who occupy a higher
rank than mankind,[51] and he says that their circuits are effortless
both because of their proximity to the divine nature and because
of their superior fiery nourishment (again a Stoic view).[52] The
pagan *topos* that the stars are one of several species of rational
creatures, related to us and yet superior, is uncritically adopted
into Philo's cosmology.

The difficulty which pagan philosophy had distinguishing
between stars and daemons is repeated now in Philo with stars
and angels. In one passage Philo follows the usual view which
puts angels (which he equates with daemons)[53] below the
ethereal region.[54] The stars are thus ontologically superior to the
angels.[55] He also has a different interpretation in which the
angels are the attendants of the heavenly bodies. This section is
tantalizing, for Philo here refers to these attendant angels as a
chorus (χορός), a word which he uses elsewhere to refer to the
stars in accordance with common Hellenistic practice, but he also
states that these angels are without bodies.[56] Does this mean that
angels are the invisible movers of the stars? The same may also be
implied in *De Specialibus Legibus*, where the stars are said to be the

[49] *Gig.* 60, *Plant.* 12, *Op.* 73.

[50] *Plant.* 12, *Somn.* 1. 135, *Gig.* 7 f. Cicero attributes this idea to Aristotle in *DND*
2. 15. 42 = *De Philosophia* frag. 21a (Ross). But the passage is again heavily
Stoicized, see Moraux, 'Quinta', 1213 and 1223; Achilles *Isag.* (35. 7–11 Maass);
Posidonius frag. 358b (Theiler, cf. his note). The idea then passes into later
Platonism: see Plotinus 2. 9. 8. 30; Porphyry *In Tim.* frag. 84 (77.30–78. 9
Sodano, frag. dub.). It has its origin in Plato *Tim.* 39e 10–40a2.

[51] *Op.* 143 f., *Conf.* 78.

[52] *Prov.* 2. 74. This section has survived only in Armenian translation. Aucher's
Latin version (published in 1822) is followed here. For problems with the use of
the large Armenian Philo corpus ('wildly underestimated by most scholars') see
Runia, *Philo*, 63.

[53] *Somn.* 1. 141, *Gig.* 6, 16, *QG* 4. 188.

[54] *Plant.* 14.

[55] *QG* 4. 188 assumes the superiority of the stars to the daemons just mentioned.

[56] *Conf.* 174; chorus: *Mos.* 2. 239, 2. 271, *Cher.* 23, *Fug.* 62, *Op.* 54, 70, *Congr.* 51,
Migr. 184; see ch. 4 n. 33.

offering that is made in the temple which is the cosmos, while the angels, who again are unembodied souls, are described as the priests of this temple.[57] Unfortunately, Philo never is more clear than this in describing the relationship of stars and angels.

What is clear is that Philo, like his pagan contemporaries, holds the stars and planets in high regard. On a number of occasions he interprets the seven minorah candles (Exodus 25:37) as symbolizing the seven planets because of the role the planets play in bringing about sublunary generation.[58] He also goes as far as to suggest that the heavenly bodies are divine images (ἀγάλματα).[59] This is understandable in light of his interpretation of reason as constituting the divine image in humanity—if this is so then it is true *a fortiori* of angel and star—but the similarity of his language to pagan astral religion in the *Epinomis* and elsewhere is striking.

And Philo appears just as close to his pagan counterparts in his depiction of the stars as divine. Harry Wolfson attempts to distance Philo from these passages by noting that Philo often puts these remarks in the third person, and he suggests that Philo is merely passing along someone else's opinion.[60] This, however, is not convincing[61] since Philo in fact often refers to the stars in this way when he speaks in his own voice. The stars are more divine (θεῖος) than we are,[62] and they are divine souls, or divine natures.[63] The stars are 'that mighty host of visible gods (αἰσθητὰ θεῖα) whose blessedness from of old has been recognized',[64] and referring to the stars as the gods perceived by the senses is very common in Philo.[65] In short, Philo does much to accommodate himself to the prevailing philosophical climate. His universe is populated by mighty beings who, though not standing apart from God's sovereignty (as we shall see), were nevertheless distinct,

[57] 1. 66.
[58] *QE* 2. 78, *Her.* 221, *Mos.* 2. 102 ., cf. *QE* 2. 75 with Marcus's notes.
[59] See Runia, *Philo*, 333. Philo phrases this more cautiously in *Op.* 82, cf. also *Migr.* 40.
[60] Harry Austryn Wolfson, *Philo* (Cambridge, Mass.: Harvard University, 1947), 1. 363–5, 398.
[61] John Dillon reaches this same conclusion for different reasons, 'Philo's Doctrine of Angels', *Two Treatises of Philo of Alexandria*, Brown Judaic Studies 25 (Chico, Calif.: Scholars Press, 1983), 200.
[62] *Op.* 84, *Migr.* 184, cf. *Abr.* 162, *Dec.* 64.
[63] Souls: *Gig.* 8; natures: *Op.* 144, *Prov.* 2. 50, *QG* 4. 188.
[64] *Aet.* 46, trans. LCL.
[65] *Spec.* 1. 19, *Aet.* 112, *Op.* 27, *QG* 1. 42, 4. 157.

superhuman entities. In the bustling heavenly court of late antiquity the stars were one more set of divine beings, but a particularly important one because all acknowledged their power and importance to at least some degree.

Philo's respect for the visible heaven, so in keeping then with the spirit of the age, made him tolerant of those who worshipped heaven. Again and again Philo suggests that, though astral worship is not correct, it is better than the worship of images made by human hands, and is in fact part of a divine plan to move pagans toward true religion.[66] The worship of heaven is second best to the worship of God, and exercises a good influence on the pagan mind. Coming as he did from a city famous for its scholarship and learning, Philo (like Clement and Origen after him), emphasizes the soul's (even the pagan soul's) ability to progress and develop to higher levels of understanding, and the recognition of the honourable position occupied by the stars was a part of this learning process. It was the ultimate natural achievement of all that which is beneath the moon.

On the other hand, Philo was continually aware of possible religious misinterpretation even as he employed language which almost invited it. Throughout all his corpus, the characteristically Jewish fear is expressed that honour might be given to the creature rather than the creator. Thus although he agreed that planets did affect the life below, he adopted numerous pagan arguments in opposition to astrology and astral determinism.[67] He continually emphasizes that aspect of Platonism which identifies a reality which transcends the stars. The heavenly bodies are exalted among all creation, but they are only second best, or even third best since they are below the purely immaterial and intelligible world, which is in turn below God.[68] The soul is divinized, not by its ascent to ether or heaven, but only by rising up to God, who is utterly beyond them.[69] Abram

---

[66] *Dec.* 66 and the sources collected by Henry Chadwick in 'Philo and the Beginnings of Christian Thought', in A. H. Armstrong (ed.), *Cambridge History of Later Greek and Early Medieval Philosophy* (Cambridge: Cambridge University 1970), 149, cf. 165.

[67] See Paul Wendland, *Philos Schrift über die Vorsehung* (Berlin: K. Gaernters, 1892), 24 n. 1 and *passim*.

[68] *Congr.* 51, *QG* 3. 42.

[69] Rising: *QE* 2. 40; beyond: *QG* 2. 54, *QE* 2. 47; see further Harl *Quis rerum* 121 n. 3.

did study the heavens before the divine call, but later he left this occupation for the higher way of the wise man and lover of God.[70] The individual who has gained a thorough mastery of the heavens but not self-knowledge has acted foolishly,[71] for an interest in heaven for its own sake which does not lead the individual to a higher understanding is useless.

As if to counter his own emphasis on heaven, Philo often takes away its usual prerogatives. He notes that Genesis says that plants were created before heaven, and takes this as evidence that sublunary generation is not controlled by heaven but directly by God, who has arranged the creation in this sequence because of his foreknowledge of the error of the astrologers in attributing generation to the stars instead of to God.[72] The destruction of Sodom and Gomorrah showed that it was not heaven or sun which brought about the times and seasons, but the power of God.[72] At times Philo speaks as if the stars were not autonomous but were simply instruments of the divine will:

He [sc. God] has set each star in its proper circuit as a driver in a chariot, and yet He has in no case trusted the reins to the driver, fearing that their rule might be one of discord, but He has made them all dependent on Himself, holding that thus would their march be orderly and harmonious.[74]

Elsewhere he suggests that the movements in heaven are simply extensions of God's own divine power.[75] Even when he affirms the autonomy of the stars, Philo often seems eager to downplay their importance. In contrast to God who acts completely impassively, the sun, moon, heaven, and the whole world are not free (οὐκ ὄντα αὐτεξούσια) but are subject to a power which is

[70] *Cher.* 7.
[71] See Walther Völker, *Fortschritt und Vollendung bei Philo von Alexandrien*, TU 49. 1 (Leipzig: J. C. Hinrichs, 1938), 183 f., and Monique Alexandre, 'La Culture profane chez Philon', in Roger Arnaldez *et al.* (eds.), *Philon d'Alexandrie* (Paris: Éditions du Centre national de la recherche scientifique, 1967), 116.
[72] *Op.* 45 f. Cf. *Sibylline Oracles* 3. 218–30, with J. J. Collins's note in James H. Charlesworth, *The Old Testament Pseudepigrapha* (Garden City, NY: Doubleday, 1983), 1. 367.
[73] *QG* 4. 51, cited by Chadwick 'Philo' 139 n. 4, who refers to the Greek fragments in the LCL Philo supplement (2. 217 f. Marcus).
[74] *Cher.* 24, trans. LCL (slightly adapted). Cf. *Op.* 46, *QE* 2. 55, and also *1 Enoch* 43: 1.
[75] *QE* 2. 51; cf. *Mos.* 2. 238.

beyond their control.[76] Again, after discussing how the heavenly
bodies provide us with knowledge of time and number and
innumerable other benefits, Philo adds that these operations in
nature 'are invariably carried out under ordinances and laws
which God laid down in His universe as unalterable'.[77] They rule
what is below the moon, but are themselves subordinate to God,
acting as his lieutenants (ὕπαρχοι).[78] The heavenly bodies have
not created themselves and are not self-sufficient, but have come
into being by the perfection of the creator.[79]

Therefore Philo repeatedly makes plain that it is wrong to
worship heaven,[80] in keeping with a longstanding polemic of
Hellenistic Judaism.[81] Though he is unsure of the stars' precise
ontological status, he knows that they are part of the created
order and so on a footing with us rather than with God.

Let us then reject all such imposture and refrain from worshipping those
who by nature are our brothers, even though they have been given a
substance purer and more immortal than ours, for created things, in so
far as they are created, are brothers, since they have all one Father, the
Maker of the universe.[82]

And so Philo takes away with his right hand what he gives us
with his left. He follows the conventions of his day in honouring
the stars, but he is both too good a Jew and too good a Platonist to
take this to its logical consequences. For all their glory, the stars
are distinctly inferior to God, who is above heaven. The
cosmological inconsistencies which were present individually in
Plato, Aristotle, and the Stoa come to a crescendo in Philo, and
this happens in part because he is not able to criticize and correct
his teachers, and because he has sometimes combined his sources
in a clumsy way, but it has also happened because of his
philosophical and religious integrity: he refuses to put anything

[76] *Cher.* 88, *Spec.* 1. 14.
[77] *Op.* 60 f., trans. LCL.
[78] *Spec.* 1. 13 f., 19, *Conf.* 173, *QG* 4. 51.
[79] *Cont.* 5, *Dec.* 58.
[80] *Congr.* 51. 133, *Her.* 97, *Dec.* 52 f., 66, *Deus* 62, *Conf.* 173.
[81] Deut. 4: 19; *1 Enoch* 80: 7; Wisdom of Solomon 13: 1–3; Apocalypse of
Abraham 7: 9; ps.-Clem. *Rec.* 5. 16. 4 (173. 20–3 Rehm). For rabbinic sources see
Joseph Barbel, *Christos Angelos*, Theoph 3 (Bonn: Peter Hanstein, 1941), 218 f.,
Johann Maier, 'Die Sonne im antiken Judentum', *ANRW* 2. 19. 1 (1979), 366,
388 f.
[82] *Dec.* 64, trans. LCL.

(even the stars) on the same level as God. His efforts are of great importance for students of Origen, because Origen will follow him both in attempting to present a scriptural cosmology, and in placing strict limitations on the usual pagan religious under-standing of heaven.

One idea, however, which Origen adopts and which is not present in Philo or any of the classical philosophical schools is the recognition of the possibility of evil in heaven. This view, which is of great importance for Origen in understanding the place of the stars in the divine economy, gradually developed in Hellenism, and exerted a great influence on early Christianity. That the heavenly bodies affected the life below was a philosophical commonplace, but our sources in the early imperial era are sharply divided about the nature of this influence. The attempts to reach some evaluation of the astral powers in moral terms and the subsequent impact of these debates will be the topic of the next chapter.

6

THE HEAVENLY POWERS

HEAVENLY POWERS AS GOOD OR AS MORALLY NEUTRAL

We have already seen that interpretation of how the soul enters upon generation is a problem in this era since Plato's *Timaeus* says that it is the result of the goodness of the demiurge while the *Phaedrus* links it to the sin of the pre-existing soul. There was therefore a good deal of disagreement among the later Platonists about the character of the cosmos and the soul's incorporation. Was the world and our life part of a divine plan? Those who adopted this understanding of Plato interpreted the soul's incorporation as providential and the heavenly bodies as assistants to a kindly design. Another interpretation of Plato stressed that this life has come about because of sin and error, and so took a very different view of the cosmos. Plato's own attitude no doubt was nearer the former than the latter,[1] but the negative understanding of the universe is also an extension of Platonic thought, and gained a great following.

The positive interpretation of Plato's discussion of the descent of the soul in the *Timaeus* interpreted it as a necessity arising out of divine goodness.[2] Plotinus writes simply in his treatise *Against the Gnostics*, 'To ask why the Soul made the world, is to ask why there is a Soul and why a Maker makes.'[3] The emphasis of this interpretation, following Plato both in the *Republic* and in the *Timaeus*, is that God is innocent of any evils that beset human life.[4] The world of generation, which is maintained and governed

---

[1] C. J. de Vogel, 'Was Plato a Dualist?', *Rethinking Plato and Platonism*, MnSuppl 92 (Leiden: E. J. Brill, 1986), 159–212.
[2] A. J. Festugière, *Révélation*, 3. 76, Dodds, *Proclus*, 305.
[3] 2. 9. 8. 1 f., trans. Stephen MacKenna (adapted).
[4] Plato *Rep.* 379c2–7, 617e5, *Tim.* 42d3f., Alcinous *Did.* 16 (172; 8 Hermann); Maximus of Tyre 41. 5 (482, 1 ff. Hobein); Plutarch *De An. Procr. in Tim.* 1015c (6. 151. 1–4 Hubert); Hierocles *In Aur. Pythag. Car.* 25. 15 (109. 10 ff. Köhler); *CH* 4. 8 (1. 52. 7 f. N/F). For Philo see Völker, *Fortschritt*, 50.

by the stars, may be the occasion for the soul to be overwhelmed by the passions, but it is not evil in itself. According to this interpretation, the inheritance of mankind from the stars is not negative; indeed, under Stoic influence many claimed that the mind or soul was a portion of the celestial essence.[5] This view became a part of Hellenistic folklore and is evident in the mass of epitaphs in antiquity which express the hope that the departed soul will return to its home in the stars.[6]

Those who remained closer to Plato knew that the highest part of the soul was not made of the heavenly substance. However, the existence of a substance which literally was on the boundary between the incorporeal noetic realm of God and the corporeal world of becoming helped explain how it was possible for the incorporeal soul to be joined to the corporeal body. The stars became a model for how humanity's divine rationality was related to the irrationality of the sublunary world. The belief began slowly to evolve that the soul was joined to the body through the medium of an 'astral body'. The fundamental discussion of this question in modern scholarship is by E. R. Dodds, who opposes the older scholarly view that this teaching represents an oriental influence on Hellenistic thought and explains the concept of the astral body as part of a development within Greek philosophy.[7] What apparently happened is that a group of eclectic philosophers in the second and third centuries AD combined passages in Plato and Aristotle which were very close to the Stoic view of the soul. Plato had written that corporeal vision occurs as a result of a fine, smooth, non-destructive fire which is emitted from the eye and combines with light, which is akin to it, forming a bond between the soul and that which is seen.[8] Light then is the medium between soul and the world.[9] In an isolated passage Aristotle once suggested that there is a psychic material in the *pneuma* in human sperm which

[5] See above ch. 3, n. 34.
[6] The idea predates Plato, see Euripides *Hel.* 1016 and frag. 961 (Nauck), the famous inscription at Plataea (*CIA* 1. 442), and ch. 1 n. 10, but was further spread by Platonism. The literature on this topic is considerable, see among others A. J. Festugière, *L'Idéal religieux des grecs et l'Évangile* (2nd edn., Paris: Librairie Lecoffre, 1981), 143–60.
[7] *Proclus*, 313–21.
[8] *Tim.* 45b4–d3.
[9] See also *Rep.* 507e6–508a2.

is analogous to the stars.[10] Both these views are easily confused with the Stoic view that the soul is made of ether or *pneuma*, and that ether and *pneuma* have some close relationship with each other and with the stars (and indeed are often said to be one and the same). The later Platonic astral body theory suggests that the star which in the *Phaedrus* myth acts as the soul's vehicle ($ὄχημα$)[11] is in fact a reference to the luminous body which joins the soul and the physical body. The gap between mind and matter is bridged by positing a body of *pneuma* or light which is somehow related to both, just as physical vision unites the mind to the world.

It was an idea whose time had come. Heraclides Ponticus already may have been working toward a similar solution in his view that the soul's nature was luminous,[12] a view followed by Plutarch and others.[13] Such attempts are not surprising since the ancient association of soul or mind with the heavens continually caused philosophers to discuss them in terms of an astral substance. The difficulty for Platonists and Peripatetics was to do so without falling into Stoic materialism—a snare into which Philo stumbled and could not escape. The view that the astral substance was not the substance of the rational soul but its vehicle retained the idea that the best part of humanity was related to the stars—an opinion now shared on all sides—while preserving an immaterialist psychology. The star, which is physically visible and moves in the world of generation but which also is commanded by a purely noetic essence, becomes the paradigm of the human soul.[15]

The identity of the first representative of this synthesis is not clear. Dodds cites a passage from Galen (late second century AD) as the earliest extant discussion of the pneumatic vehicle,[15] but he notes similar passages in a variety of writers from around the same era, some of whom are hard to date.[16] It seems that the

[10] See ch. 2, n. 17.

[11] 247b2, cf. *Epin.* 986b4.

[12] See ch. 1 n. 151.

[13] *Aetia Rom. et Graeca* 281b (2. 313. 22 f. Titchener), *De Sera Num. Vind.* 565c (3. 437. 5–9 Pohlenz), *De Lat. Viv.* 1130b (6. 221. 18–22 Pohlenz/Westman = Heraclides frag. 100 Wehrli); ps.-Clementine *Hom.* 9. 9. 5 (135. 11 f. Rehm).

[14] See Moraux, 'Quinta', 1173, 1249.

[15] Dodds *Proclus*, 316.

[16] Ibid. 317, and also *Oracula Chaldaica* frag. 120 (des Places). The *Oracula* date from about the same time as Galen.

philosophical potential of this idea went largely unnoticed for a long time. Origen's opponent Celsus (*c.*AD 178) knows the idea in connection with claims about the bodies of ghosts, but dismisses it,[17] and later Plotinus is familiar with the notion of an astral body but is not particularly interested.[18] Only after Origen, in the tradition of interpretation which begins with Porphyry and his student Iamblichus, does Platonism begin to clarify the precise nature of the astral body both in heaven and existing as the vehicle for the human soul. At this later point, the astral soul becomes a tenet in systematic, neo-Platonic philosophy.[19] But in Origen's day, the concept of the soul's astral vehicle was still an intellectual experiment which could be developed in several different ways.

A particularly important development in this experiment is the theory of a planetary component in the structure of the soul. The growth of interest in astrology in the Hellenistic era led to a special emphasis on the influence of the planets on the soul, since astrology is very much concerned with the effects of the various planetary positions on all generation. The part that Plato had assigned to the 'young gods' in the creation of the two lower parts of the soul[20] was seen, as in astrology, as the influence of a particular planetary characteristic on the soul as it came into generation. This approach to the understanding of the soul's relation to heaven was popular in a variety of philosophically eclectic movements just before and after the beginning of the common era. The texts which are extant from these movements could be classified in many ways, but the most important one for the current problem is between approaches which reflect cosmic optimism and an important tendency to cosmic pessimism.

The positive interpretation of planetary influence needs little explanation since it is a continuation of the traditional philosophical understanding of the heavenly bodies as a divinely

[17] *CCel.* 2. 60 (1. 183. 7–16 K.).
[18] Dodds, *Proclus*, 318.
[19] Ibid. 319 f. See also Robert Christian Kissling's 'The *Ochema-Pneuma* of the neo-Platonists and the *De Insomniis* of Synesius of Cyrene', *AJP* 43 (1922), 318–30; for Porphyry: Andrew Smith, *Porphyry's Place in the Neoplatonic Tradition* (The Hague: Martinus Nijhoff, 1974), 152–8; for Iamblichus: John F. Finamore, *Iamblichus and the Theory of the Vehicle of the Soul* (Chico, Calif.: Scholars Press, 1985); Proclus: J. Trouillard, 'Reflexions sur l'ochéma dans Proclus', *REG* 70 (1957), 102–7.
[20] See ch. 1 n. 93.

ordained part of the cosmos. To the planets were assigned a
variety of roles which preserved this traditional view that they
were not to be thought of as evil or inferior. There are many
examples among the Hellenistic philosophers. Iamblichus says
that the 'older philosophers' think that the visible gods, especially
the sun, purify the ascending soul,[21] and many Platonists shared
the idea that the planets guarded the heavens against unworthy
souls and aided the ascending souls of the virtuous.[22] Some
believed that the planets each added something of their own
essence to the descending soul, and in many cases again the
planetary effect is either positive or at least no worse than mixed.
Plutarch says that the moon provides the individual with soul
and the sun provides him with mind,[23] and beginning with
Porphyry it becomes common in later Platonism to suggest that
the soul's astral body (or pneumatic vehicle) was from the
planetary spheres and was reabsorbed by them in the soul's
ascent.[24] Porphyry and a number of other sources describe our
inheritance from the planets in terms which are neither wholly
positive nor wholly negative. For example, Porphyry writes that
souls descending from the moon are both hot-tempered and
gentle.[25] Or again, Servius (late fourth century) says that the
natural scientists (*physici*) teach that we receive *spiritus* (i.e.
pneuma) from the sun, body from the moon, blood from Mars,
inventiveness from Mercury, desire for honours from Jupiter,
passions from Venus, and tears from Saturn.[26] One Hermetic
fragment says that all seven planets are in us, since we receive
tears from Saturn, birth from Jupiter, speech (λόγος) from
Mercury, anger from Mars, sleep from the moon, desire from

[21] *De Anima* ap. J. Stobaeus *Ecl.* (1. 455. 1 f. Wachsmuth).
[22] Plutarch *De Genio Socr.* 591c (3. 496. 1–8 Sieveking); J. Lydus *De Mens.* 4.
149 (167. 21–168. 9 Wünsch).
[23] *De Fac.* 943a (5. 2. 82. 22–4 Pohlenz); cf. Porphyry *Sent.* 29 (19. 6–10
Lamberz).
[24] Porphyry ap. J. Stobaeus *Ecl.* (2. 171. 2 Wachsmuth), *Sent.* 29 (18. 7
Lamberz), *In Tim.* frag. 16 (10. 6 f. Sodano); reabsorbed: 'followers of Porphyry' in
Porphyry *In Tim.* frag. 80 (68. 16–69. 6 Sodano; for this phrase see Andrew Smith,
'Porphyrian Studies since 1913', *ANRW* 2. 36. 2 (1987), 765 n. 300). The common
source of Proclus *In Tim.* (3. 69. 14–23 and 3. 355. 9–18 Diehl) and Macrobius *In
Somn. Scip.* 1. 12. 14 (50. 15–24 Willis) is probably Porphyry: note the attribution
of imagination to the sun in Porphyry (*Sent.* 29, and ap. Stobaeus *Ecl.* 1. 430. 7–9
Wachsmuth) and in the parallel Proclus/Macrobius passages.
[25] *In Tim.* frag. 22 (14. 1–6 Sodano).
[26] *In Aen.* 11. 51 (2. 482 f. Thilo).

Venus, and laughter from the sun.[27] Three other passages in the *Corpus Hermeticum* speak of the soul's ascent through the heavenly bodies without suggesting that there is anything wrong with them—they just happen to come between the soul and the transcendent God.[28] There is evil in the world, but there is no indication here that this is the fault of the planets, who are here (as in the *Timaeus*) instruments of a higher purpose which is good.

The adherents of Mithraism taught that the ascending soul needed to deal with good but somewhat more menacing heavenly beings. Their appreciation of the planets' fearful powers may well be linked to their strong interest in astrology.[29] Reinhold Merkelbach observes that though Mithraism has its roots in Persian religion, it has been so deeply penetrated by Greek ideas that one must speak of it as a new religion; he also notes that its teachings have been particularly influenced by Platonism.[30] That Origen was familiar with their teaching on the descent and ascent of the soul through the planetary spheres is apparent in one of Origen's lengthy citations from Celsus, who describes this teaching in some detail.[31] Celsus says that the Mithraic doctrine (which he regards as essentially Platonic) is

---

[27] Frag. 29 (4. 99 N/F). Probably the influence of classical astrology (which again spoke of both positive and negative planetary attributes) is important here: the claim that Saturn brings tears is also in Vettius Valens 1. 1 (2. 7 Pingree, cf. N/F 3. cxcvi).

[28] *CH* 4. 8 (1. 52. 8–11), 11. 19 (1. 155. 2–5), frag. 23. 28 (4. 8 . N/F). At a later date, Hermias of Alexandria *In Phaedr.* (130. 4–7 Couvreur).

[29] Mithraic astrology has been much discussed in recent literature, see Michael P. Speidel, *Mithras-Orion: Greek Hero and Roman Army God*, EPRO 81 (Leiden: E. J. Brill, 1980), Roger Beck, *Planetary Gods and Planetary Orders in the Mysteries of Mithras*, EPRO 109 (Leiden: E. J. Brill, 1988), and David Ulansey, *The Origins of the Mithraic Mysteries* (New York: Oxford University, 1989).

[30] *Mithras* (Königstein: Anton Hein, 1984) vii and 230–44. Caution is necessary since most of the literary sources of Mithraism are by Platonists. R. Turcan argues that they have Platonized their material, *Mithras Platonicus*, EPRO 47 (Leiden: E. J. Brill, 1975), but he goes too far: see Beck, *Planetary*, 81 f.

[31] *CCel.* 6. 22 (1. 92 f. K.). Turcan (*Mithras*, 50) notes that the planets listed by Celsus correspond with the days of the week and not with any of the usual ancient planetary orders, and suggests that they had a non-spatial interpretation and did not imply an ascent of the soul through the heavens. We shall see that non-spatial use of astronomical imagery does occur in Jewish and gnostic texts. And yet two factors argue against that as an exclusive interpretation (though it is surely part of the picture): (1) the ladder image itself suggests a spatial understanding (cf. e.g. Philo *Somn.* 1. 150–3), and (2) the parallels of this text with many other texts in which the interpretation is spatial is not likely to be just coincidental.

symbolized by a ladder with seven gates and an eighth gate on top which represent the seven planets through which the departed soul ascends to reach the eighth, fixed sphere. Celsus' account is supported by a good deal of evidence. The seven gates, each associated with a planet, appear in several Mithraic mosaics, and it is also evident that the seven ranks of believers in Mithraism are also each associated with a particular planet.[32] Porphyry adds that adherents carry symbols of the planets and the heavenly regions, and celebrate the ascent and descent of the soul in mystic rites.[33] Mithras is depicted with the planets on his cap,[34] and seven imagery (symbolizing the planets and the days of the week) is very common in the cult.[35] Vermaseren and Merkelbach have suggested that the Mithraic cave symbolizes the celestial vault, which is why the ceiling of the Mithraeum is arched and sometimes adorned with stars.[36]

The precise character of the planets in Mithraism is unclear. Presumably the planets could aid or hinder the ascending soul at death,[37] and the rites of the cult prepared the individual for the difficult journey back to his true home in the stars. Since the stars have come into being because of Mithras' sacrifice of the bull,[38] they cannot have been simply evil, for in Mithraism the cosmos is the result of a divine act, not a divine oversight. One of the principle ways Mithraism differed from both gnosticism and much of later Platonism was that it lacked a myth of the soul's fall into generation,[39] and with it a sense of heavenly tragedy or

---

[32] Mosaics: see *CIMRM* 239, 287, 299. Seven ranks: see Reinhold Merkelbach, *Weihegrade und Seelenlehre der Mithrasmysterien* (Opladen: Westdeutscher, 1982), 14, and *Mithras*, 77. The image of the ladder with seven gates also appears in the *Oracula Chaldaica* frag. 164 (des Places).

[33] *De Antro Nympharum* 6 (60. 1–4 and 9–11 Nauck).

[34] Turcan, *Mithras*, 67.

[35] There are seven stars on Mithras' cape (*CIMRM* 245, 310, 368, 390), Mithras is the 'god of seven rays' (*CIMRM* 101, 126), the cultus at Dura-Europas is reached by seven steps (see Roger Beck, 'Mithraism since Franz Cumont', *ANRW* 2. 17. 4 (1984) 2017 n. 23), etc.

[36] M. J. Vermaseren, *Mithras, the Secret God* (London: Chatto & Windus, 1963), 158; Merkelbach, *Mithras*, 201.

[37] Beck, *Planetary*, 78, says that the Mithraic rite should be seen as the realization of the soul's heavenly ascent rather than its anticipation, but in my view this need not be a case of either/or.

[38] Merkelbach, *Mithras*, 201. Hence Mithras is *genitor luminis*.

[39] See R. Turcan, 'Salut mithriaque et sotériologie néoplatonicienne', in Ugo Bianchi and M. J. Vermaseren (eds.), *La soteriologia dei culti orientali nell' impero romano*, EPRO 92 (Leiden: E. J. Brill, 1982), 180.

error. The wrath of the planets was not therefore due to their native malevolence, but perhaps was reserved for those souls which had not purified themselves during their terrestrial life and which had not participated in the Mithraic rite or learned its lore. Completion of the rite would enable the initiate to pass through the planetary gates to higher and higher levels of reality, so that the fullest members could go beyond all the planetary guardians and enter heaven.[40]

HEAVENLY POWERS AS MORALLY EVIL

(a) Pagan sources

In other circles within pagan Hellenistic thought, planetary influence on the soul was understood in completely negative terms. The emergence of the idea that the stars might be evil powers which the soul must evade or defeat is an event of great importance. Heaven had been the one place which the older philosophy thought was free of evil, and now in many separate groups it came to be regarded as in fact the source of evil in the cosmos.[41] The origins of this cosmic pessimism are obscure, but two ways of speaking about the stars contributed to their transformation from mankind's dearest friends to its bitterest enemies. First, it is probable that the growth in astrology contributed to a negative appraisal of the visible heavens. This was not because of the attitude of the more traditional and sophisticated astrologers, who adhered to the older philosophical

---

[40] Cf. 'the Magi' ap. Arnobius *Adv. Nat.* 2. 62 and 2. 13 (97. 24–7 and 58. 20–3 Reifferscheid). There are many parallels in gnosticism: see the teachings of the Naasseni with regard to entrance into the 'gate of heaven', Hippolytus *Ref.* 5. 8. 44 (164. 232–7 Marcovich), and their use of scripture in 5. 8. 18 (158. 93–6 Marcovich), or the *gnosis* of the 'Gnostics' in Epiphanius *Pan.* 26. 10. 7 (1. 288. 3–7 Holl), and of the Simonians in 21. 2 (1. 243. 5–10 Holl). Cf. also the *Book of Jeu* 2. 44 (103. 10–13 Schmidt/MacDermot), the *First Apocalypse of James* (NH 5. 33. 5–34, 20), Marcosians ap. Irenaeus *AH* 1. 21. 5 (1. 2, 304–6 R/D), the *Gospel according to Mary* (BG 16. 12–17. 7), and *PGM* 4. 585 ff.

[41] See the famous discussion in Hans Jonas, *Gnosis und spätantiker Geist*, FRLANT 51, 63 (Göttingen: Vandenhoeck & Ruprecht, 1934, 1954). Jonas suggests that the theme of an evil heavenly inheritance arose first in pagan sources and then spread to gnosticism, 1. 183 f.; Jörg Büchli argues the reverse, *Der Poimandres: Ein paganisiertes Evangelium* (Tübingen: J. C. B. Mohr, 1987), 132. The strands are very difficult to separate at this point.

idea that none of the heavenly bodies are evil.[42] The fact that the
planets had various influences did not mean that they were
malevolent; they were all good, but they sometimes inadvert-
ently had damaging effects on the life below as they went about
their dance which maintained the harmony of the universe. It
was inevitable, however, that once individual fate was believed
to be entrusted to the care of the heavenly bodies—a point on
which both astrology and the Hellenistic philosophy (with its
concept of secondary providence) agreed—the fact that human
life has bad luck as well as good would lead people to question
the powers in heaven. The strong emphasis of classical astrologers
and some philosophers[43] on the inexorability of fate and the
vanity of attempts to escape it lends itself to pessimism. By great
intellectual effort the Stoics might conclude that all things
(including evils) happen according to an overarching, beneficial
plan, but an easier conclusion to draw is that some of the
heavenly bodies are good and others are evil—and the more
pessimistic one's view of the world, the more malevolent the
rulers in heaven.

A second factor which worked in concert with the first was the
negative interpretation of Plato's difficult imagery on the creation
of the soul in the *Timaeus*. In this dialogue we have already seen
that Plato said that the body and the two lower parts of the soul
were made by the 'young gods', the stars and planets. There
certainly is no hint here that the gods in heaven impart evil to the
soul. However, Plato also said elsewhere that the body was a
prison and a tomb for the soul,[44] and suggested the possibility of
an evil World Soul,[45] and so it was perhaps not a big step for the
interpreters of Plato to ignore the passages which honour the
heavenly bodies and to decide that the stars who fashion the
body and the irrational parts of the soul are in fact the minions of
a wicked cosmic soul. The body and its passions lead us astray,
the stars made this body (but not our true, rational self),

---

[42] Julian of Laodicea (*CCAG* 4. 105. 28–31); J. Lydus *De Mens.* 4. 41 (98. 14–21
Wünsch). Iamblichus devotes a chapter to the defence of the stars' goodness, *De
Myst.* 1. 18 (52. 17–57. 3 des Places).

[43] Nechepso/Petosiris frag. 21 (370 Riess); Vettius Valens 5. 6 (210. 6–9
Pingree); Manilius 4. 14; *SVF* 2. 932; Seneca *QN* 2. 35.

[44] Prison: *Phaedo* 82d4–e4, cf. Philolaus 44 B 15 (D/K); tomb: *Crat.* 400c1–9,
Phaedr. 250c4–6, cf. *Gorgias* 493a1–3.

[45] *Laws* 896d5–9.

therefore there is evil at work in heaven. This cosmic evil force imprisons the good part of the soul made by the true, transcendent God. A pessimistic Platonism along these lines is easily joined to a pessimistic astrology where not only one's body but one's entire circumstance is governed by pitiless and unapproachable heavenly forces.

In his commentary on the *Timaeus*, Proclus considers the already ancient problem of the meaning of the Atlantis story, and mentions some of the older interpretations. One group of interpreters thought that the account of a primeval war between Athens and Atlantis was a mythological reference to certain conflicts which took place before the foundation of the world. Proclus continues,

And some of these trace the solution to the stars and planets, taking the Athenians as an analogy for the stars and the people of Atlantis as an analogy for the planets. They fight because of the contrary revolution [i.e. of the planets]; but the former conquer because of the one revolution of the world. This, at any rate, is the opinion of the noble Amelius, who strains to take these things in this way because in the *Critias* the island of Atlantis is clearly said to be divided into seven circles. If anyone else is of the same opinion on these teachings, I do not know it.[46]

Amelius is a student of Plotinus, a generation younger than Origen, but whether or not this interpretation of the Atlantis story is solely his (he may have been influenced by Numenius),[47] the idea of a war in heaven by this point is not new. Already Philo of Alexandria knows similar views, though he is careful to keep his distance:

I remember once hearing a man who had applied himself to the study [sc. of the heavens] in no careless or indolent manner say that it is not only men who have a mad craving for glory, but the stars too have rivalry for precedence and consider it right that the greater should have the lesser for their squires. How far this is true or mere idle talk is a question I must leave to the investigators of the upper world.[48]

---

[46] *In Tim.* (1. 76. 21–30 Diehl). The passage in question is Plato's *Critias* 113e6–114c4. Cf. Hans Lewy, *Chaldaean Oracles and Theurgy*, ed. Michel Tardieu (Paris: Études augustiniennes, 1978), 499–502, above, ch. 4 n. 43, ps.-Heraclitus *Hom. Probl.* 53. 3 (62 Buffière), and Plutarch *Quomodo adol. poet.* 19ef (1. 38. 18–28 Paton/Wegehaupt/Pohlenz).

[47] See below, n. 54, and Porphyry *Vita Plot.* 3. 43–5.

Even as traditionalists reaffirmed the classical view that there was a perfect harmony in heaven, voices in some quarters, especially outside the traditional philosophical schools, were beginning to suggest that perhaps things were not as tranquil as they seemed. Different thinkers began to suspect that there was something terribly wrong with the cosmos.

In particular, a number of pagan writers began to regard the beings who live in the planets or their spheres as altogether evil. The precise origins of this idea are obscure, but the second century AD once again seems to have been the critical period of growth for this theory. A key figure probably was Numenius, whose views are often close to those of the *Chaldaean Oracles* and to gnosticism (especially Valentinianism),[49] and who was used both by Clement of Alexandria[50] and extensively by Origen.[51] Numenius' name (which means 'son of the new moon') may indicate that he was reared in circles which were sympathetic to astrology,[52] and in any case such an interest is reflected in his philosophy. Proclus (who was himself interested in the relationship between Plato and astronomy/astrology) disapproved of the way he 'stitches together Platonic expressions with those of astrology and of mystic rites', and Macrobius mentions his interpretation of the Eleusinian mysteries and his attention to the occult.[53] One unusual aspect of Numenius' Platonism was his negative understanding of the planetary powers. Numenius believed the soul's incarnation is always an evil, and Aeneas of Gaza writes that Numenius and several others (probably including Amelius, whose views on Atlantis are quoted above) say that the soul can be corrupted by irrational powers even before its

[48] *Somn.* 2. 114 f., trans. LCL.
[49] See Turcan, *Mithras*, 80. Dodds notes that Numenius and Valentinus were in Rome about the same time, i.e. 136–40, *Entretiens sur antiquité classique*, 5 (Geneva: Fondation Hardt, 1960), 178.
[50] Clement *Strom.* 1. 22. 150 (2. 93. 11 St.) = frag. 10 Leemans (130. 21–3).
[51] Origen knows five of Numenius' treatises, see Numenius frag. 1c (des Places) = frag. 32 (144. 15–18 Leemans), frag. 29 (des Places) = frag. 31 (144. 3–10 Leemans). I refer to both des Places's and Leemans's editions, since the former has valuable notes, introduction, and translation, while the latter on an important point is (in my view) more accurate (see below).
[52] Cf. G. Delling, '*Mén*', trans. Geoffrey W. Bromiley, *TDNT* 4 (1967), 638 for other examples. Such births were regarded as auspicious.
[53] Proclus: frag. 35 (86. 14 f. des Places) = test. 42 (100. 18–20 Leemans); occult: frag. 55 (des Places) = frag. 39 (146. 19–26 Leemans).

incorporation.[54] Iamblichus reports that Numenius thinks that evil is attached to the soul externally from matter.[55] It appears that he believed the planets are the forces which corrupt the soul as it descends to earth from heaven. First, Numenius says that the planets ('the gods who direct the world of becoming') are mixed with matter,[56] which he identifies as non-being and the source of evil.[57] Because of this mixture with matter, there is evil in heaven among the heavenly bodies (the 'corporeal and generated gods').[58] While the Stoics placed Tartarus in the air, Numenius placed it even higher, in the planetary region. Proclus writes that Numenius

says that the fixed sphere is heaven and in it are two openings, Cancer and Capricorn, one the opening of descent for generation and the other of ascent. And he says that the planets are the rivers under the earth, for he has these refer to the rivers and even to Tartarus itself.[59]

The evil effects of the planets are described in Macrobius' *Commentarii in Somnium Scipionis*. Macrobius twice (1. 11. 11 f. and 1. 12) speaks of the soul's descent through planetary spheres, and scholars have been divided about what his sources were. Leemans links both passages with Numenius, but this was denied by Rudolf Beutler, who said that this view is not compatible with Numenius' arithmetical definition of the soul.[60] He was followed by des Places, who accordingly did not include in his edition of Numenius either of these passages which describe planetary influences in human generation. However, Hermann de Ley (a student of Leemans) has shown that Beutler's objections are not decisive after all.[61] Furthermore, M. A. Elferink has demonstrated that these discussions in Macrobius are not part of the same argument, and suggests they come from different sources.[62]

---

[54] Always evil: frag. 48 (des Places) = test. 40 (99. 21–5 Leemans); corrupted: frag. 49 (des Places) = test. 41 (99. 26–100. 4 Leemans); for the textual problem associated with Amelius' name see des Places's note.

[55] Frag. 43 (des Places) = test. 35 (98. 17–20 Leemans).

[56] Frag. 50 (des Places) = test. 26 (89. 1–7 Leemans).

[57] Frag. 4a (des Places) = frag. 13 (132. 18–133. 2 Leemans).

[58] Frag. 52 (des Places) = test. 30 (94. 16–97. 5 Leemans).

[59] Frag. 35 (des Places) = test. 42 (100. 11–15 Leemans).

[60] T 47 (104–10 Leemans); Beutler's review of Leemans, *Gn* 16 (1940), 114, and 'Numenius', *PW* Suppl. 7 (1940), 677.

[61] *Macrobius and Numenius*, ColLat 125 (Brussels: Latomus, 1972), ch. 2.

[62] *Les Descentes de l'âme d'après Macrobe*, PhAnt 16 (Leiden: E. J. Brill, 1968), 35;

The present author comes to this conclusion for a different reason, and would suggest that while 1. 12. 14 is perhaps derived from Porphyry, 1. 11. 12 comes from Numenius. This latter passage states that the soul

does not suddenly put on an earthly body from its complete incorporeality, but it swells up little by little through quiet setbacks and a very long decline from its simple and absolute purity to certain growths that derive from an astral body (*in quaedam siderei corporis incrementa*). For in each of the spheres below heaven it is clothed with an ethereal envelope, so that through the spheres it is gradually reconciled to its association with this garb. And so it passes by as many deaths as it does spheres, and comes to what on earth is called life.[63]

As de Ley notes, Numenius elsewhere refers to the swelling of the passive part of the soul,[64] and this passage is also compatible with Numenius' teaching that the planetary region is hell. It is furthermore incompatible with Porphyry's teachings on the descent of the soul, which does not speak of it as evil.[65] Since matter is evil in Numenius, the idea that the soul is completely incorporeal before entering into life would strengthen the conclusion that Macrobius' source in 1. 11. 12 is Numenius. On the other hand, Macrobius 1. 12. 14, like Porphyry and unlike Numenius, speaks of the soul's inheritance in mixed terms, and perhaps is derived from Porphyry.

Evil planetary forces are mentioned in several other pagan sources. A passage in the Latin grammarian Servius cited above mentions both good and evil planetary powers, but Servius, like Macrobius, draws on a variety of sources and also preserves an anonymous teaching that the planets are evil and impose a particular vice on the descending soul:

when souls descend, they draw with them the sloth of Saturn, the wrath of Mars, the lust of Venus, the yearning for money of Mercury, and the

cf. de Ley, *Macrobius*, 22, who agrees that the two sections are not derived from the same passage, but thinks the doctrines in 1. 11. 12 and 1. 12 both come from Numenius. See also Jacques Flamant, *Macrobe et le néo-platonisme latin*, EPRO 58 (Leiden: E. J. Brill, 1977), 546–65.

[63] *In Somn. Scip.* 1. 11. 12 (47. 21–9 Willis) = test. 47 (105. 10–18 Leemans), not in des Places.
[64] *Macrobius* 51 n. 2, Numenius frag. 52 (des Places) = test. 30 (94, 12–14 Leemans).
[65] See above n. 25.

desire to rule of Jupiter. These things cause disturbance to the souls so that they are unable to exercise their own power and properties.[66]

The late third-century Christian apologist Arnobius attacks a pagan group who teach that evil actions are determined by the heavens.[67] The identity of the sect which Arnobius attacked has been much debated, but, whoever they were, according to Arnobius they were interested in Numenius' teaching.[68] It is apparent that the pessimistic interpretation of Plato favoured by Numenius was not at all unusual in pagan circles.

This is also evident in the *Corpus Hermeticum*, a body of literature representing several different viewpoints[69] which are both pagan and close to gnosticism. The *Poimandres* says that each individual is given part of the planetary essence by the seven administrators, and yearns to rise above them to the eighth sphere.[70] Once again the perfection of the soul is the region of the fixed stars. The planets, made of fire and air, administer the world of sense, and their control is called Fate.[71] Ascending through the planetary spheres, the soul gives back the power of increase and decrease in the first sphere (i.e. the moon), evil plotting in the second (Mercury), lust in the third (Venus), the proud desire to rule in the fourth (the sun), impiety and audacity in the fifth (Mars), greed for wealth in the sixth (Jupiter), and malevolent falsehood in the seventh (Saturn),[72] and escapes the rule of Fate. The planets exercise a baleful influence over us, and our ultimate goal is to escape their power. The most traditional pagan approach to the heavenly bodies was to regard them as good, but many in the Hellenistic era regarded them as having a mixed character, and a few even went so far as to suggest that they were altogether evil (and so 'demons' in the Christian sense of the word).

---

[66] *In Aen.* 6. 714 (2. 98. 21–4 Thilo).
[67] *Adv. Nat.* 2. 16 (60. 10–15 Reifferscheid), cf. 2. 28 (71. 17 f.).
[68] 2. 11 (55. 13 Reifferscheid).
[69] There have been a number of attempts to classify the tractates of the *Corpus Hermeticum*, see Karl-Wolfgang Tröger's summary in *Mysterienglaube und Gnosis in Corpus Hermeticum XIII* (Berlin: Akademie, 1971), 5 f.
[70] 1. 13 (1. 11. 2–5 N/F) and 1. 16 (1. 12 N/F). The date of the *Poimandres*, is uncertain; Büchli, *Poimandres*, 207, suggests the mid-third century AD.
[71] 1. 9 (1. 9. 17–20 N/F).
[72] 1. 25 (1. 15 f. N/F).

(b) Apocalyptic and gnostic sources

It is the phenomenon called gnosticism which is especially
known for teaching that there are evil powers in heaven.[73] As
has often been noted, the word 'gnostic' is unsatisfactory. In
modern scholarship the term (following the usage of the early
heresiologists) often lumps together under the same heading
different individuals and groups which (as Origen himself
observed) strongly disagreed with each other.[74] At this point, the
terminological problem has not yet been resolved, mainly
because there is still no consensus among modern scholars about
what this phenomenon is and how it began.[75] The word 'gnostic'
will be used in what follows to describe those groups whose
language and imagery has been strongly influenced by Jewish or
Christian cosmologies, who even more than Plato (contrast
Origen) are drawn to mythology as a mode of expression, and for
whom the belief that esoteric knowledge ($\gamma\nu\hat{\omega}\sigma\iota\varsigma$) delivers the
individual from evil powers in heaven is of special importance.

Before the gnostic understanding of the life in the heavenly
bodies or spheres is presented, a digression is necessary to
consider two topics: (1) the background of gnostic ideas on
heavenly demons in Jewish literature from the Hellenistic era
with a strong interest in cosmological themes ('Jewish apocalyptic'),
and (2) the means by which gnostic texts more relevant to the

[73] Several Nag Hammadi texts are notable for not reflecting an explicitly
Christian theology, but the view that gnosticism ever existed apart from
Christianity remains unproved. See further Simone Pétrement, *Le Dieu séparé*
(Paris: du Cerf, 1984), especially 573–628, 'Les Ouvrages dits non chrétiens'.

[74] *In Matth*. Comm. Ser. 35 (11. 66. 12–15 Kl.). This is evident within the Nag
Hammadi treatises. In contrast to many of the works in this find, the *Melchezidek*
(NH 9) and the *Gospel of Truth* (NH 1, 20, 10–14) are not docetic, the *Silvanus* (NH
7. 116. 5–9) warns against denigrating the demiurge, and the *Apocryphon of John*
(NH 2. 22. 11–15) regards the serpent as evil.

[75] Some have suggested that the teachings of an early gnostic sect can be isolated
in a certain group of treatises, many of which were discovered at Nag Hammadi, and
that this sect was foundational for later gnosticism, especially Hans-Martin Schenke,
'Das sethianische System nach Nag-Hammadi-Handschriften', *Studia Coptica*, ed.
Peter Nagel (Berlin: Akademie, 1974), 165–73, and id. 'The Phenomenon and
Significance of Gnostic Sethianism', in Bentley Layton (ed.), *The Rediscovery of
Gnosticism*, SHR 41 (Leiden: E. J. Brill, 1981), 2. 588–616. If this were true, such a
group could arguably be defined as 'gnostic' in a strict sense. And yet questions
remain about whether such a group ever existed, see Frederick Wisse, 'Stalking those
Elusive Sethians', in Layton, *Rediscovery*, 2. 563–76.

theme of astral souls can be separated from texts which are only of secondary importance.

Discussion of gnosticism, however it is defined, must include some consideration of contemporary Jewish speculation. This Jewish literature (especially 'apocalyptic') is of special interest for the present topic, because in addition to being integral to the development of gnosticism, Origen on many occasions refers to Jewish apocalyptic texts (some of which are only known through his references).[76]

This body of literature does not explicitly identify the home of the soul after death as the stars, but it frequently uses language which stops just short of such an identification. For example, it is a commonplace to say that the righteous after death will shine,[77] a practice which probably is related to the older Hebrew tradition of linking divine epiphanies with light (Exodus 3: 2, Deuteronomy 4: 15), but which can readily take on new meaning in a setting in which theological speculations are routinely combined with astronomy. Thus when *1 Enoch* says the righteous receive 'garments of glory' and *3 Baruch* says they gather in 'choirs',[78] we are on the verge of the view that the souls ascend to the visible heavens. Again, since angels are often described as fiery,[79] it is significant that the fate of the righteous is linked to that of angels.[80] So when the *Testament of Moses* says that Israel will be set in the stars, or when *4 Maccabees* says the same of the martyrs, this may well be more than metaphorical.[81]

As there is a connection between daemons and stars in many Hellenistic pagan texts, so too in apocalyptic demons (or angels) and stars are often linked, especially in the Enoch literature. Here

[76] Integral: A. D. Nock, 'The Milieu of Gnosticism', *Essays on Religion and the Ancient World*, ed. Zeph Stewart (Cambridge, Mass.: Harvard, 1972), 1. 446 f., and Kurt Rudolph, *Gnosis*, trans. Robert McLachlan Wilson (New York: Harper & Row, 1983), 277–80. Origen: see Harnack *Ertrag*, part 1, pp. 17–19, part 2, pp. 48–50.

[77] Daniel 12: 3; 4 Macc. 17: 5; *1 Enoch* 39: 7; 104: 2; *2 Enoch* 42: 5, 65: 10, 66: 7 ('J'); *2 Baruch* 51: 3; *4 Ezra* 7: 97; cf. *Odes of Solomon* 21: 3. All references to Jewish apocalyptic texts (except Daniel) are taken from Charlesworth (ed.) *Pseudepigrapha*.

[78] *1 Enoch* 62: 15 f.; *3 Baruch* 10: 5.

[79] See Barbel, *Christos*, 213–15, J. Michl, 'Engel I–IV' *RAC* 5 (1962) 85. So also in gnosticism: *Hypostasis of the Archons* (NH 2. 95. 9), Iren. *AH* 2. 19. 6 (2. 2. 192 R/D).

[80] *2 Baruch* 51: 10. See further Hans C. Cavallin, 'Leben nach dem Tode im Spätjudentum', *ANRW* 2. 19. 1 (1979), 267.

[81] *Test. of Moses* 10: 9; 4 Macc. 17: 5

the angels are as numerous as the stars,[82] and frequently are said to regulate their courses and hence the seasons of the year.[83] The author of *2 Enoch* refers to 'the rulers of the stellar orders' and 'the angels who govern the stars and the heavenly combinations'.[84] In *3 Enoch*, there is an angel in charge of each of the seven heavens, while their numerous angelic subordinates move the heavenly bodies.[85] The *Testament of Adam* likewise says that the fourth of the six orders of heavenly beings, namely the 'authorities', administers all the heavenly body.[86] Another common image is the heavenly body as a chariot pulled by angels.[87]

What is of particular interest is the importance of the idea that there is conflict in heaven. Occasionally in apocalyptic literature wars between the stars are a sign of the world's end,[88] and it is not uncommon to see the stars described as sinners. According to *1 Enoch*,[89] the 'chiefs of the stars' are said to err in their courses,[90] and this leads to the punishment of the 'seven stars' (i.e. the planets),

And I saw there the seven stars (which) were like great, burning mountains. (Then) the angel said (to me), 'This place is the (ultimate) end of heaven and earth: it is the prison house for the stars and the powers of heaven. And the stars which roll over upon the fire, they are the ones which have transgressed the commandments of God from the beginning of their rising because they did not arrive punctually. And he was wroth with them and bound them until the time of the completion of their sin in the year of mystery.'[91]

This apparently means that the seven planets are to be punished for their retrograde rotation. Another passage in *1 Enoch* which speaks of the punishment of the stars is more ambiguous,

---

[82] *1 Enoch* 43: 2.

[83] *1 Enoch* 75: 3 (the stars are under the angel Uriel); 82: 9 f.; 19: 2, 4.

[84] *2 Enoch* 4 (trans. F. I. Andersen).

[85] *3 Enoch* 17; cf. 'the spirits of the stars', 46: 1.

[86] 4: 4.

[87] See *3 Baruch* 9: 3 (Slavonic) with H. E. Gaylord's note, *2 Enoch* 11: 4, cf. Ps. 67 (68): 5.

[88] *Sibylline Oracles* 5. 512–31; cf. Rev. 12: 7 f.

[89] Origen often cites the Enoch literature, see Klaus Berger, 'Henoch', *RAC* 14 (1988), 534–6.

[90] 80: 6.

[91] 18: 13–16 (trans. E. Isaac). See Isa. 24: 21–3, and in the New Testament Jude 13. Cf. also ps.-Clementine *Hom.* 8. 12 f. (126. 16–127. 11 Rehm).

And I came to an empty place. And I saw (there) neither a heaven above nor an earth below, but a chaotic and terrible place. And there I saw seven stars of heaven bound together in it, like great mountains, and burning with fire. At that moment I said, 'For which sin are they bound, and for what reason were they cast in here.' Then one of the holy angels, Uriel, who was with me, guiding me, spoke to me and said to me, 'Enoch, for what reason are you asking and for what reason do you question and exhibit eagerness? These are among the stars of heaven which have transgressed the commandments of the Lord and are bound in this place until the completion of ten million years, (according) to the number of their sins.'[92]

In *3 Baruch* the moon is said to have been punished by being given its dimmer light because it provided Satan with light in Eden,[93] and the *Testament of Solomon* suggests that an evil demon (named Onoskelis) travels with the moon.[94] *The Apocalypse of Abraham* reports that the fallen angel Azazel rules the stars.[95] All of these images, but particularly the concept of evil powers which govern the heavenly bodies, are important background to the gnostic concept of astral demons.

The impact of astrology and also of Jewish apocalyptic in giving impetus to a negative interpretation of Plato helps explain gnostic hostility to heaven, but gnosticism's attitude toward the stars is complicated by other factors specific to it. Gnostic references to heavenly powers are at times intertwined with astrology, numerology, and its own mythology, and in such cases individual heavenly bodies are often only of secondary interest. This may sound like an odd claim since astrology is concerned with nothing but the meaning of the stars, and gnostic myth speaks repeatedly about events in heaven. Astrology, however, is a technique which describes the significance of stellar phenomena for mortal life, and is not necessarily interested in whether the stars as individuals are good or bad, or their physical composition, or their ontological relationship to God. Only when astrological teachings are combined with a philosophical interest are the heavenly bodies discussed as living beings. In the absence of such

[92] 21. 1–6 (trans. E. Isaac). Cf. also *1 Enoch* 86 and 88.
[93] 9: 7.
[94] 4: 9; see also 2: 2, 8: 2–4.
[95] 14: 6. Rubinkiewicz notes the parallels with *1 Enoch* 1–36 in Charlesworth, *Pseudepigrapha*, 1. 685.

an interest, the stars are seen merely as the instruments of Fate (εἱμαρμένη). Some gnostic texts accordingly subordinate the heavenly bodies to this superior power of Fate, while on the other hand other texts maintain (as the philosophers traditionally had) that the stars and planets (or their spheres) were vital forces in shaping terrestrial life.

The concern for the visible heavens is at times further diluted by gnostic myth, which has a spiritualizing tendency that is at odds with more physically orientated speculations. Gnosticism will use themes such as the flight of the soul through heaven, or astronomically significant numbers,[96] without necessarily giving them settings which are physically located. Numerology in this period is especially important in weakening the astronomical significance of this language. Thus themes or language which had their origin in astronomy in many cases become conventional and no longer have any real astronomical reference.

This is evident in the way that astronomical language is used, and again the influence of Jewish apocalyptic is probably key. Pétrement suggests that Jewish interpretation of the seven days of Genesis was of more central importance in Jewish and gnostic speculations on the number seven than the planets.[97] Though Pétrement's argument is slightly exaggerated—apocalyptic texts do at times show a strong astronomical interest—this is an important point which is borne out in many passages. Specific-ally, Jewish apocalyptic texts sometimes put God's seat in seventh heaven,[98] but this makes little sense in purely astro-nomical terms: it was thus a common pagan error to believe that the God of the Jews, 'the most High', was Saturn, the seventh planet away from the earth.[99] The number of the days in the

[96] 7, 8 (7 heavens and an eighth sphere), 12 (from the signs of the zodiac), 28, 30 (the days in a lunar and solar month), 36 (the number of decans), 52 (weeks), 72 (weeks in the Babylonian calender), 360 (= 72 weeks × 5 days, 12 months × 30 days (i.e. minus the intercalary days), and also 360 degrees, cf. the Marcosians ap. Iren. *AH* 1. 17. 1, 1. 2. 268 R/D), and 365.

[97] *Séparé*, 100.

[98] The *Book of Baruch* ap. Origen *Prin.* 2. 3. 6. Seventh heaven as the final destiny of the soul: *Ascent of Isaiah* 8: 14 f., and further Pétrement, *Séparé*, 106.

[99] Tacitus *Hist.* 5. 4 (206. 10–15 Halm/Andresen/Köstermann); Celsus ap. *CCel.* 6. 19 (2. 89. 18–20 K.); J. Lydus *De Mens.* 4. 53 (110. 7–10 Wünsch). Others thought this because the Jews rested on the Sabbath, which in the pagan world was Saturn's day (i.e. because of speculations on the calendar rather than because of speculations on the physical bodies): Tacitus loc. cit., Augustine *De Cons. Ev.* 1. 22. 30 (*PL* 34. 1055).

week has been applied by the writers of apocalyptic to the heavens without any connection being made between heavens and planetary circuits: for of course if there had been such an awareness, God would have been placed in a higher heaven. Another example of this is that the number of heavens in apocalyptic and gnostic literature is very often unrelated to planetary positions.[100] This in turn often affected the way that later literature discussed heavenly powers, which were often not tied to particular spheres or given any definite location in heaven.

One important instance of this is the way the terms 'hebdomad' and 'ogdoad' are later used in gnosticism and the magic papyri. As Walter Scott notes, if these terms referred to astral powers, 'hebdomad' would stand for the seven planets, and 'ogdoad' would refer to the seven planetary spheres together with the enclosing eighth sphere, but gnostics and magicians often use these terms as if they were the name of a single heavenly power without specific location. For example, the second-century Alexandrian Christian Basilides says that the Archon of the Hebdomad is Ῥητός ('Spoken') while the Archon of the Ogdoad is Ἄρρητος ('Unspoken').[101] 'Ogdoas' is frequently used as a name of an evil heavenly power in the magic papyri. Two magic formulas quoted by Reitzenstein exemplify this:

Child, when you have learned the power of the book you must keep it secret. For in it is the powerful name, which is the name Ogdoas, which directs and administers all, for the angels, archangels, male and female daemons, and all under creation are subordinate to it,

and again,

You must use the great name, which is the name Ogdoas, which administers all things that are according to nature.[102]

'Ogdoas' here does not refer to eight planetary demons, or even

---

[100] e.g. in the *Apocalypse of Abraham* 19: 9, the stars are all said to be in fifth heaven. In *2 Enoch* 11, sun, moon, and stars are all in fourth heaven (for the question of whether the heavenly bodies are thought of as alive in this latter treatise, see F. I. Andersen's note in Charlesworth, *Pseudepigrapha*, 1. 120 f.). Cf. *The Second Treatise of the Great Seth* (NH 7. 58. 18–21).

[101] Hippolytus *Ref.* 7. 25. 4 (295. 20 f. Marcovich), cf. 10. 14. 7 f. (392. 32–8).

[102] Richard Reitzenstein, *Poimandres* (Leipzig: Teubner, 1904), 54 (from *PGM* 13. 741–6, 752–4), quoted by Walter Scott, *Hermetica* (Oxford: Clarendon, 1925), 2. 64 f. n. 5. See also the *Sophia Jesu Christi* 95. 12 f. (230 Till/Schenke), and Sagnard's note to Clement of Alex. *Exc. ex Theod.* 63. 1 (184–7).

to a demon in the fixed sphere, but has simply become a conventional way of referring to heavenly authority. Once 'Hebdomad' or 'Ogdoad' refer to a single entity rather than a group of individual beings, the connection of this hebdomad or ogdoad to particular planets or spheres becomes rather hazy. Language which may once have had an astronomical meaning has been transformed into something different. A central part of this process (again with reference to the days of the week) was early Christian discussion of the significance of the numbers seven and eight, where 'eight' becomes a symbol of perfection because the Christian sabbath is the 'eighth day' replacing the Jewish sabbath, which accordingly is a symbol of imperfection.[103] The net result is that the importance of the visible heavens fades into the background, even if it does not quite disappear.

Thus two very different attitudes about the heavens are found in that large body of texts which are called gnostic. On the one hand, gnosticism was influenced by astronomical speculation, with the result that some gnostics certainly did link heavenly demons with definite heavenly bodies. In these cases, the concept of evil powers located in certain stars or planets is integrated with gnostic myth. On the other hand, the idea that such souls inhabit or inhere in certain heavenly bodies is sometimes only present in a secondary way, overlaid by more central numerological, mythological, or astrological speculations.

Different recensions of the *Apocryphon of John* exemplify both tendencies. The *Apocryphon* states[104] that the first archon, Ialtabaoth, brought forth twelve authorities (ἐξουσίαι). Seven kings were established, one over each firmament up to the seventh heaven, and five over the depth of the abyss. The upper archons created seven powers for themselves, and these in turn created angels until there were 365 in all. This was the hebdomad of the week, which was united in Ialtabaoth's thought with seven (of the twelve) authorities, and each of the seven powers was placed over a heavenly firmament. Each archon thus has two names, one by which he is powerful and one by which he can be

---

[103] See Franz Dölger, 'Zur Symbolik des altchristlichen Taufhauses', *AuC* 4 (1934), 165–82, and Waszink, *De Anima*, 429 f. In Origen: *In Ps.* 118 (21. 28–35 Dev.).

[104] NH 2. 10. 27 ff. I cite from codex 2, but have checked 3, 4, and the Berlin codex (BG).

overcome.[105] That this account is connected with teachings on the existence of planetary demons is confirmed by parallels of the seven masculine names of the seven powers with the names of demons in Ophite sources, where the association of these demons with planets is explicit.[106] The Berlin text of the *Apocryphon*, however, says that the first archon together with the powers produced Fate (εἱμαρμένη), and 'bound the gods of heaven, angels, demons, and humanity through measures, seasons, and times, so that they might be lords over all'.[107] In this recension, we see that the role of specifically planetary or astral beings is in fact quite humble, for they are subordinated to higher powers which are not clearly located. This astrological approach which subordinates the stars to the powers of fate is common both in the *Corpus Hermeticum* and in gnosticism.[108]

In other texts astral demons are less important simply because they are only one myth among many. Here allusion may be made to heavenly demons, but they may also have little importance. For example, in an untitled work from Nag Hammadi (now called *On the Origin of the World*) there arise in chaos as part of the creation seven androgynous powers of the seven heavens, each with masculine and feminine names. Each is said to dwell in a heaven, and so may have been thought of as planets, but again their leader, the demiurge Ialtabaoth, is called the Hebdomad. Since 'Hebdomad' is taken as the name of a demon rather than as a reference to the seven planets, it is likely that another myth is in effect.[109] Similarly, the Valentinians said that the seven heavens

[105] That planets have secret names is also asserted in *Pistis Sophia* 4. 137 (357. 10–17 Schmidt/MacDermot), in *CCAG* 8. 2. 154–7, and frequently in the magic papyri, e.g. *PGM* 1. 148–95.

[106] See R. van den Broeck, 'The Creation of Adam's Psychic Body', *Studies in Gnosticism and Hellenistic Religions*, FS Gilles Quispel, EPRO 91 (Leiden: E. J. Brill, 1981), 38–57. Van den Broeck puts the *Apocryphon* in the tradition of texts in which the soul's pneumatic body is made by the planets. For the Ophites see below n. 128.

[107] In codex 2 fate only 'mixes with' the gods, which are not referred to as heavenly (i.e. heaven is not subordinated to the powers), and the first archon acts with the authorities (i.e. the twelve) rather than with the powers, BG 72. 3–11 (184 Till/Schenke), NH 2. 28. 17–32.

[108] See CH frag. 12 (3. 61 N/F), 13. 12 (2. 205 N/F); ps.-Apuleius *Asclep.* 19 (2. 319. 5–8 N/F), frag. 6. 5 (3, 35 N/F): Hermetica ap. J. Lydus *De Mens.* 4. 7 (70. 20 ff. Wünsch), *Trimorph. Prot.* NH 13. 43. 15–26; Clement *Exc. ex Theod.* 70. 2 (194 Sagnard); Bardesanes ap. René Cadiou, *Introduction au système origène* (Paris: Les Belles Lettres, 1932), 33, and further Nock, 'Hermetica', *Essays*, 1. 27.

[109] NH 2. 101 f. and 125. 19 ff.

are noetic angels. Once more they are subordinated to the demiurge, who is called the Hebdomad, and to another individual who is called the Ogdoad, who is the demiurge's mother Achamoth.[110] In view of the complicated mythologies of these groups, it is hard to imagine that when the individuals who used these texts referred to the demiurge Ialtabaoth they all thought of Saturn, and when they referred to Achamoth they all thought of the fixed sphere. Other sets of problems appear to have had much greater importance. Again, when the Valentinian Marcus says that each of the seven heavens utters a vowel, and these create the world below, this may appear to suggest that the planets are living, demiurgic powers, but Marcus' thought is concerned mainly with numerology and shows little interest in speculations on the planets.[111]

We have seen (and shall see) many texts which speak of the soul's ascent through the seven planets, but it is important to recognize that a number of very diverse religious and philosophical concepts have contributed to the development of this theme in the Hellenistic era, and have greatly complicated its analysis.[112] In some texts the planets have an important role, but in many others their significance is difficult to determine.

The *Apocalypse of Paul* from Nag Hammadi illustrates the kind of problem which sometimes occurs in trying to understand gnostic myths in astronomical terms. Paul ascends to the third heaven in the Spirit (following 2 Corinthians 12: 2–4), and then passes toll collectors in the fifth and sixth heavens, again by the help of the Spirit. These toll collectors cast down the souls of those who had sinned in their earthly lives back into bodies (and so, as in the *Timaeus* myth, compel a transmigration of souls). Finally, in the seventh heaven Paul meets an old man who attempts to block his path. Instructed by the Spirit, Paul delivers a formula and then a sign to the old man, and so is enabled to rise to the ogdoad. There Paul is greeted by the twelve apostles. Then they rise to the ninth and tenth heavens and Paul greets his fellow spirits, and so

---

[110] Iren. *AH* 1. 5. 2 (1. 2. 80 R/D), 1. 5. 4 (1. 2. 84 R/D).

[111] Iren. *AH* 1. 14. 7 (1. 2. 226–8 R/D).

[112] See J. Flamant, 'Sotériologie et systèmes planétaires', in U. Bianchi and M. J. Vermaseren (eds.), *La soteriologia dei culti orientali nell' impero romano*, EPRO 92 (Leiden: E. J. Brill, 1982), 223.

achieves the ultimate goal of pneumatic perfection, at which point the treatise ends.[113]

There is obviously room here for an astronomical interpretation. Paul's 'third heaven' of 2 Corinthians is expanded to seven, with each heaven guarded by malevolent spirits past which Paul may travel since he possesses the knowledge (γνῶσις) of the Spirit. The twelve apostles are probably put in the ogdoad (rather than in the ninth or tenth heavens, as one might have expected) so that they can be identified with the signs of the zodiac, a common practice in early Christianity, following the earlier Jewish identification of the zodiac with the twelve patriarchs.[114] One can readily imagine a mythic interpretation in which a perilous journey through the seven planets is followed by a happy trip through the twelve signs located in the fixed sphere. But again there are features which are not part of such a myth: the one dominant evil figure is not identified with the dominant planet, the sun, but instead with the Jewish God, Daniel's 'ancient of days', located (as often in apocalyptic),[115] in the seventh heaven. The most dangerous figure in heaven is depicted less as a planet, and more as the Hebdomad and demiurge, and as God of the despised Old Testament. An astronomical myth has been overlaid by a new and very different myth.

In short, it is often simply hard to tell how important the stars or planets are in a given passage. When Saturninus and Menander say the world was made by seven angels, do they mean the planets?[116] When the *Gospel of the Hebrews* says Christ was in Mary's womb for seven months, does this allude to a descent through the seven planets?[117] When in the *History of Joseph the Carpenter* Joseph travels through seven aeons of darkness,[118] is the author making a conscious reference to a heavenly journey through the evil planets on the way to the fixed sphere, or is he adopting a conventional way of speaking about the departed soul which is no longer connected with

[113] NH 5. 17. 19–24. 9.
[114] See Jean Daniélou, *Primitive Christian Symbols*, trans. Donald Attwater (Baltimore: Helicon, 1964), 124–35.
[115] See above n. 98.
[116] Iren. *AH* 1. 24. 1 (1. 2. 320–2 R/D).
[117] Frag. 1 (Hennecke/Schneemelcher, trans. Wilson 1. 163).
[118] 22. 1 (18 Morenz). Cf. the soul's ascent through the seven powers of wrath in the *Gospel of Mary* (BG 16. 1 ff.).

speculations on the physical heavens? This type of judgement is
not easy to make, but it would appear that in this era
astronomical language is often used for purposes which are not
astronomical.[119]

But even if the role of the visible heavenly bodies is not always
clear or central in gnostic speculation, there are many texts which
do speak openly of astral demons. Some texts, influenced by a
more general application of astrological teachings, personify and
demonize the stars. The *Paraphrase of Shem* says that Nature gives
each of the winds and demons a star, and through the stars they
control life on earth.[120] It also juxtaposes 'demons and stars' with
'powers and authorities'.[121] Or again, the Valentinian *Excerpta ex
Theodoto* claims that invisible powers guide the stars and specifically the zodiac, and that these powers are in some cases good, in
other cases evil, and in other cases mixed.[122] An early Christian
sect called the Peratae believed that the stars were gods of
destruction, symbolized in scripture by the serpents who attacked
the Israelites in the wilderness.[123] Our world of generation and
corruption is ruled by emanations from these evil stars.[124] The
book of Elchasai, which was central to a Jewish sect in eastern
Syria, warns against the power of evil stars and regulates the
group's characteristic baptismal rite in accordance with astrological observations.[125]

More common once again than the treatment of stellar
demons, however, is the discussion of planetary demons, similar
to the discussion of Mithraic texts above, but now (as with
Numenius and some of the *Hermetica*) with a distinctly negative
interpretation. As many scholars have noted, the idea that the
soul descends into generation at birth and ascends to the fixed
sphere at death through evil planetary demons which burden

---

[119] In this context it should be noted that the στοιχεῖα referred to in Col. 2: 8, 20
probably are not evil planetary powers but simply elements, see Eduard
Schweizer, 'Slaves of the Elements and Worshipers of Angels: Gal. 4: 3, 9 and Col.
2: 8, 18, 20', *JBL* 107 (1988), 455–68, and Festugière, *L'Idéal*, 107 n. 1.

[120] NH 7. 27. 25 f.

[121] NH 7. 34. 7.

[122] 69–71 (192–4 Sagnard). Cf. also *CH* 16. 14–16 (2. 236 f. N/F).

[123] Hippolytus *Ref.* 5. 16. 6 f. (183. 30–9 Marcovich).

[124] Ibid. 5. 15. 2 f. (181. 4–13 Marcovich).

[125] *Ref.* 9. 16 (362. 7–20 Marcovich). For Origen's knowledge of this group and
its literature see Eusebius *HE* 6. 38 (2. 140 Bardy).

and obstruct it is important in gnosticism.[126] One gnostic group which had such teachings about planetary demons was the Ophites, who were known both to Celsus and Origen.[127] The Ophites believe there are seven evil archons, which are each given Hebrew names and called the superior holy Hebdomad. Already we see that the word 'hebdomad' is given a more literal meaning, referring to seven beings rather than one. Furthermore Irenaeus says that the Ophites explicitly identify the 'holy Hebdomad' with the planets,[128] and similarly Origen writes that there is a 'sympathy' between the archons and the planets in Ophite thought.[129] They are themselves invisible, but each rules in its own region in heaven, i.e. in its own planetary sphere, controlling life in heaven and on earth.[130] Since they are altogether evil, they continually incite mankind to apostasy, idolatry, and contempt for all things.[131] The Ophites taught that Christ descended through the seven heavens at the time of Jesus' baptism disguised as the sons of each of the archons, and by degrees took away their powers.[132] After the Resurrection he remained on earth for eighteen months and passed on knowledge from above to his disciples.[133] This knowledge probably again included the formulas which the initiate had to recite in order to get through the heavenly gates which are guarded by these archons.[134]

Such journeys were not uncommon in the literature of the period. The *Pistis Sophia* speaks of the defence (ἀπολογία) which

---

[126] W. Anz regarded this as the central characteristic of gnosticism, *Zur Frage nach dem Ursprung des Gnostizismos*, TU 15. 4 (Leipzig: J. C. Hinrich, 1897), especially 58 f. n. 2, though few go this far. On planetary demons see Hans Jonas, *Gnosis* 1. 181–5, and Nilsson, *Geschichte*, 2. 618 f.

[127] Origen disapproves of them, *CCel*. 6. 24 (2. 94. 22–4 K.) and thinks they are few in number, 6. 26 (2. 96. 22 f. K.); cf. frag. 47 in 1 Cor. 13: 3 (30. 31–5 ed. Jenkins), In Matth. Comm. Ser. 33 (11. 60. 30–61. 1 K1.).

[128] *AH* 1. 30. 9 (1. 2. 376 R/D).

[129] *CCel*. 6. 31 (2. 101. 10 f. K.); cf. Wilhelm Bousset, 'Gnosis, Gnostiker' *PW* 7. 2 (1912), 1511.

[130] 'per ordinem sedentes in caelo secundum generationem ipsorum, non apparentes, regere quoque caelestia et terrestria . . .', Iren. *AH* 1. 30. 5 (1. 2. 368 R/D).

[131] *AH* 1. 30. 9 (1. 2. 376 R/D).

[132] *AH* 1. 30. 12 (1. 2. 380 R/D). Jesus' baptism: 1. 30. 14 (1. 2. 382 R/D).

[133] *AH* 1. 30. 14 (1. 2. 382–4 R/D); cf. the *Apocryphon of James* (NH 1. 2. 19–21).

[134] See the formulas (in reverse order) ap. Origen *CCel*. 6. 31 (2. 100. 32–102. 4 K.), and above n. 40.

the soul gives before five evil planetary archons.[135] In the *Ascent of Isaiah* (a text which Origen used), after passing through the top two heavens which were not evil, Jesus descends through the next five heavens disguised as the angels of those heavens, and gives the proper formulas to pass through each of their heavenly gates.[136] Epiphanius reports that a group called the Archontics, who use the *Ascent of Isaiah*, have a book called the *Harmony* which claims there are archons in each of the seven heavens ruled by 'the shining mother' in the eighth, 'as in other heresies'. This group believes that the uninitiated soul becomes the food of these archons, but again by giving the proper defence ($\dot{\alpha}\pi o\lambda o\gamma \acute{\iota}\alpha$) before them the soul may escape and rise beyond the heavens to the 'Mother and Father of all things'.[137] There were instruction books on what the soul should say to the powers in its ascent through the heavens—Epiphanius refers to a revelation discourse in the *Gospel of Philip* (apparently different from the Nag Hammadi text) in which Christ teaches this knowledge to his followers.[138]

The *Testimony of Truth* also knows about planetary malevolence. It says that the 'old leaven' is 'the errant ($\pi\lambda\acute{\alpha}\nu\eta$) desire of the angels and the demons and the stars'.[139] Disapproving of those Christians who seek salvation through martyrdom, the *Testimony* says that their boasts are in fact made 'through the agency of the wandering stars' (the planets).[140] And it too knows of the inability of evil souls '[to pass by ($\pi\alpha\rho\acute{\alpha}\gamma\omega$)] the archon of [darkness]'.[141] Mention could also be made of a Christian gem, described by Reitzenstein (who dates it to the third century AD), in which a shepherd carries one lamb and has six other lambs at his feet, with seven stars in the sky, which is probably meant to

---

[135] Defence: 3. 113 (292. 12–14 Schmidt/MacDermot); planets: 4. 136 (356. 2–14), cf. 1. 22 (32. 14–20).

[136] 10 (2. 659–61 Hennecke/Schneemelcher, trans. Wilson); cf. the *Epistula Apostolorum* 13 (in ibid. 1. 198), *The Second Treatise of the Great Seth* (NH 7. 56. 21 ff.), *Pistis Sophia* 1. 7 (12. 1–6 Schmidt/MacDermot), and the *Trimorphic Protennoia* (NH 13. 49 f.). Origen's use: see *In Jesu Nave* Hom. 2. 1 (7. 297. 12 B.).

[137] *Pan.* 40. 2–8 (2. 82. 14–83. 10 Holl); food: also the Gnostics in 26. 10. 8 (1. 288. 8 f. Holl). Mother: see Bousset 'Gnosis', 1513–15.

[138] *Pan.* 26. 13. 2 (1. 292. 13–20 Holl).

[139] NH 9. 29. 15–18 (trans. Giversen/Pearson).

[140] 9. 34. 7–10 (trans. ibid.).

[141] 9. 30. 16 (trans. ibid., who note that $\pi\alpha\rho\acute{\alpha}\gamma\omega$ is here a technical term).

represent Christ the Good Shepherd preserving his flock from the evil planetary powers.[142]

The reaction of Plotinus to an unknown group of gnostics is particularly interesting, since he may have had the same teacher as Origen, namely Ammonius, and in any case Plotinus had a comparable philosophical training.[143] In his treatise *Against the Gnostics* Plotinus complains that the gnostics do not call sun, stars, and World Soul their brethren, though they were willing to do so with the very worst people.[144] The idea that their souls might be more free from passion and more divine than the stars outrages Plotinus.[145] The gnostics (he says) claim they are better than heaven without having had to do anything meritorious, in stark contrast to the Plotinian view that the heavenly bodies are the clearest image of the intelligible world.[146] They believe there is a 'tragedy of terrors' in the heavenly spheres,[147] and that learning certain spells would enable their souls to pass by the evil planetary archons and return to their supercelestial home. Plotinus describes their rites:

For when they write spells to say to them [the heavenly powers] . . . they are simply uttering charms and enchantments and persuasions in the idea that these powers will obey a call and be led about by a word from any of us who is in some degree trained to use the appropriate forms in the appropriate way—certain melodies, certain voices, roughly breathed and hissed sounds, and all else to which is ascribed magic potency upon them.[148]

Thus Origen wrote in a time when many spoke in dread of the evil which awaited us in heaven, and especially of wicked planetary powers. A key goal of many influential religious tracts in this setting was to provide the initiate with protection from evil forces located in particular heavenly bodies or spheres.

[142] *Poimandres*, 113, Festugière, *L'Idéal*, 115, and in general J. Quasten, 'Der gute Hirte in frühchristlicher Totenliturgie und Grabeskunst', *SeT* 121 (1956), 373–406.

[143] See Porphyry ap. Eusebius *HE* 6. 19. 6 f. (2. 114 f. Bardy). Heinrich Dörrie, however, argues that Origen's Ammonius and Plotinus' Ammonius were two separate people: 'Ammonios, der Lehrer Plotins', *Hermes* 83 (1955), 439–77.

[144] 2. 9. 18. 17–20.

[145] 2. 9. 5. 1–16. Cf. Arnobius *Adv. Nat.* 2. 19 (63. 10–14 Reifferscheid).

[146] 2. 9. 9. 56–9; clearest image: 2. 9. 4. 26–32, cf. 2. 9. 13. 14–20, Porphyry *In Tim.* frag. 52 (39. 18–27 Sodano).

[147] 2. 9. 13. 6–8.

[148] 2. 9. 14. 2–8, trans. Stephen MacKenna (adapted). Hippolytus says that the Carpocratians use incantations, charms, spells, and mediums to gain power over 'the rulers', Hippolytus *Ref.* 7. 32. 5 (316. 24–8 Marcovich); cf. Arnobius *Adv. Nat.* 2. 13 (58. 20–3 Reifferscheid).

7

CLEMENT OF ALEXANDRIA

One test for the importance of these views for Origen is to see their influence on Clement of Alexandria, who was active in Alexandria during Origen's youth, and who also represents a similar theological approach. Both were very interested in classical pagan culture (though Origen pursued philosophy more seriously and, in sharp contrast to Clement, virtually ignored literature and poetry), and both used allegory to understand Christian scripture in its terms. One of Origen's early writings (now lost) was a *Stromateis*, which must have been influenced by Clement's lengthy work of the same title. Eusebius says that Origen was Clement's student, but regardless of whether Origen studied under him in some type of school setting (which is open to question), he certainly has been influenced by him theologically.[1]

In all three of the great Alexandrians, Philo, Clement, and Origen, there is an attraction to speculations on the stars, but also an awareness that these issues are easily misunderstood. There was a great curiosity about cosmological matters, and yet also warnings about potentially dangerous conclusions. This is obvious in Clement, who is an uncompromising opponent of the Hellenistic religion of the heavens, particularly in his *Protreptikos*, which is addressed to pagans. He attacks Alcmaeon of Croton for believing that the stars are gods and alive, and Xenocrates for suggesting that the planets and the cosmos are eight gods.[2] The heavenly bodies are not gods but are at best administrators[3] and instruments established by God to measure time.[4] Like Philo, he is also a strong opponent of astrology. Those who say that the

[1] Eusebius *HE* 6. 6 (2. 94 Bardy, see his note).
[2] *Protr.* 5. 66 (1. 50. 20–4 St.), cf. 2. 26 (1. 19. 12–16 St.), 6. 67 (1. 51. 21–3 St.), 10. 102 (1. 73. 22 f. St.).
[3] *Strom.* 6. 16. 148 (2. 508. 1 St.).
[4] *Protr.* 4. 63 (1. 48. 7–10 St.), 10. 102 (1. 73. 22 f.).

stars are the primary cause of growth and change in the universe take away what is in fact a prerogative of the Father.[5] The stars do not cause events, but because of the sympathy which binds together all the parts of the cosmos,[6] the stars act as signs of what is to come.[7] The claim, so frequently made, that the stars are powerful and deserving of worship is totally false. Therefore Clement not only passes on Philo's view that Abraham began as an astrologer but then proceeded to higher insights,[8] he also suggests that Psalm 18: 3 (19: 2), 'night proclaims knowledge to night', indicates the teaching of Enoch that evil angels taught the human race astonomy, divination, and the other dark arts.[9]

The discoveries made in Egypt, especially in this century, of many Coptic gnostic texts which have survived both persecution and time confirms the power of gnostic (and, at a later point, Manichaean) speculation in early Christian Egypt. This influence is evident in Clement, who habitually uses gnostic terminology,[10] and indeed calls himself a 'gnostic' more than any other extant Christian writer of this era. Clement, however, transforms gnostic language, giving it quite a different meaning (as in fact he does with ecclesiastical language).[11] In Clement's theology gnostic ideas are used like a vaccine: he transmits a dilute form of them in order to render the more developed gnostic faith powerless. For Clement could never be the type of gnostic who wrote and used any of the diverse texts in the Berlin and Nag Hammadi codices, since he strongly disapproves of the radical asceticism practised by groups such as these. He calls himself a gnostic, but at the same time attempts to distance himself from 'heresy', and this includes all of what modern scholars would normally call gnosticism.

[5] *Strom.* 6. 16. 148 (2. 507. 30–4 St.).
[6] *Protr.* 1. 5 (1. 5. 33–6. 1 St.). The idea is a commonplace, see Moreau, *L'Âme*, 164, W. and H. Gundel, 'Planeten', 230.
[7] *Ecl. Proph.* 55 (3. 152. 15–19 St.): neither events nor dreams, cf. *Exc. ex Theod.* 70. 2 (194 Sagnard). This again is very common in philosophical circles, see Utto Riedinger, *Die heilige Schrift im Kampf der griechischen Kirche gegen die Astrologie* (Innsbruck: Wagner, 1956), 177–82.
[8] *Strom.* 5. 1. 8 (2. 331. 1–9 St.), 6. 10. 80 (2. 471. 27–30 St.), 6. 11. 84 (2. 473. 20 f. St.); see above ch. 5 n. 70.
[9] *Ecl. Proph.* 53. 4 (3. 152. 8f. St., citing *1 Enoch* 8: 3).
[10] Such as γνῶσις, ἀνάπαυσις, ἐγκράτεια. See n. 12 below.
[11] Einar Molland, *The Conception of the Gospel in the Alexandrian Theology* (Oslo: Jacob Dybwad, 1938), 6.

Clement believes that there are angels who oversee the ascent of souls and see to it that souls which are still attached to a desire for material things do not reach heaven. To get past these angels, the soul must show some sign of its own purity.[12] This is similar to many gnostic views, and the lack of any clear connection of the angels with visible heavenly phenomena is not unusual in gnostic cosmologies. Now, however, the guardians in heaven are no longer evil. Because this is so, Clement avoids the assumption that the fire which Jesus in the New Testament often says awaits the unworthy soul is a reference to a physical fire, which some gnostics identified with the heavenly bodies, saying instead that it was a reference to the fire of wisdom.[13] Clement does not see this world or the heavens as demonic, and this is a critical distinction between his theology and that of gnosticism.

A more important influence for Clement's teachings on the stars are the speculations of contemporary philosophical literature. Echoes of the Hellenistic schoolroom and of Philo abound in his writings. In Platonic fashion he regards astronomy as a propaedeutic for philosophy[14] (which, turning the tables on the philosophers, he regards as a preparation for true knowledge),[15] and so as leading to the knowledge of God.[16] Like so many of his predecessors, Clement believes that humanity had its origins in heaven, and that salvation is a return there.[17] With Philo (and also Justin Martyr), he proposes that God allowed the pagans to worship the heavenly bodies so that they might be spared from atheism and might have at least some knowledge of the divine.[18] Again with Philo, he passes on the Stoic commonplace that man was given an erect posture in order to contemplate heaven.[19] As

[12] See Lilla, *Clement*, 182 f., who cites 4. 18. 116 (2. 299. 18–21 St.) and 117 (2. 299. 24–8 St.). The Christian 'passes through the spiritual beings' onto heaven by his knowledge, *Strom.* 7. 13. 82 (3. 59. 2 f. St.).

[13] *Strom.* 7. 6. 34 (3. 27. 5–8 St.), cf. *Paed.* 1. 6. 46 (1. 117. 28–118, 4 St.); gnostics: see Plotinus 2. 9. 13. 9–14.

[14] *Strom.* 6. 11. 90 (2. 477. 7–19 St.), 6. 10. 80 (2. 471. 27–30 St.).

[15] 6. 14. 108 (2. 487. 11–14 St.). See Walther Völker, *Der wahre Gnostiker nach Clemens Alexandrinus* TU 57. 2 (Berlin: Akademie, 1952), 86 and 350 n. 2.

[16] See Lilla, *Clement*, 169 f., 172.

[17] Origins: *Protr.* 25. 4 (1. 19. 9–12 St.); return: *Dives* 3. 6 (3. 162. 6–9 St.).

[18] *Strom.* 6. 14. 110 (2. 487. 11–14 St.); Justin *Dial.* 55. 1 (154 Goodspeed).

[19] *Strom.* 4. 26. 163 (2. 320. 22 f. St., see his note), cf. Seneca *Ep.* 92. 30 (358. 22–359. 3 Reynolds); Philo: see Runia, *Philo*, 325. The idea is attacked by Galen, *De Usu Part.* 3. 3 (1. 133. 14–134. 3 Helmreich).

in Stoic/Peripatetic cosmology, he believes that the four elements are arranged as spheres and make up the world beneath the moon,[20] and accepts the standard classroom view that there are seven heavens surrounded by a fixed eighth sphere.[21] With some reserve he even suggests that the fixed sphere borders on the noetic, superheavenly world of God familiar from Plato's *Phaedrus*.[22] As part of his argument that pagan culture is a preparation for the gospel, Clement interprets the myth of Er (whom Clement identifies with Zoroaster) from the end of Plato's *Republic*, and suggests (evidently with approval) that Plato means that the soul at birth descends through the twelve signs of the zodiac and again ascends through them at death. In the standard fashion of contemporary pagan philosophy, which often used the figure of Hercules as an illustration, Clement also writes that the twelve labours of Hercules symbolize the difficulties which the soul must go through before winning freedom from this world.[23] In another passage, he says that the five stones and two carbuncles on the high priest's robe are the seven planets, which are controlled by powers established by divine providence, and that these were responsible for creation. Clement thinks that these powers and creation as a whole are good, which sounds like the classical Hellenistic teaching that the seven planets are benevolent demiurgic powers.[24]

An interest in both philosophical and gnostic speculations seems to have led him to a new interpretation of Christian eschatology which influenced Origen. It is preserved in the *Eclogae Propheticae*, which are a series of notes that were not meant to be published in their present form, but which by some strange turn of events are still extant. Another set of notes which survived along with it, the more famous *Excerpta ex Theodoto*, was apparently a preparation for a work on Valentinianism, and mainly represents Valentinian views. On the other hand the *Eclogae* are rough notes apparently made in preparation for a work on the interpretation of scripture, and mostly reflect

---

[20] *Strom.* 5. 14. 106 (2. 397. 16 f. St.).
[21] *Strom.* 4. 25. 159 (2. 318. 28–319. 2 St.).
[22] Ibid.
[23] *Strom.* 5. 14. 103 (2. 395. 17–396. 4 St.); Er as Zoroaster: see already Colotes ap. Proclos *In Remp.* (2. 109. 8–14 Kroll).
[24] *Strom.* 5. 6. 37 (2. 351. 8–17 St., see his note).

Clement's own position. One passage is particularly interesting. In it Clement says that the stars are 'spiritual bodies, in communion with and governed by their appointed angels'.[25] He follows this with a long interpretation of Psalm 18: 5 (19: 4), 'He set his tent in the sun.' Clement denies the gnostic interpretation of Hermogenes that Christ's body is taken from the sun,[26] and passes on his own teacher Pantaenus' view that Old Testament prophecy has a future as well as a past reference, so that this passage in fact looks forward to the Resurrection. In the end the righteous all return to the same unity, where in different ways they will be, as Clement says, ' "gleaming like the sun" [cf. Matthew 13: 43], or rather in the sun, since a ruling angel is in the sun'. Here they are put in charge of days with the angels who are in the sun, under the rule of a commanding angel (cf. Revelation 19: 17), and so provide light to the earth. Eventually, however, they progress to 'the first abiding place', the place of rest (ἀνάπαυσις), and are replaced by those who are ontologically subordinate.[27] The identification of the heavenly bodies with angels is thus put forward, and combined with two speculations found elsewhere in pagan Platonism, first that the planets might serve as an intermediate dwelling for the soul on its way to its final resting place,[28] and second that the soul might ascend at death to the sun.[29] The suggestion that this might represent a stage in the soul's moral progress, which would continue after death, is apparently Clement's (or perhaps Pantaenus') own. It is not certain how serious Clement was about this idea that the soul ascended to a higher ontological position within the sun, especially since in the next section he puts forward another interpretation in which the sun (ἥλιος) is taken as a reference to the Hebrew word for God, *El*, so that the passage in question is interpreted to mean 'he set his tent in God'. But this adoption of pagan imagery clearly was not a random note of Clement's since Origen similarly will propose that the heavenly bodies (and the different angelic ranks, which Clement treats in the following

---

[25] 55. 1 (3. 152. 14 f. St.). Cf. also *In Epistola Iudae* frag. (3. 207. 7–12 St.).

[26] Hermogenes: see Hippolytus *Ref.* 8. 17. 3 f. (337. 14–23 Marcovich). Hermogenes' view may be connected with exegesis of 2 Cor. 5: 1–4.

[27] *Ecl.* 56 (3. 152 f. St.).

[28] Calcidius *In Tim.* 200 (220, 10–17 Waszink).

[29] Iamblichus *De Comm. Math. Sc.* 6 (28. 1–16 Festa), and above ch. 6 n. 21.

section) might serve as stages on the soul's progress to its ultimate goal beyond the fixed sphere.[30] So although the stars are not discussed as often in Clement as in Philo, and though the influence of pagan and gnostic astral speculation only surfaces occasionally in his thought, theories on the special place of the heavenly bodies are present in non-gnostic Christian circles and waiting for a fuller treatment. This is where Origen begins his work on the stars.

The relation of the soul to the star was a matter of debate in the Hellenistic period, and though there was a wide consensus that the stars represented some power greater than humanity but less than God, there was little agreement on how these beings should be described. The positions of Plato, Aristotle, and the Stoics on the physical nature and religious function of the stars were in many ways incompatible, and the tendency of later Hellenistic philosophers to confuse and harmonize rather than resolve these differences complicated efforts to speak of the stars in philosophically coherent terms.

In the second and third centuries of our era, a number of thinkers explained the soul's relation to the stars (which everyone presupposed) by claiming that the soul had an 'astral body'. This was composed during the soul's descent into generation, and the manner of its composition was a matter of debate. An optimistic interpretation of Plato saw the role of the heavenly bodies as essentially positive, and this was the view of the classical tradition of Platonism and astrology (and of Mithraism, which was a cross between the two). This tradition of cosmological interpretation passed on many of the ideas of the classical period, without making coherent many of the proposals that had been put forward by the great philosophers of the past. The stars were honoured—often extravagantly. But the questions of who they are and what they do remained without consensus or even clear exposition, as Porphyry pointed out in his letter to Anebo.

Hellenistic interpretation of the stars was further complicated

[30] See below ch. 9 with n. 57. Note that in the next paragraph, *Ecl.* 57 (3. 154. 5–13 St.), Clement speaks of the training individuals receive after death for a thousand years from ontologically superior angels. This is again similar to Origen's view.

in this period by a new and definitely negative tendency in Platonism. This was the path of Numenius, some of the Hermetica, and of 'gnosticism', and was the result of the fusion of popular philosophy and astrology with a negative appraisal of humanity's place (and options) in the universe. This cosmic pessimism (which was also strengthened in its polemic against the visible heavens by some aspects of Jewish apocalyptic) was a prolific source of cosmological discussion, even though the connections of these discussions to visible phenomena are at times hazy. It clearly was a source with which Origen, in the peculiar context of Alexandrian Christianity, had to come to grips.

But Origen's intellectual development is not only a matter of trends and tendencies, but also of individuals. Philo is of great importance to Origen because he combined a great respect for Hellenistic philosophy with Jewish religion and the interpretation of scripture. His example as an apologist and exegete, his discussions of 'sympathy', his condemnation of astrology and the worship of heaven, and yet at the same time his essentially pagan cosmological framework, were an important example to Origen.

Clement is somewhat more guarded than Philo in cosmological matters, but is no less important in the development of Origen's own views on the heavens. Clement is aware of the pagan and gnostic depiction of the stars as either gods or evil demons, and rejects both. Most important, he also sees the opportunity to incorporate contemporary lore on the stars into the Christian doctrine of life after death. The views of these two Alexandrians together with the speculations on the heavens from a wide range of pagan, Jewish, and gnostic sources provide the background to Origen's theological appropriation of the stars, which will be the subject of the third and final part.

PART III

8

ORIGEN AND THE STARS

It is one of the paradoxes of the Christian religion that its saviour is the *Logos*, or Reason incarnate, and yet its doctrines are 'folly to Greeks' and in conflict with the wisdom of this world. Christians claimed Reason as their own, but had to defend themselves against pagan philosophers who were full of scorn and (even worse) of damaging criticisms about the Bible and its teachings. Justin Martyr wore the philosopher's cloak and Clement of Alexandria regarded 'the love of wisdom' as a preliminary stage in the promulgation of the gospel, but it was far more common for early Christians to regard philosophy as a source of error and heresy. Even Marcion and the gnostics, who were often accused of being compromised by the teachings of pagan philosophy, frequently attacked it.[1] Scholars have long been interested in Origen's obvious use of the classical pagan tradition, but he wrote at a time when such expertise was more of an accusation than a boast, and this colours his attitude toward it. Waszink notes that Origen differs from Philo in never seeing philosophy as a divine gift to the Greeks, and from Clement in never describing it as a factor within divine providence.[2] Throughout his writings Origen was almost instinctively hostile to philosophy, regarding it as a seducer and as inevitably mixed with folly.[3] Granted there is something conventional about this attitude—in fact, some pagan

[1] Marcionite/gnostic errors are due to philosophy: Hippolytus *Ref.* 7. 29 (304. 6 f. Marcovich) and *passim*; Tertullian *De Praescr.* 7 (1. 192 Dekkers). See already in the New Testament Col. 2: 8. For Marcion's attacks on philosophy see Gerhard May, *Schöpfung aus dem Nichts*, AKG 48 (Berlin: Walter de Gruyter, 1978), 58 n. 72, and Adolf von Harnack, *Marcion* (Berlin: Akademie, 1960), 125*. Gnostic attacks: see Carl A. Keller, 'Das Problem des Bösen in Apokalyptik und Gnosis', in Martin Krause (ed.), *Gnosis and Gnosticism*, NHS 8 (Leiden: E. J. Brill, 1977) 89.
[2] 'Bemerkungen' 159 f.
[3] See Henri de Lubac, *Histoire et esprit* (Paris: Aubier, 1950), 80 f., Henri Crouzel, *Origène et la philosophie*, ML. T 56 (Paris: Montaigne, 1962), 67 and *passim*. Like his later opponents, he regarded it as an arrogant enemy to the simplicity of faith, *In Sam.* Hom. 1. 10 (8. 19. 14–19 B.).

philosophers struck the same pose—his feelings about this discipline are cooler than Clement's, and much cooler than Philo's. For Origen philosophy was no more than a tool within a distinctly Christian theology, and its terminology was accordingly used in a new way.[4]

In Origen's view the only proper use for philosophy was strictly to help understand scripture,[5] for it was scripture and not philosophy which was the means to true knowledge.[6] Christian apologists had always said this, but Origen's most eloquent affirmation of the importance of scripture was the amount of time and attention he gave to its interpretation. Origen adopts the philosophical assumption that the stars are alive, but when he does so his mind is always on how it might help explain thorny biblical passages or doctrinal problems which arose out of conflicts in scripture. His overriding interest is in biblical exegesis within the context of preaching and of practical theological issues.

And yet despite his mixed feelings about Hellenistic learning, Origen was strongly drawn to it. One of the best indications of a scholar's interests is the curriculum he prepares for his students, and we are fortunate to have a report about Origen's curriculum from his student Gregory Thaumaturgus. Here Origen devotes considerable attention to secular learning, including astronomy. As usual in a Platonic course of education, geometry and astronomy were propaedeutic studies—a bow to a philosophical tradition which had also been followed by Clement but which had been spurned by Origen's theological predecessor Justin Martyr.[7] For Origen, however, astronomy (like all pagan learning) was a propaedeutic, not to philosophy, but to the study of scripture.[8] Thaumaturgus says that Origen's knowledge about the natural sciences was based partly on what he had learned, but also on his own discoveries,[9] and if this report can be trusted, it

---

[4] Crouzel, *Philosophie*, 186 f.

[5] Ibid. 147.

[6] *In Ps*. 36 Hom. 3. 6 (PG 12. 1342cd), *In Ps*. 63: 6 (PG 12. 1492bc). See Clement in ch. 7 n. 15.

[7] Gregory *Orat. Pan*. 8. 113 f. (142. 18–27 Crouzel); Justin *Dial*. 2. 4 f. (92 Goodspeed). For astronomy and mathematics in philosophical education in this era see Alcinous *Did*. 7 (161. 28–162. 20 Hermann), Taurus ap. Aulus Gellius *Noc. Att*. 1. 9. 7 f. (56. 15–24 Marshall).

[8] *Ep. ad Gregorium* 1 ap. *Philocalia* 13. 1 (64. 21–65. 2 R.).

[9] *Orat. Pan*. 8. 111 (142. 14 Crouzel).

would indicate that he had a curiosity about the world which was very rare in the early church. The second-century apologist Tatian asks what good it is to know the size of the earth, the position of the stars, or the course of the sun,[10] a sentiment echoed even by Clement of Alexandria,[11] but Origen's attitude is very different. His teachings on the elements, meteorology, comets, planets, and stars display a wide knowledge of contemporary science[12] which is all the more impressive in light of the time he must have devoted to his scriptural studies and his vast literary output. As a result of these broad interests, his cosmology encompasses a degree of astronomical detail previously unknown in Christian (including gnostic) theology.

Much of this knowledge was mediated through Origen's careful study of contemporary philosophical literature. As a number of recent scholars have noted, an important influence on Origen in these speculations was middle-Platonism, a loosely bound and eclectic group of schools and individuals who emphasized the study of Plato (especially the *Timaeus*) but also drew heavily on Stoic ideas. An investigation of Origen's concept of the universe, beginning with the human mind and rising through the elements and heavenly bodies to the highest portion of creation, shows how Origen incorporates this pagan philosophical tradition into a scriptural cosmology.

Though no one has used the word 'banalité' to describe Origen's cosmology (people may like or dislike Origen but they never find him boring), much of Origen's understanding of the heavens is once again a repetition of commonplaces familiar in Hellenistic schoolrooms. Therefore discussions of Origen in philosophical terms are certainly valuable because he has been influenced by these traditions, even though it should be remembered

---

[10] *Orat.* 27 (29. 13–17 Schwartz); cf. Tertullian *De Praescr.* 14 (1. 198 f. Dekkers). There are again parallels for this attitude in pagan philosophy, see Marcus Aurelius 1. 17 (10. 23 Dalfen).

[11] *Strom.* 6. 11. 93 (2. 478. 14–21 St.).

[12] Meteorology: see *In Jer.* Hom. 8. 5 (3. 60. 1–16 Kl.); comets: *CCel.* 1. 58 (1. 109. 27–110, 2 K.); other sciences, mineralogy: *In Matth.* 10. 7 (10. 7. 2 ff. K1.), *In Ps.* 118 (67 f. Dev.), Jerome [Origen] *In Amos* 3 (318 f. Adriaen), cf. Max Wellmann, 'Die Stein- und Gemmenbücher der Antike', *Quellen und Studien zur Gesch. der Naturwissenschaft* 4 (1933), 87; zoology: *In Jer.* Hom. 17. 1 (3. 143 f. Kl.), and further Max Wellmann, *Der Physiologus*, Philol Suppl. 22 (Leipzig: Dieterich, 1931), 7, D. S. Wallace-Hadrill, *The Greek Patristic View of Nature* (Manchester: Manchester University, 1968), 31.

that he has also been deeply influenced by other, very different interests.

As in Hellenistic philosophy, so for Origen discussion of the nature and destiny of the soul and discussion of the physical heavens are intertwined. Following the Stoics, Origen speaks about rational souls (νόες or πνεύματα λογικά) in terms of fire.[13] He is distinctly Christian in his division of soul in its highest sense into mind (νοῦς), which is fallen and capable of sin, and an unfallen portion of mind, namely spirit (*pneuma*). He is, however, clearly part of the Platonic tradition in regarding this spirit as incorporeal.[14] Origen accepts the Stoic understanding of ether as made of some type of material which is very fine and subtle[15] and its view of ether as a pure type of fire naturally located at the periphery.[16] He distinguishes the invisible and unquenchable fire of punishment (Isaiah 66: 24, 2 Corinthians 4: 18) from the material fire familar on earth, though he does not identify this immaterial fire with the ether found at the edge of the cosmos.[17] Ether is the body in which soul in its higher sense makes its home before the Fall, and where it will make it again after its resurrection from the dead.[18] This ethereal body is likened (as often) to fire, and the ethereal heavenly body of e.g. the sun is said to have the same nature as light,[19] a view which is connected by Origen, as it was in contemporary speculations on the astral body, with the understanding of the human soul. As with them, the existence of a substance which was physically located at the end of the material world and on the boundary of complete incorporeality helped explain the relation of the immaterial to the material through the medium of soul.

[13] See Rüsche, *Blut*, 417.
[14] Mind/spirit: see Stephanus Tauress Bettencourt, *Doctrina Ascetica Origenis*, StAns 16 (Vatican City: Libreria Vaticana, 1945) 9, Henri Crouzel, *Théologie de l'Image de Dieu chez Origène* (Aubier: Éditions Montaigne, 1956), 131; incorporeal: *Prin.* 1. 7. 1. 10–14 (C/S), Verbeke, *Pneuma*, 453.
[15] *Prin.* 1. 7. 5. 156 f. (C/S), *CCel.* 4. 56 (2. 329. 11–16 K.).
[16] *In Prov.* 23 (*PG* 17. 221d), cf. the Peratae ap. Hippolytus *Ref.* 5. 14. 10 (180. 55 f. Marcovich).
[17] *In Matth.* Comm. Ser. 72 (11. 171. 25–32 Kl.). See further Pierre Nautin, *Origène: Homélies sur Jérémie*, SC 232 (Paris: du Cerf, 1976), 174.
[18] See below ch. 9 n. 46.
[19] Ethereal bodies: see below ch. 9 n. 46; fire: *In Rom.* 9. 41 (*PG* 14. 1244a); light: see H. Cornélis, 'Les Fondements cosmologiques de l'eschatologie d'Origène', *RevSciPhilTheol* 43 (1959), 77 n. 139. This makes ether almost immaterial, as Porphyry notes ap. Stobaeus *Ecl.* (1. 430. 6 f. Wachsmuth).

world within which soul operates is a unity of heaven and
Origen therefore rejects the Peripatetic doctrine that there
fifth element and that the physical nature of heaven differs
in all that which is beneath the moon, and he asserts the
additional elements of earth, air, fire, and water.[20] With some
hesitation, Origen suggests that the interpretation of John 4: 35
('there are still four months before the harvest comes') is, with
Philo and classical philosophy, that the four elements are
arranged by weight in spheres beneath 'the ethereal nature'.[21]
The earth is (as usual) at the centre of the cosmos, water settles
naturally on top of it, then air on top of water and earth, and fire
(in which is included ether) on top of air. Elements which are not
mixed with one another stabilize naturally in these four regions.
Following Peripatetic/Stoic cosmology, the four elements pass
into one another by their natural affinity. The type of bodies
which are formed by the combination of the elements is once
again determined by the mixture of qualities (hot, cold, dry, and
moist).[22]

Moving from earth to the heavenly regions, we again see much
that is familiar. The heavenly regions are for Origen as for all of
his pagan contemporaries a place of great beauty. The regularity
of movement in the heavenly bodies is recognized, and as with
Plato and the Stoics it serves as an argument for the existence
both of God[23] and of divine providence.[24] As in Plato and a host
of others, the planets are said to be wrongly so called since they
do not really 'err' ($\pi\lambda\alpha\nu\acute{\alpha}\omega$). Instead, they move in an orderly way
in the opposite direction of the fixed sphere.[25]

What is surprising is not the opinions but their Christian
setting. Origen is the first Christian theologian to discuss the
physical composition of the stars. With Philo, he rejects Anaxagoras' contention that the stars are fiery metal,[26] but he thinks

[20] *CCel.* 4. 56 (1. 329. 11–16 K.), *In Jo.* 13. 21. 126 (4. 245. 4 f. P.), *Prin.* 3. 6. 6.
196–205 (C/S).
[21] *In Jo.* 13. 40. 266 (4. 266. 13–18 P.). Philo: see ch. 5 n. 19; classical: see ch. 3
n. 36.
[22] *Prin.* 4. 4. 6. 236–8, 2. 1. 4. 110–14 (C/S).
[23] *CCel.* 8. 52 (2. 267. 19–268. 5 K.).
[24] *Prin.* 4. 1. 7. 188 f. (C/S, Greek), *In Ps.* 1 ap. *Philocalia* 2. 4 (39. 9–12 R.).
[25] *CCel.* 6. 22 (2. 92. 3 f. K.), 8. 52 (2. 267. 19 f. K.), *Philocalia* 23. 6 (193. 23 f.
R.). Unless otherwise stated, all extracts from the *Philocalia* are from the third
book of Origen's lost *Commentarii in Genesim.*
[26] *CCel.* 5. 11 (2. 12. 7 f. K.); see ch. 5 n. 48.

they are still made of some type of body which is ethereal in
nature.[27] And some of Origen's astronomical knowledge is fairly
sophisticated. For example, he is familiar with Hipparchus'
theory that the fixed stars move around the pole of the ecliptic
one degree every one hundred years, and that this movement is
governed by a separate, ninth sphere located above the fixed
sphere.[28] Like Philo, he also knows the scientific name of Jupiter,
'the radiant one' (ὁ φαέθων).[29] It is no surprise to see that Origen
is aware of the vast size of the cosmos, as this again was widely
recognized. He is rare among early Christian writers, however, in
knowing how to demonstrate this: he notes that unless the stars
were very far off, they would not be seen as being in the same
place in the heavens by people who were far apart on the earth.[30]

Origen's astronomical knowledge is only evident in asides that
are buried in much larger arguments, and is all the more
impressive considering that this was only a secondary interest for
him. Since Origen saw pagan learning as a preparation for
understanding the gospel, much of his cosmology comes out only
incidentally in doctrinal discussion and scriptural exegesis.
Following the view of contemporary astronomy that the sun is
the leader of the other planets, Origen interprets this in a
Christian sense, saying that the superiority of the sun illustrates
the place that the *Logos* has in the spiritual world.[31] Like most
Hellenistic philosophers he realizes that the moon reflects the
light of the sun, but he then compares this again and again to the
Church's relationship to Christ: the only light which the Church
has is that given it by the Sun of Righteousness, who is Christ.[32]
Origen passes on the standard scientific view that the earth lies at
the absolute centre of the universe, not set upon any other body,
and connects this with the exegesis of Job 26: 7 ('in the most
accurate copies', he tells us) that the earth rests on nothing but

[27] *Prin.* 1. 7. 5. 155–7 (C/S), cf. Philo *Som.* 1. 22, *Aet.* 47.
[28] *Philocalia* 23. 18 (206. 29–7. 6 R.), *Prin.* 2. 3. 6. 274–80 (C/S); Heath,
Aristarchus, 172 f. For the ninth sphere see below n. 45.
[29] *In Jer.* Latin hom. 3. 4 (8. 314. 25 f. B.). See above ch. 4 n. 29. Philo knows
this too, *QE* 2. 75; cf. also the Ophites ap. *CCel.* 6. 31 (2. 101. 11 K., referring to
Saturn).
[30] *In Matth.* Comm. Ser. 49 (11. 102. 20–5 Kl.).
[31] See Cornélis, 'Fondements', 79.
[32] *In Jo.* 1. 25. 163 (4. 31. 10–14 P.), 6. 55. 287 (4. 164. 19–21 P.), *In Gen.* Hom.
1. 5 (6. 7. 14–19 B.), *In Num.* Hom. 23. 5 (7. 217. 24 f. B.), *In Ezech.* Hom. 9. 3 (8.
411. 22–7 B.). See C. Schmitt, 'Lune (Symbolisme)' *DSp* 9 (1976), 1192 f.

the power of God.[33] Origen is familiar with the advances of contemporary astronomy, but he only uses them in a highly restricted role.

Used in this way, pagan learning could at times have an important function. A dictum of Origen's scriptural interpretation (common in his day to Jews, Christians, and pagans) was that if the literal interpretation of a passage was impossible, an allegorical interpretation must be necessary. One of the functions of pagan learning for Origen was to help determine what was possible. Interpreting Philippians 2: 10 ('that at the name of Jesus every knee should bow, in heaven and on earth and under the earth'), Origen said that this cannot be taken literally since 'the experts' have shown that the stars are spheres.[34] Or again, the stars cannot literally fall from heaven onto earth (Matthew 24: 29), because many or all of the stars are greater than the earth, and so they could not possibly fit.[35] The current state of astronomical research could be ancillary to an exposition of Christian doctrine.

Astronomy and astrology are of course sharply distinguished in modern thought, but in antiquity the two words were used interchangeably. Most experts in one tended also to be experts in the other—Ptolemy is the classic example. Thus it is not surprising that Origen, who shows an interest in astronomy, is also familiar with astrology, even though he was strongly opposed to it. He knows astrological terms like zodiac, degree, hour, minute, second,[36] conjunction,[37] meridian, and opposite meridian.[38] He realizes the importance of the Eastern horizon in casting nativities,[39] and how benign planets can blunt the power of malevolent ones.[40] It is true that most of this information probably comes from philosophical (especially Academic) attacks on astrology, but it is nevertheless unusual in the context of early

---

[33] *In Jer.* Hom. 8 (3. 55. 17–20 Kl.).

[34] *De Orat.* 31. 3 (2. 397. 4–7 K.), cf. *In Rom.* 9. 41 (PG 14, 1244a). For pagan sources see K.'s note.

[35] *In Matth.*, Comm. Ser. 49 (11. 102. 25–103, 6 Kl.); de Lubac *Histoire* 199. Greater than the earth: see Arist. *Meteor.* 339^{b}6–9, Posidonius frag. 261b (Theiler), etc.

[36] *Philocalia* 23. 17 (206. 5 f. and 16 f. R.).

[37] Ibid. 23. 18 (207. 9 f. R.).

[38] Ibid. 23. 14 (202. 18 f. R.).

[39] Ibid. 23. 17 (206. 9–12 R.).

[40] Ibid. 23. 18 (207. 9–20 R.).

Christian polemic that Origen has an informed opinion about the
astrological views he opposes.

The reason his interest in the visible heavens was only
secondary was that he believed a more important reality was to
be found above the stars. In the tradition of Plato's *Phaedrus,*
Origen refers to a celestial vault and to a purely noetic supercelestial region.[41] Origen regards this as the fourth major portion
of the world (along with heaven, earth, and that which is below
the earth); Psalm 148: 4f., which speaks of the waters above
heaven that praise the name of the Lord, is a reference to this
supercelestial region.[42] In contrast to the Valentinians, this
invisible and superheavenly world was seen as part of our own
universe and as created by God.[43] The highest heavens are the
supreme portion of this world, but are still part of creation and
subordinate to God's will.[44]

Origen refers to this region above the visible heaven (which he
once again regards as a ninth sphere above the eighth, fixed
sphere) as the celestial earth (*terra coeli*), which is the inheritance
of the blessed.[45] This is the earth of Genesis 1: 1 which God
created in the beginning, while the earth we inhabit is the 'dry
land' created on the third day according to Genesis 1: 10. So too
the heaven above the ninth sphere is the heaven created on the
first day, while the fixed sphere (which is also called 'heaven') is
the firmament made on the second day. There are thus two
earths and two heavens.[46] This is the solution he offers to the
ambiguity of the Christian term 'heaven', which in scripture is
used both in a physical and in a spiritual sense.

This brief description of Origen's view of the physical universe
shows that his affirmation of the life of the heavens is part of a
wide-ranging series of speculations on cosmology and on the
world's elemental forces. It is with Origen above all other

[41] *CCel.* 7. 44 (2. 196. 1–5 K.), cf. 5. 44 (2. 47. 29–48. 1) and 6. 19 (2. 89. 32–90.
18 K.).
[42] *In Ezech.* Hom. 1. 15 (8. 339. 17–21 B.), *CCel.* 6. 20 (2. 91. 3–8 K.). See Philo,
above ch. 5 n. 18.
[43] See Henri Crouzel and Manlio Simonetti, *Origène: Traité des principes,* SC 253
(Paris: du Cerf, 1978), 2. 151 n. 32.
[44] *In Ezech.* Hom. 1. 15 (8. 339. 18–21 B.).
[45] *In Ps.* 36 Hom. 5. 4 (*PG* 12. 1362d–1363a); cf. Porphyry ap. Stobaeus (2. 170.
11 Wachsmuth). Ninth heaven: see above n. 28.
[46] *Prin.* 2. 3. 6, 286–94,. *In Ps.* 36 Hom. 2. 4 (*PG* 12. 1333a), cf. *In Gen.* Hom. 1.
2 (6. 3. 2–4 B.), *In Num.* Hom. 26. 5 (7. 251. 31–252. 1 B.).

Christian writers of the patristic period that the cosmos comes alive—not only in the literal sense which is the focus of the present work, but in the figurative and general sense that the physical cosmos becomes an important area of speculation within Christian theology. The failure of this approach to win acceptance in later ecclesiastical tradition had important consequences in the development of Christian theology which, after Origen as before him, tended more strongly to separate theology from physics and astronomy.

Origen's contribution is therefore impressive and unique. Four reservations, however, must be made about his combination of physical and theological speculations. First, Origen's work has been misrepresented in the past because of an unsatisfactory use of the fragments (so-called) of his *De Principiis*. In particular his work has often been treated as if it were intended to be systematic and definitive in cosmological matters, and this is doubtful. Many scholars in this century have noted that the word 'system' is not the right term to characterize Origen's work.[47] Origen does have a consistent sense of theological direction in his speculations on the heavens. In particular, John Dillon notes the ongoing importance of the idea of a cosmic fall and return in Origen's thought.[48] This, however, is too general a concept to be the basis of a system. Furthermore, as we shall see, Origen had very little interest in the internal consistency of his propositions—and that, after all, is not the attitude of the truly systematic. Such an approach would have required more time and theological precedent than Origen had (his most important predecessors after all were Philo and Clement—the former often strays into self-contradiction and the latter's *magnum opus* is quite literally a 'Patchwork'). Later thinkers influenced by Origen may have had a more internally consistent (and radical) cosmology which was inspired by the *De Principiis*, but the accomplishments of Evagrius in the fourth century and later of sixth-century Origenist monks should not be confused with Origen's own

[47] Walther Völker, *Das Vollkommenheitsideal des Origenes*, BHTh 7 (Tübingen: J. C. B. Mohr, 1931), 83 n. 3, and Crouzel, *Philosophie*, 195–205, against E. de Faye, Hal Koch, and Hans Jonas. See further appendix A.

[48] 'Looking on the Light: Some Remarks on the Imagery of Light in the First Chapter of the *Peri Archon*', in Charles Kannengiesser and William L. Petersen (eds.), *Origen of Alexandria* (Notre Dame, Ind.: University of Notre Dame, 1988), 216 n. 1.

views. Origen was a theologian who was not so much working
from an overall master plan as putting his ideas together as he
went along—a style nearer that of St Augustine than that of St
Thomas. This seems to have been true even in the *De Principiis*
(allegedly the showpiece of Origen the systematic Platonist):
Dillon observes that Origen himself seems to have thought of this
work not as a self-contained unity but 'as a collection of essays'.[49]

Second, Origen was far from regarding himself as a free thinker
in cosmological matters. He describes himself as a man of the
Church (*vir ecclesiasticus*)[50] and, as de Lubac notes, frequently uses
phrases like 'rule of the Church', 'faith of the Church', 'teaching
of the Church', 'tradition of the Church', etc.[51] As we shall see,
this causes Origen to limit some of his speculations and to adapt
others to doctrinal and scriptural requirements. There were thus
more controls on the direction of his work than either his ancient
enemies or some modern admirers would like to admit.

Third, it is important to observe that Origen himself is acutely
aware that his cosmological speculations are innovative, and he
frequently expresses his views hesitantly. He writes that unless
he had been called by Christ to make his theological enquiries, he
would have withdrawn from them, conscious as he was of his
own lack of sufficient spiritual insight.[52] Before discussing the
question of whether heaven is part of this world, Origen remarks
that the matter is too high for a human being to comprehend.[53]
Before asking if God is glorified more in himself than in the Son,
he says that the question is bold and beyond his abilities[54]—one
could multiply examples. It is true that Origen cannot resist
speculating on all of the questions about which he has so gravely
warned us (here again he is like St Augustine), but this does not
mean that the warnings are simply conventional: he means these
flights of intellect or fancy to be taken as speculation and not as
dogma. Origen (like Irenaeus) felt that many questions could
only be decisively answered in the next life, believing that, since
the visible world was only an image of an intelligible and invisible

---

[49] 'Remarks' 217, citing *In Rom*. 7. 15 (*PG* 14. 1145a).

[50] *In Luc*. Hom. 16 (9. 97. 28–98, 2 Ra.), *In Jesu Nave* Hom. 9. 8 (7. 353. 17 B.).

[51] De Lubac, *Histoire*, 56 and 62.

[52] *In Gen*. ap. Pamphilus *Apol*. Praef. (*PG* 17. 544b). See further Henri Crouzel,
Origen, trans. A. S. Worrall (San Francisco: Harper & Row, 1989), 164–6.

[53] *Prin*. 2. 3. 6. 249–58 (C/S).

[54] *In Jo*. 32. 28. 349 f. (4. 473. 25–34 P.).

one, many problems could be better understood when we were in the kingdom of the heavens.[55] This also was true of theories on the life of the stars:

When . . . the saints have reached the heavenly places, then they will clearly see the nature of the stars one by one, and will understand whether they are living beings or whatever else may be the case.[56]

Origen recognizes an uncertainty here which he does not allow in other doctrinal issues.

This brings us to the fourth point, which is that Origen weighs his teachings very differently, putting forward many ideas as conjectures, and it is sometimes difficult to know how seriously he takes these views. Though Origen certainly thought the stars are alive, it should be stated at the outset that there is some room for doubt in his mind. He notes that the tradition does not make clear whether the stars have life or not,[57] and elsewhere he says that Job 25: 5, 'the stars are not clean in his sight', proves that the stars are capable of sin 'unless this is a hyperbole'.[58] The view that the stars possess life is not one to which Origen feels completely committed.

Along these same lines, it is also important to recognize that Origen's speculations are often prefaced by the frank admission that he is only expressing his own opinion in a matter which is still open to question. Origen thought there was no harm in discussing possible answers to questions not fixed by dogma (an attitude strongly contested by his opponents). At the beginning of a passage where he directly discusses the question of whether sun, moon, and stars are living and rational, whether their souls come into existence with their bodies or pre-exist, and whether their souls will leave their bodies at the end of the age, Origen admits that his enterprise is adventurous, and asks for indulgence:

It is true that to inquire into these matters seems somewhat daring, yet impelled as we are by a keen desire to ascertain the truth, we see nothing unreasonable in examining and testing, by the grace of the Holy Spirit, all that lies within our power.[59]

---

[55] *In Ps.* 38. 7 (*PAS* 3. 30), *In Ps.* 118 (68. 41 f. Dev.), *In Rom.* 5. 9 (*PG* 14. 1044c), Irenaeus *AH* 2. 28. 3 (2. 2. 274 R/D).
[56] *Prin.* 2. 11. 7. 241–4 (C/S), trans. Butterworth (slightly adapted).
[57] *Prin.* Praef. 10. 186 f. (C/S), cf. Pamphilus *Apol.* 9 (*PG* 17, 607b).
[58] *In Jo.* 1. 35. 257 (4. 45. 24 f. P.).
[59] *Prin.* 1. 7. 3. 71–82 (C/S), trans. Butterworth.

Aware that he was almost unique among ecclesiastical Christians in his serious theological interest in astronomy and in his view that the stars were alive, Origen often hedged his speculations and conceded the tentative nature of his conclusions.

Compared to the gnostic and Valentinian speculations which were eagerly embraced in second- and third-century Alexandria, Origen's cosmology (like Clement's) is restrained. Scholars ancient and modern regard him as a bold and innovative thinker, but much of his energy is spent warning against even more daring proposals. Like Philo, Origen is accordingly a thinker whose praise of heaven—by this point a standard feature of philosophical treatises—is circumspect and at times even diffident. Origen points out that at the Incarnation Christ became a human being rather than any other creature because he honoured the human race before all others, even before all the life in heaven.[60] Similarly, he writes that the light of the stars, though worthy in its own right, only came into existence on the fourth day of creation and is not to be confused with the true light which has come into the world, Jesus Christ, who enlightens the soul.[61] Referring to the motif of the heavenly journey which is so strong in some of the apocalyptic and gnostic literature, Origen says concerning Ephesians 4: 10 that Christ's ascent to heaven is mystical rather than spatial.[62] His understanding of the stars and their importance is more conservative than that of many of his contemporaries.

Furthermore, Origen often ends up being less radical than the initial tendency of a particular argument. For example, discussing the opening verses of Genesis, Origen remarks that only heaven, earth, sun, moon, stars, and humanity are directly made by God, while everything else in creation is made at God's command. He notes also how redeemed humanity is honoured by being promised that it will shine like the sun and the moon. He sees it as a mark of the human race's greatness that it is put on the same footing as such exalted parts of creation.[63] We seem to be on the verge of that Hellenistic veneration of the heavens that Cumont called 'astral mysticism'. Then, however, Origen immediately

---

[60] *In Jo.* 1. 26. 175 (4. 32. 27–9 P.).
[61] *In Jo.* 1. 25. 161 (4. 30. 31–31, 5 P.).
[62] *In Jo.* 19. 22. 145 (4. 323. 27–31 P.).
[63] *In Gen.* Hom. 1. 12 (6. 14. 16–15. 3 B.).

shifts his ground and notes that it is the human being (or rather, as he goes on to say, the inner, incorporeal human being) who is made in the image of God, and that this honour is not attributed to heaven, earth, sun, or moon.[64]

This caution extended to the way he assessed astronomical theories in light of biblical revelation. It has not always been noted how often scriptural teachings prevented Origen's acceptance of an aspect of pagan cosmology. He writes that 'some' believe that there are seven heavens, and appeals to the *Apocalypse of Baruch* for support,[65] but he doubts the scriptural basis of this very common teaching (2 Corinthians 12: 2 was a sticking point), and usually prefers with Paul to set their number at three.[66]

Furthermore, many of Origen's ideas flew in the face of the usual honours which the ancients had given the stars. Origen reports that even some Christians regard sun, moon, and stars as immutable and everlasting, which is the almost universal pagan philosophical view, but he remarks that they cannot be eternal since they are created and visible, neither of which would be possible in that which is eternal.[67] Psalm 118 (119): 89 says that the Word of the Lord endures 'until the *age*' and not 'until the age of the ages' or 'until the age of the age' (other common scriptural idioms), because after this *age* in which we now live 'heaven and earth will pass away' (Matthew 24: 35).[68] Recalling the tradition of the *Epinomis* that the stars are the guardians of divine providence, Origen says that the eyes of the God's heavenly watchmen are on the poor (Psalm 10 (11): 4), but he then promptly denies that this is true in any physical sense.[69] Origen believes the stars and planets are alive, but he holds something back; he is not cautious enough to satisfy his later opponents, but his speculations on the stars would not have honoured the heavenly bodies enough to please contemporary pagan philosophers.

---

[64] 1. 13 (6. 15. 4–13 B.).

[65] *Prin.* 2. 3. 6. 268–94 (C/S). For the relation of what Origen was reading to the extant apocalypse (now called *3 Baruch*) see H. E. Gaylord in Charlesworth, *Pseudepigrapha*, 1. 655 f.

[66] See C/S *Principes*, 2. 152 n. 34, and P. A. Recheis, *Engel, Tod und Seelenreise*, TeT 4 (Rome: Edizioni di storia e letteratura, 1958), 95 n. 115.

[67] *Prin.* 1. 7. 2. 46–51, 3. 6. 4. 114 f. (C/S); cf. *In Rom* 8. 11 (*PG* 14. 1192b).

[68] *In Ps.* 118 (51. 17–20 Dev.).

[69] *In Ps.* 10. 4 (*PG* 12. 1197c).

And yet even when one acknowledges that Origen's approach is not systematic, that his proposals are often tentative, and that frequently his devotion to scripture overrules a philosophical commonplace, pagan cosmological traditions nevertheless play an important role in Origen's thought. A danger that Origen's admirers have always faced is that their efforts to defend his orthodoxy may lead them to portray Origen as fundamentally untouched by Hellenistic speculation and (despite appearances) theologically tame. This, however, is just as false as the approach which sees him as nothing but another Hellenistic Platonist. Origen was deeply influenced by a variety of Hellenistic philosophical speculations, and used this inheritance to ask questions which had never been asked before in the history of Christian theology. The composition and life of the stars had a firmly established place in pagan philosophy and religion, even if their role was not always clearly understood, and Origen (like Philo) would try to understand them in his attempt to lay out a biblical cosmology.

Origen follows Plato in seeing movement as a sign of the presence of rationality, but (like Plato in the *Laws*)[70] Origen realizes that rationality can be present in different ways. He accordingly divides movement into three categories: (1) the lifeless motion of that which is moved externally, (2) soul in a lesser sense, such as the growth of plants, or the movement of elements (as in fire's upward motion, earthquakes, winds, and water currents), and (3) soul in its higher sense: the more sophisticated, self-movement of living creatures, who not only move 'by themselves' but 'through themselves'.[71]

Origen refers to both the first and third categories of movement in his discussion of elemental and astral movements at several points, without coming to a definite conclusion. Following the Stoic concept of a World Soul, Origen says that the world is a great animal which is maintained by the immanent power of God. Several scriptural passages which speak of God's presence in heaven and on earth are adduced as evidence. Here, as often, Origen interjects a note of caution: 'I think' (*puto*) that the world is held together by God 'as if by a single power' (*quasi ab una*

---

[70] See above ch. 1 n. 127.
[71] *De Orat.* 6. 1 (2. 311. 16–312. 10 K.).

virtute).[72] It was common philosophical practice to say that the elements have souls,[73] and Origen follows this view, and also passes along the opinion of certain others (who are unnamed) that veins of metals and stones possess a vital force, and that fire and perhaps water are ensouled.[74] Since divine judgement is truly universal, scriptural references to the judgement and sin of the earth presuppose that it is alive.

And so it will be that on Judgement Day not only humanity but also the universe will be judged; indeed, 'all creation groans and grieves' [Romans 8: 22]. If 'all creation groans and grieves', and furthermore earth, heaven, ether, and whatever are under the heavens and also above them are a portion of creation, and all creation 'will be freed from the slavery of corruption to the freedom of the glory of the sons of God' [Romans 8: 21], who knows whether the earth also, according to its own nature, is accountable for some sin?[75]

We shall see that Origen makes this same type of argument on behalf of the idea that the heavenly bodies sin, and here again the scriptural reference to sin presupposes *a fortiori* the possession of life and soul.

Moving up from elemental movements to higher forms of life, the same principle holds true: self-movement and life do not arise from body but from soul.[76] Like Philo, Origen in some passages links the lower soul with blood, in accordance with the Hebrew idea that blood is life. He explained the ensouled self-movement of insects and sea creatures as arising from a different type of blood which did not happen to be red in colour.[77] He is, however, too good a Platonist to link all soul with something so unabashedly material. He explains that if the equation that blood is life

---

[72] *Prin.* 2. 1. 3. 60–81 (C/S).

[73] Alcinous *Did.* 15 (171. 13–18 Hermann); Varro frag. 24 (Cardauns); Celsus ap. *CCel.* 8. 31 (2. 246. 19–22 K.). The elements are also personified in Judaism, see Recheis, *Engel*, 45, *Jub.* 2. 2.

[74] Elements: *CCel.* 8. 31 (2. 246. 26–247. 1 K.); see below n. 81. Veins: *Prin.* 3. 1. 2. 29–48 (Latin), 21–34 (Greek), *De Orat.* 6. 1 (1. 311. 19–312. 1 K.). A passage attributed to Origen suggests that when Psalm 76: 17 (77: 16) says that the waters have seen God, 'the waters' signify rational natures, *In Ps.* 76 (*PAS* 3. 108). This passage, however, is probably from Evagrius, see Marie-Josèphe Rondeau, 'Le Commentaire sur les Psaumes d'Évagre le Pontique', *OCP* 26 (1960), 339.

[75] *In Ezech.* Hom. 4. 1 (GCS 8. 361. 4–13).

[76] *CCel.* 6. 48 (2. 120. 1–3 K.).

[77] *Prin.* 2. 8. 1. 22–31 (C/S).

were generally made, the resurrected soul could not live outside
of the tomb and so could not 'be with Christ' after death
(Philippians 1: 23).[78] Furthermore, Paul had said (1 Corinthians
15: 20) that flesh and blood could not inherit the kingdom of
heaven.[79] Therefore where it is linked with rational soul 'blood'
must be understood in a spiritual sense. This is an important
distinction, since Origen concedes that the ethereal living beings
in heaven also do not have blood in the ordinary physical way.[80]
In like manner, the ethereal, psychic bodies of angels and of
humanity in the Resurrection are not identical with physical
matter, a distinction which will be discussed below. On the
borderline between Hebrew and Greek, physical and spiritual,
Origen hesitates. Soul is blood, but it is also something more; the
ether of star and soul is material, but in a sense that is so subtle
that the framework of his immaterialist Platonic psychology is
unaffected.

Origen has another, rather different explanation of movement
in other passages (which again indicates how unsettled his
opinion is in these matters). Along with positing a lower soul to
explain elemental movements, Origen accounts for them by
suggesting that they are governed by spiritual powers:

But as for my own opinion, I think it should also be boldly said about
those powers which have taken on the administration of this world that
it is not by fortune or chance that one power presides over the
germinations of the earth and trees, another adequately accounts for
(*exhibeat*) springs and rivers, another presides over rains, another over
winds, one over sea animals and another over terrestrial animals, or over
each of the individual things which grow from the earth. In each one of
these there are ineffable mysteries of the divine economy so that
everything is divided according to its own rank and according to the duty
assigned to each power. For the apostle Paul says the following, 'Are not
all ministering spirits sent to serve those who receive the inheritance of
salvation?' [Hebrews 1: 14].[81]

In one passage, Origen toys with the idea, familiar in Jewish
apocalyptic,[82] that the heavenly bodies likewise are guided by an

[78] *Entretien d'Origène avec Héraclide* (23. 12–15 Scherer).
[79] *In Ps.* 1. 5 (*PG* 12. 1096a).
[80] See below n. 96.
[81] *In Jesu Nave* Hom. 23. 3 (7. 444. 5–15 B.), see also *CCel.* 8. 31 (2. 246. 26–
247. 2 K.).
[82] See ch. 6 nn. 83–7.

angel. He discusses this at length in one of his homilies on Jeremiah:

'How long will the earth mourn, and the grass of every field wither because of the wickedness of its inhabitants' [Jeremiah 12: 4]. The prophet here speaks as if the earth was alive when he says the earth mourned because of the wickedness of those who walked upon it. For each of us the earth either 'mourns' or rejoices, for either it mourns 'because of the wickedness of its inhabitants' or rejoices because of the virtue of its inhabitants. In each of us then this same element (στοιχεῖον) either rejoices or grieves, and if it is so for the earth it is also true for the other elements. Similarly I shall say: there is water and an angel in charge of water [Revelation 16: 5], so that I may also describe the earth which is grieving and that which is not grieving. For it is not the body earth that grieves 'because of the wickedness of its inhabitants', but understand that for the administration of the universe an angel is assigned for the earth, and another for the waters, and another for air, and a fourth for fire. Thus rise up by reason to all the order that is in animals, in plants, and in the heavenly stars. An angel is assigned to the sun, and another to the moon, and ‹another› to the stars. These angels, whom we accompany as long as we are on the earth, either rejoice or grieve with us when we sin.[83]

Taken seriously, this would mean that the heavenly bodies (and the elemental forces), like other objects strictly moved externally, were not alive at all. They would not have a soul, but would be controlled by a being who did have a soul (the first type of life of the three enumerated above). Such a view would eventually prevail in Christian theology, but not in Origen's own thinking. His usual understanding of the heavenly bodies is that they have their own source of life (the third category of life listed above).

For Origen, the movement of the stars is the most important evidence for this life. In light of pagan speculations, the following argument to prove that the stars are living and rational is by this point very familiar:

[83] *In Jer.* Hom. 10. 6 (3. 76. 8–26 Kl.). In SC 232, *Origène: Homélies sur Jérémie*, ed. Pierre Husson and Pierre Nautin (Paris: du Cerf, 1976), 410, the editors conjecture 'others', so that the last line would be translated 'another to the moon, and *others* to the stars'. Klostermann's conjecture ('another'), however, agrees with the ancient Latin translation, and is in line with Origen's suggestion that one angel watches over an entire element; moreover, there is precedence in Platonism to suggest that a single soul could govern multiple heavenly bodies, see above ch. 1 n. 128.

And since the stars move with such majestic order and plan that never
have we seen their course deflected in the slightest degree, is it not the
height of stupidity to say that such order, such exact observance of rule
and plan, is accomplished by things without reason?[84]

The order of the stars is made possible by divine creation (as is the
order of human rationality), but it is maintained by the heavenly
bodies and their souls. This rationality of heavenly movement
was a weapon in his battle against Christian heretics who denied
the goodness of creation. These opponents (Marcionites and
Valentinians) cited scripture to prove that the world was evil. In
his commentary on Genesis Origen replied that the term 'world'
(κόσμος) is used in several different ways in scripture:

Through not knowing that the term 'world' can be used as a homonym,
people have fallen into the most impious opinions concerning the
Creator: I mean those who have not cleared up the question in what
sense 'the world is in the power of the evil one' [1 John 5: 19], and have
not realized that the 'world' there denotes earthly and human affairs.
Supposing the 'world' to be literally the complex whole of heaven and
earth and things therein, they exhibit the utmost audacity and impiety in
their conceptions of God, for with all their efforts they cannot show how
the sun, moon, and stars, with all their wonderful orderly movements,
are 'in the power of the evil one.'[85]

Similarly, discussing John 1: 10, 'the world (κόσμος) did not
know him,' Origen remarks that

. . . it is foolish to say that the world here means the whole compounded
of heaven and earth and that which is in them, as if someone would say
that the sun, moon, chorus of stars, and the angels in the whole world
did not recognize 'the true light', and in their ignorance preserved the
order assigned them by God.[86]

Thus in several different contexts Origen adopts the traditional
philosophical view that the orderly motion of stars and planets
was proof of their immanent intelligence and high ontological
status.

Other important arguments for the life of the stars are also
deduced from scripture: the stars are said to receive divine

[84] *Prin.* 1. 7. 3. 93–8 (C/S), trans. Butterworth.
[85] *Philocalia* 14. 2 (69, 6–16 R.), trans. George Lewis (adapted).
[86] *In Matth.* 13. 20 (10. 235. 22–33 Kl.); cf. *Test. Naphtali* 3. 2.

commands, and commands are only made to living and rational beings.[87] Origen gives Isaiah 45: 12, 'And I have commanded all the stars,' as an example.[88] He also points to Jeremiah's description of the moon as the queen of heaven as additional proof, suggesting that the scriptural idea that the moon rules the night as the sun rules the day is not simply a metaphor.[89] The Bible says that sun and moon praise God, and the fact that they are able to praise is proof that they possess free will.[90] When in Philippians 2: 10 Paul says that every knee in heaven shall bow to God, this means that sun, moon, stars, and angels are subject to the worship of God.[91] To counter the pagan philosopher Celsus' charge that Christians stripped all dignity away from sun, moon, and stars, Origen quotes Psalm 148: 3 f. (LXX), 'Praise him sun and moon; praise him all you stars and light, praise him you heavens of heavens,' to show that the Bible recognizes the worth of astral and planetary life.[92] Their visible light is the work of God, but the intellectual light which they possess probably (his caution surfaces again) comes from their own free will.[93] Here as with the elements, free will and culpability for sin are *a fortiori* signs of life and rationality, so that the freedom of the heavenly bodies puts them on the same footing as human beings.

Though believing that the heavenly bodies are spiritually comparable to humanity, Origen never doubts that the stars have a much happier life. Following a long philosophical tradition, Origen thinks that the life of the rational bodies in heaven must be one of great peace and order, in contrast to the troubles which plague the life below:

it must be said concerning those on earth, that certain impressions arising from attendant circumstances induce our instability or inclination to the worse course, so as to do or say such and such things. But in regard to those in heaven, what impression can arise to divert or remove from that course which is beneficial to the universe any of those beings who possess a soul that is perfected by reason and alien to the influence

---

[87] *Prin.* 1. 7. 3. 83–5 (C/S), *In Rom.* 9. 41 (*PG* 14. 1244a).
[88] *Prin.* 1. 7. 3. 85 f. (C/S).
[89] *Prin.* 1. 7. 2. 35–8 and 1. 7. 3. 98 f. (C/S).
[90] *De Orat.* 7 (2. 315. 28–316. 4 K.), cf. *CCel.* 8. 67 (2. 283. 19 K.).
[91] *In Rom.* 9. 41 (*PG* 14. 1244a).
[92] *CCel.* 5. 13 (2. 14. 9–23 K.), *De Orat.* 7 loc. cit.
[93] *CCel.* 5. 10 (2. 11. 15–18 K.).

of these impressions, and make use of a body whose quality is ethereal and absolutely pure?[94]

Occasionally, Origen seems to suggest in a traditional philosophical manner that this serene life is a mark of ontological superiority, and thus that we are inferior to the heavenly bodies.[95] Elsewhere, though, in keeping with his emphasis on the supreme dignity of humanity in creation, he suggests that this serenity is not the result of natural superiority but simply of circumstance:

> There are more pains and a more precarious life for beings of flesh and blood than there are for those who are in an ethereal body, and if the luminaries of heaven put on earthly bodies they would not complete the life here free from danger and sin.[96]

Origen's position is nuanced: the stars are living and rational, and they lead an orderly and undistracted life, but they are still creatures, and indeed the biblical understanding of Creation and the Incarnation show that in some ways their dignity is comparable to (and even less than) that of humanity. Plato had spoken of the stars as gods and (at least mythically) as in some sense the soul's master. Origen agrees that they are alive, but brings them down ontologically much nearer our own level.

This new understanding of the stars' rank is evident in his polemic against the worship of heaven. Like Philo, Clement of Alexandria, and Justin Martyr, Origen concedes that the worship of sun, moon, and stars is a superior error to that of worshipping graven images,[97] but he leaves no doubt of his opposition to a religion of the heavens. He adopts Academic arguments to show that this practice does not make any sense,[98] adding that since sun, moon, and stars pray to God, it did not make sense to pray to them.[99] While showing as much sympathy to the widespread pagan practice as he could, he retained God's claim to undivided

[94] *De Orat.* 7 (2. 316. 11–19 K.), trans. Oulton. See also Philo ch. 5 n. 43; Posidonius frag. 400b (Theiler); Seneca *Ad Marc.* 26. 4 (165. 7–11 Reynolds); Apuleius *De Deo Socr.* 12 (20. 8–15 Thomas); Plotinus 2. 3. 3. 21–5, 2. 9. 8. 35; Porphyry *De Regressu An.* (32*. 23–5 Bidez).
[95] *CCel.* 5. 11 (2. 12. 22–9 K.). Ontological superiority would also appear to be implied by the passage quoted above in this chapter, see n. 85.
[96] *In Jo.* 1. 25. 173 (4. 32. 14–17 P.).
[97] *In Jo.* 2. 3. 27 (4. 56. 23–7 P.); see ch. 7 n.18.
[98] *CCel.* 5. 7 (2. 7. 8–26 K.), with the note in Henry Chadwick's translation, 268 f.
[99] *CCel.* 5. 11 (2. 12. 11–16 K.), *Exh. Mart.* 7 (1. 9. 9 f. K.).

worship and rejected the adoration of the physical heavens which was the common inheritance of contemporary philosophy.

As part of his attack on the widespread veneration of the stars, Origen focuses on the contrast between the sensible and the noetic in heaven—a contrast which was the source of some embarrassment to adherents of the Platonic 'astral mysticism'—to make absolutely certain that the stars and God cannot be confused. Origen claims on the authority of the Old Testament that 'the true things all have the same name as the earthly things which are more generally given these names,' and as examples refers to the true Light, which differs from the visible heaven, and the 'sun of righteousness' (Christ), which differs from the visible sun.[100] The sun, moon, and stars only give light to the earth, but the true light, who is the Saviour, illumines the mind.[101] When scripture calls God 'light' (1 John 1: 5), corporeal light is used as a metaphor for that which is invisible and incorporeal, and to ascend to God one must go beyond that which is merely visible.[102] In thus rejecting the worship of the heavenly bodies, Origen is part of a long tradition in Jewish and Christian apologetic.[103]

And yet denying that the heavens were divine led to a new type of difficulty. Like all his contemporaries, Origen thinks that the universe was filled with rational, spiritual beings who had powers and responsibilities which were much greater than anything in the human race. Like his predecessors in Hellenistic philosophy, he divides these beings into angels (the Jewish and Christian equivalent of a daemon) and heavenly bodies without making clear how these two groups were related to each other, a problem which would persist in Augustine's theology.[104] Each (once again) was seen as somehow an intermediate being between the human race and God. Having rejected the worship of these beings, Origen was faced with the problem of giving some theological account for this situation. Why were some

---

[100] *CCel.* 7. 31 (2. 182. 9–13 K.), trans. Chadwick; cf. Philo *Spec.* 4. 192.

[101] *In Jo.* 1. 25. 160 f. (4. 30. 29–31, 5 P.), *Prin.* 1. 1. 1. 14–24 (C/S).

[102] *In Jo.* 13. 23. 139 (4. 247. 7–9 P.); ascend: see below ch. 9 nn. 67–71.

[103] See Aristides *Apol.* 6 (119 f. Vona); Theophilus of Antioch *Ad Aut.* 35 (84 Grant); Lactantius *Inst.* 2. 5. 6 ff. (1. 115. 9–121. 18 Brandt); *Odes of Solomon* 16: 14–19, *Constitutiones Apost.* 5. 12. 1 f. and 5 (266–9 Funk). Jewish: see also ch. 5 n. 81.

[104] Aug. *Enchir.* 58 (37. 26–30 Scheel).

beings, such as angels and stars, endowed with superior faculties and a more blessed life?

Origen's answer was that the differing positions in which all creatures found themselves was a consequence of sins that they committed before they were born. Because every rational being is created free, there exists within each one the possibility of ontological advance or decline, and the exercise of these choices explains one's current state in life.[105] With the exception of Christ,[106] all the pre-existent souls fell away from God in varying degrees. Pre-existent merits or sins establish the position of each one in the world,[107] a view which Origen defends on several occasions with reference to the biblical account of Jacob and Esau, where God is said to favour Jacob even before he was born.[108] Life may appear to be unfair, but merit is in fact more important in establishing the status of the individual than appearances would suggest. Evil does not come from either God above us or matter below us, but strictly from the improper use of our freedom,[109] and the consequences of our decisions cause beings to enter upon higher or lower estates in the world.[110]

After birth as before it, souls are ontologically transformed in accordance with ethical decisions. The free exercise of the will enables the soul to become angelic even in this life (Origen's influence on the Christian ascetic tradition is key on this point), or to become more bestial: there is a possibility of noetic rising or falling for the soul.[111] Depending on its choices, the soul either becomes more like flesh or more like spirit (*pneuma*).[112] In no case does it remain stable: life is a process in which we either

[105] *Prin.* 2. 9. 6. 190–5 (C/S). See further Jonas, *Gnosis*, 2. 191.

[106] *Prin.* 2. 6. 3. 96–106, 2. 6. 5. 159–76 (C/S); cf. *In Rom.* 5. 9 (*PG* 14. 1044a).

[107] For sources on the different consequences of different falls see Pépin, *Théologie*, 324 f. n. 1. For precedent for this in paganism see Plato above ch. 5, n. 32; for the later period, Cicero *Consolatio* frag. 8 f. (Mueller), cited by Pierre Boyancé 'La Religion astrale de Platon à Cicéron', *REG* 65 (1952), 337 n. 3.

[108] *In Jo.* 2. 31. 191–2 (4. 89. 2–16 P.), *Prin.* 1. 7. 4. 119–36, 3. 1. 21 f. 930–44 (C/S); Cadiou, *Introduction*, 30.

[109] Not God: *CCel.* 6. 55 (2. 126. 10 f. K.); not God or matter: *CCel.* 4. 66 (1. 336. 24–31 K.); free will: *In Jer.* Hom. 17. 4 (3. 148. 1–9 K1.).

[110] *In Jer.* Hom. 8. 2 (3. 58. 5–10 K1.), *In Luc.* Hom. 20 (9. 123. 16–124. 6 Ra.), *In Lev.* Hom. 12. 2 (6. 457. 1–4 B.).

[111] *In Jo.* 19. 22. 144 (4. 323. 24–6 P.).

[112] Jacques Dupuis, SJ, *L'Esprit de l'homme: Étude sur l'anthropologie religeuse d'Origène*, ML. T 62 (Toulouse: Desclée de Brouwer, 1967), 180.

become more like God or less like him.[113] The redemption of the soul is the point when it is transformed into spirit (*pneuma*).[114]

As this world is a moral testing ground for the human soul, so also it is for angelic souls. Both pagan philosophy and Jewish biblical exegesis (particularly of Genesis 6) had concluded that ontological superiority did not necessarily mean moral superiority. Angels/daemons could be evil as well as powerful.[115] Origen Christianized this *communis opinio*. Temptation and moral decision are the universal condition of rational creatures, and each of them, even the superior ones, had fallen into sin.[116] Jude 6, which speaks of the imprisonment of evil angels, and Revelation, which reproaches the angels who are set over the seven churches, prove that even beings who are superior to humanity are not without guilt.[117] The differences among angels and demons which we are described in scripture are not the result of their essence at creation but of moral (and immoral) decisions freely made.[118]

Just as it is a mistake to think that all heavenly beings are good, so it is equally erroneous to think they are all in the same location or all doing the same task. According to Origen there are angels in every part of the cosmos,[119] and the responsibilities they have and the attitudes they take to the human race differ widely. Following Clement of Alexandria and the combined traditions of Platonism, Jewish apocalyptic, and gnosticism, Origen thought that an angel stood watch over every nation,[120] and he believes

[113] See Dupuis, *L'Esprit*, 43–51.
[114] *In Luc.* Hom. 36 (9. 207. 15–18 Ra.), *Prin.* 2. 8. 3. 109–11 (C/S).
[115] Pagan: already Xenocrates frag. 24 (Heinze) = *SVF* 2. 1104; Jewish: see Gerald Bostock, 'The Sources of Origen's Doctrine of Pre-existence', in Lothar Lies (ed.), *Origeniana Quarta*, (Innsbruck: Tyrolia, 1987), 261.
[116] *In Rom.* 3. 1 (*PG* 14. 924c).
[117] Jude: *In Rom.* 3. 6 (*PG* 14. 939b); Revelation: *In Luc.* Hom. 13 (9. 80. 20–8 Ra.), *In Num.* Hom. 20. 3 (7. 194. 15–18 B.) and 20. 4 (7. 197. 8–14 B.).
[118] *Prin.* 1. 5. 3. 131–7, 1. 8. 4. 125–60, 1. 6. 2. 64–84 (C/S).
[119] *In Ezech.* Hom. 1. 7 (8. 331. 30 B.). Cf. Proclus *In Tim.* (3. 306. 15–18 Diehl), *De Magia* ap. *CMAG* 6. 149. 28 (see Festugière, *Révélation*, 1. 134–6).
[120] Clement *Strom.* 6. 17. 157 (2. 513. 6 f. St.), 7. 2. 6 (3. 6. 16 ff. St.); Porphyry *In Tim.* frag. 17 (11. 7–9 Sodano); Iamblichus *De Myst.* 5. 25 (236. 6–8 des Places); Origen *Prin.* 3. 3. 3. 101–4 (C/S), *In Jo.* 13. 50. 333 (4. 278. 19–22 P.), *CCel.* 5. 30 (2. 32. 8–19 K.). Jewish: see Jean Daniélou, 'Les Sources juives de la doctrine des anges des nations chez Origène', *RSR* 38 (1951), 132–7. Gnostic: *On the Origin of the World* (NH 2. 105. 14–16), Basilideans ap. Irenaeus *AH*. 1. 24. 4 (1. 2. 326 R/D).

that these responsibilities are handed out according to merit; the same holds true for those angels who watch over individual souls and the elements.[121] Again as in Jewish apocalyptic, the angels too are accountable for their acts at the Last Judgement, where they will be rewarded or punished according to their merits in keeping human beings from temptation and sin.[122]

The theological result of this was that God could not rightly be accused of injustice for any of the evils that beset life.[123] Evil is entirely the result of decisions made within the created order, and is not from God. This interest in theodicy is also noticeable in Plato and subsequent Hellenistic philosophy,[124] but was especially important to Origen because the problem of the origins of evil was often a source of conflict among early Christians.[125] Furthermore, Origen's astrological opponents had an influential explanation for the presence of evil in the world in their theory of the workings of Fate. It was therefore of the utmost importance to explain how evil was possible in a world made and ruled by God.

For Origen, a correct evaluation of the place of the stars in the divine economy was critical to the proper understanding of this problem, and a wrong assessment was an important obstacle to belief in the doctrine of creation. He asks how it is possible if creation is ruled by Providence that 'some inherit a happier lot' (*aliis nascendi sors felicior evenit*), and why the various peoples of the world have such diversity in their condition at birth.[126] Here and elsewhere Origen acknowledges that the vastly different conditions and societies into which people are born affect every aspect of their lives, a diversity which astrologers claimed was due to the rule of different heavenly powers.[127] Origen is also well aware of how the disciples of Marcion, Valentinus, and Basilides argue that the existence of various types of life in

[121] *In Jesu Nave* Hom. 23. 3 (7. 443. 5–444. 16 B.).
[122] *In Num.* Hom. 11. 4 (7. 82. 16–25), 20. 4 (7. 197. 5–8), 24. 3 (7. 231. 21–5 B.), *In Luc.* Hom. 35 (9. 198. 17–23 Ra.). Jewish apocalyptic: see Pétrement, *Séparé*, 86.
[123] *Prin.* 3. 5. 4. 135–7 (C/S).
[124] See ch. 6, n. 4.
[125] Tertullian *De Praescr.* 7. 5 (1. 192. 15 f. Dekkers); cf. ps.-Clem. *Rec.* 3. 75. 6 (145. 10–13 Rehm). For theodicy in Origen see Koch, *Pronoia*, 96–162.
[126] *Prin.* 2. 9. 5. 152 f., 164 f. (C/S).
[127] See also *CCel.* 5. 27 (2. 27 f. K.), *Philocalia* 23. 16 (205. 4–16 R.), *Prin.* 2. 9. 3. 69–92, 4. 3. 10. 265–71 (Latin), 263–7 (Greek).

heaven is additional proof that the cosmos was not fashioned by a good creator:

> They ask how it is consistent with the righteousness of God who made the world that on some he should bestow a habitation in the heavens, and not only give them a better habitation, but also confer on them a higher and more conspicuous rank, favoring some with a 'principality', others with 'powers', to others allotting 'dominions', to others presenting the most magnificent seats in the heavenly courts [i.e. the angels Paul calls 'Thrones'], while others shine with golden light and gleam with starry brilliance, there being 'one glory of the sun, another of the moon, and another glory of the stars, for one star differeth from another star in glory' [1 Corinthians 15: 41]. To sum it up briefly, they ask what reason there could be, supposing that God the Creator lacks neither the will to desire what is good and perfect nor the power to produce it, that when creating rational natures, that is, beings of whose existence he himself is the cause, he should make some of higher rank and others of second and third and many still lower and less worthy degrees?[128]

In a theological context in which the stars were either regarded as the cause of evil in this life or as proof that the affairs of this cosmos were not justly arranged, it was necessary to show the true place the stars occupied in God's creation.

Before Origen, some had pictured the stars as good, others as neutral, and still others as completely evil. Origen set forth a new understanding of the stars in which their current exalted position was traced to their superior merit, but their possession of corporeal bodies was explained by positing some type of preexistent sin of their souls. We have already seen that Origen argues with some hesitation in his commentary on John that Job 25: 5, 'the stars are not clean in his sight' shows that the stars have indeed sinned,[129] and he repeats the same argument at greater length and without hesitation in *De Principiis*:

> Now Job appears to show that not only is it possible for the stars to be subject to sins, but that they are in fact 'not clean' from the pollution of sin. For he writes as follows: 'The stars also are not clean in his sight.' This is certainly not meant to refer to the brightness of their body, as if, for example, one were to say that a certain garment was not clean. Were it to be understood thus, an injurious reflection would undoubtedly be

---

[128] *Prin.* 2. 9. 5. 137–51 (C/S), trans. Butterworth. At least some Marcionites are interested in astrology, see Cadiou, *Introduction*, 106.

[129] See above in this chap. n. 58.

cast upon the Creator by the charge that there was something unclean in the brightness of their body. For if the stars are unable either by their own diligent efforts to assume for themselves a clearer body or by their slackness a less pure one, why are they blamed for being 'not clean', since they would receive no praise even if they were clean?[130]

Origen apparently thought a good deal of this argument and repeated it in other works.[131] As the different positions of human beings and angels are determined by the degree of severity in previous sin, so too it appears that for Origen the various arrangements of the stars have the same cause. In one passage Origen says that in this world 'supercelestial beings' differ in position and brightness according to their use of free will, but he then quotes as evidence 1 Corinthians 15: 41, which refers to sun, moon, and stars.[132] His meaning is not altogether clear, since 'superheavenly beings' refers to creatures who exist in the region above the fixed sphere and so not to sun, moon, and stars. Thus when Jerome accuses Origen of teaching that the heavenly bodies give light in different degrees according to their sins,[133] he puts forward this view more clearly than Origen did. But there can be little doubt that this is substantially an accurate representation of what Origen thought. This same view appears to be the thrust of another passage from *De Principiis* quoted above,[134] and Origen is close to such a view in a homily on Joshua. Here he refers to the distribution of the stars as inexplicable, and then writes that as the stars are in different parts of heaven, so the children of Abraham inherit a different lot.[135] Since Origen refers elsewhere to the different fates of the children of Abraham in a discussion of how variety in position is traceable to free decisions of the will,[136] it would appear that he thought of the distribution of the stars in the same way.

As with the angels, so too the stars' capacity for evil could be great. We saw above that though the stars are fallen, they are

---

[130] *Prin.* 1. 7. 2. 58–70 (C/S), trans. Butterworth.
[131] *In Rom.* 3. 6 (*PG* 14. 940d). In his note to *Prin.* 1. 7. 2, Crouzel adds Jerome *In Eph.* 1 (*PL* 26. 493), which was very likely taken from Origen's commentary.
[132] *Prin.* 2. 9. 3. 63–9; free will: 2. 9. 6. 190–207 (C/S).
[133] *Ep.* 124. 4 (3. 99 Hilberg). Augustine repeats the charge in his *Contra Prisc. et Orig.* 9 (175. 289–95 Daur).
[134] In this ch. n. 130.
[135] *In Jesu Nave* Hom. 25. 4 (7. 457. 1–21 B.).
[136] *Prin.* 2. 9. 5 f.

often seen as being ontologically superior to humanity. In a couple of passages, however, demonic beings are identified as stars who sinned and fell from their great heights to their present wicked condition. In two different passages Origen speaks of this fall of the stars in very strong and dramatic terms. In each passage he is commenting on Isaiah 14: 12, which exclaims 'How the morning star, arising at dawn, fell from heaven!' In his commentary on Ezekiel, Origen suggests that Satan, who according to Luke fell from heaven (10: 18), is a fallen star, and the redeemed will take his place 'among the stars of heaven' (cf. Genesis 15: 5).[137] In a scholion which is probably by Origen there is a very similar interpretation. Commenting on Revelation 12: 7–9, which says that Michael and his angels cast down the dragon and his angels from heaven, Origen writes:

Do you not see that the dragon fought with the angels, and when he was hard-pressed he was thrown down from heaven. As he fell he drew with him a third of the stars. ‹It is likely that› these stars were divine powers which had revolted with him, and they were borne down with the dragon, as Isaiah said, 'How the morning star fell from heaven!'[138]

All the stars visible in the sky are less evil than the human race, but a third of the demons had also once been stars. Their superior ontological status enabled them to enter into a more blessed state, or to fall into a more wretched one.

Even for the two-thirds of the stars which did not fall as far as Satan, there still was a loss of an original harmony with God. The most obvious result of this for both humanity and stars was the type of bodies in which we were incorporated. Corruption is possible because of the bodies we possess; but the inner person who is made according to the image of God is incorruptible, incorporeal, and invisible.[139] In heaven a visible and tangible

---

[137] *In Ezech.* 12. 2 (8. 444. 18–21 B.).

[138] *Scholia in Apocalypsem* 38 (15. 1–4 Turner). Turner notes (vs. Harnack) that a word is needed to govern the infinitive and conjectures εἰκός. In light of Origen's caution in such matters this seems plausible. Irenaeus has the same interpretation, *AH* 2. 31. 3 (2. 2. 330 R/D).

[139] Incorruptible: *In Rom.* 7 (*PG* 14. 1110ab); incorporeal: *In Gen.* Hom. 1. 13 (6. 15. 11–13 B.). It is important to see that Origen tends to use the word 'incorporeal', not in its strict sense, but only to indicate the absence of an earthly body. Thus he can equate 'incorporeal' with 'invisible', *Prin.* 3. 6. 7. 224, see Herwig Görgemanns and Heinrich Karpp, *Origenes vier Bücher von den Prinzipien* (Darmstadt: Wissenschaftliche Buchgesellschaft, 1976), 117 n. 23, and C/S, *Principes*, 4. 144 n. 41.

body (as opposed to incorporeality) is a sign of a lower ontological status. It is because of this principle that Origen writes that the incorporeal powers in heaven are true, but that those visible on earth and corporeal are what the Letter to the Hebrews (9: 24) calls 'imitations of the true' and not 'the true'.[140] Satan fell from his body of light to a body of this world, which is why Satan is called the Prince of this world (John 12: 31).[141]

The stars and planets are bodies of light, as Satan was before his fall, and like humanity are not as bound up with the merely corporeal and material as Satan, but in their own way these heavenly beings are also tied to bodies and subject to their limitations. Denying that it is possible to have a body and not to be subject to 'the reproach of angels' mentioned in Job 40: 19 (LXX), Origen suggests that the soul of the sun was placed in a body together with the rest of creation against its will, and that those who are in the body unwillingly do the things of the body.[142] Or again, he says elsewhere that the sun is now subject to corruption and needs to be freed from its bondage.[143]

This did not mean (as Origen's enemies would charge) that he believed the body was nothing more than a punishment, a view which Origen specifically denied.[144] The physical world (including the body) was a gift of Providence given to help train rational creatures so that they might regain their lost sanctity, for as the possession of body increased the temptation to sin, it also provided the opportunity for virtue, and also acted as an aid to the soul.[145] As even our thick and tangible bodies were given to us as a consequence of sin (even if they are not intrinsically evil), so the visible bodies of stars and planets probably were given to these souls after they had turned away from God. Origen does consider the possibility that God made the bodies of the stars at the same time as their souls, but definitely inclines to the view that their spirit (*spiritus*) was placed in the stars after the creation

---

[140] *In Cant.* Hom. 2 (8. 160. 18–20 B.); Recheis, *Engel*, 85.

[141] *Prin.* 1. 5. 5. 270–8 (C/S). Evagrius says of demons, 'leur substance est coextensive avec la substance du monde,' *KG* 4. 35, trans. (from the Syriac) Guillaumont p. 151.

[142] *In Jo.* 1. 17. 98 f. (4. 21. 21–7 P.).

[143] *Exh. Mart.* 7 (1. 9. 11–14 K.).

[144] Opponents charge: Epiphanius *Pan.* 64. 4. 6 (2. 411. 4 f. Holl, see his note); denied: *CCel.* 4. 66 (1. 336. 28–30 K.).

[145] The world a gift: *In Jo.* 19. 20. 132 (4. 321. 23–5 P.); train: *Prin.* 3. 5. 4. 131; virtue: see in this ch. n. 96; aid: *In Jud.* Hom. 6. 5 (7, 502, 24 f.).

of their bodies. Intending to prove this from scripture, he cites various passages in which infants had received divine favour when they were still in the womb.[146] Arguing that God would be unjust or show favouritism (cf. Romans 9: 14, 2: 11) if this were arbitrary, he says that this proves the pre-existence of souls, and that what reason and scripture say holds true for human beings must also hold true for heavenly life,[147] so that the assignment of this body also to a higher type of soul is the result of sin. Origen argues frequently that the current usefulness of the stars in identifying the times and the seasons is their consciously expressed penance for these pre-existent misdeeds, a topic which will be discussed in greater detail below. Stars, like people, were rational beings who had sinned and for whom their present bodies were fashioned as a result of their sin, and this life was a time in which they, like humanity, attempted to recapture that more spiritual life which had been enjoyed by them before the foundation of the world.

Since Origen believed that the stars were free rational beings who had fallen into sin, it is not surprising that he included them in his doctrine of Redemption:

It would indeed be absurd to say that he [sc. Christ] tasted death for human sins and not for any other being apart from man who had fallen into sin, such as the stars . . .[148]

Christ's blood was shed not only for humanity but also for 'the church of the first-born' which is in the heavens (Hebrews 12: 23).[149] The crucifixion is twofold: there is Christ's visible sacrifice as a human being for other human beings, and an invisible sacrifice for all of rational creation. This is the meaning of Origen's claim that Christ came as a human being to save human beings and as an angel to save angels:[150] Christ's sacrifice was

---

[146] Gen. 25: 22–6; Luke 1: 41; Jer. 1: 5.

[147] *Prin.* 1. 7. 4. 104–40 (C/S).

[148] *In Jo.* 1. 35. 257 (4. 45. 24–7). He goes on to cite Job 25: 5.

[149] *In Lev.* Hom. 1. 3 (6. 284. 21–285. 5 B.). See further Barbel, *Christos*, 289–97, and Marcel Borret's note in *Origène: Homélies sur le Lévitique* (Paris: du Cerf, 1981), 1. 363 f. This is not a separate sacrifice, or one that would have to be repeated, as Origen's enemies charged: see C/S, *Principes*, 2. 148 f. n. 24.

[150] *In Jo.* 1. 31. 217 (4. 38. 30–3 P.), *In Gen.* Hom. 8. 8 (6. 83. 12–14 B.); cf. the catena on Hebrews, no. 363 in Hans Urs von Balthasar, *Origen: Spirit and Fire*, trans. Robert J. Daly, SJ (Washington, DC: Catholic University, 1984), and Jerome *In Eph.* 1. 1 (*PL* 26. 493); see also the Valentinian *Gospel according to Philip* 23 (NH 2. 57. 27–58. 2), and *Pistis Sophia* 1. 7 (12. 2–6 Schmidt/MacDermot).

cosmic in nature and included all the beings in heaven and in the regions above heaven, as well as those on earth. Therefore Origen says that when we read that the gospel is to be declared to the whole universe (κόσμος, Mark 16: 5), we must understand that this includes the earth and all of the heavens.[151]

And yet, despite the fallen condition of the stars and their need for redemption, Origen regards the stars visible in the sky (i.e. and not those who have fallen and become demons) as in no way a menace to the human race. This does not mean that there were no malevolent forces located above. Like many of his contemporaries, Origen believed that forces located above inspect the ascending soul and, under certain circumstances, would prevent it from reaching its heavenly goal.[152] In a homily on Numbers, Origen wonders if the ascending soul will struggle with evil powers in heaven,[153] and says that the 'spiritual hosts of wickedness in the heavenly regions' (Ephesians 6: 12) must yet be conquered in spiritual battle.[154] He also alludes to this in one of his homilies on Joshua:

You have heard who they are whom you must drive out of the heavenly places by war and by force so that you may be able to receive these places of the kingdom of the heavens as your legitimate inheritance.[155]

In his commentary on Luke Origen has an interpretation which is influenced by the myth of the soul's ascent through evil heavenly powers. He writes that the tax-collectors who come to be baptized by John the Baptist in Luke 3: 12 are the Prince of this world and his minions, who scrutinize the ascending soul to see 'if there is anything in it that is their own',[156] i.e. to see if the ascending soul is still bound to that which is material and worldly. Since Satan and one-third of the stars were 'borne down' by their sins and no

---

[151] *In Jo.* 1. 15. 87 (4. 19. 20–3 P.).

[152] *In Ezech.* Hom. 7. 3 (8. 393. 8–13 B.), *Exh. Mart.* 48 (1. 44. 6–14 K.).

[153] *In Num.* Hom. 27. 4 (7. 262. 16–18 B.).

[154] *In Num.* Hom. 7. 5 (7. 47. 5–19 B.).

[155] *In Jesu Nave* Hom. 12. 1 (7. 368. 9 f. B.). See Jerome *Ep.* 124. 11 (3. 113. 26–114. 6 Hilberg).

[156] *In Luc.* Hom. 23 (9. 144. 16–21 Ra.); similarly *In Ps.* 36 Hom. 5. 7 (*PG* 12. 1366bc), *In Ps.* 118 (29 Dev.), and Clement of Alex. (see Ra.'s note). See also above in this ch. n. 141. The same term which Origen uses for 'tax-collectors' (τελῶναι) is used in a number of gnostic sources: *The First Apocalypse of James* (NH 5. 33. 5–34. 20); the *Apocalypse of Paul* (NH 5. 20. 17); the *Acts of Thomas* 148 (257. 11 f. Bonnet); and in the gnostic-influenced ps.-Macarius Aegyptius *Hom.* 43. 9 (290. 134–9 Dörries).

longer had a body of light but a body of this world, they lived in a region below heaven. In the following passage, in which Origen assures a congregation familiar with stories about the terrors in the heavens, the implication is that these evil powers are located in the air and fire which surround the earth beneath heaven. After describing how the waters of the Jordan river parted to allow the people to cross into the promised land, Origen continues:

And you should not be surprised when these things are related to you about an earlier people. It is to you, Christian, who through the mystery of baptism have crossed the river Jordan, that the word of God has promised a way much better and higher: it promises you a journey and passage through the air itself. For hear Paul when he says of the righteous, 'we shall be taken up in the clouds to meet Christ in the air, and so we shall always be with the Lord' [1 Thessalonians 4: 17]. There is nothing at all that the righteous person should fear: every creature serves him. Hear finally how God, again through the prophet, makes him a promise, saying, 'if you should pass through fire, the flames would not harm you, for I am the LORD your God' [Isaiah 43: 2].[157]

There were demons above, but they were not stars (at least not any longer). Instead, comparable to the Stoic view, the domain of these evil powers was in the proximity of the earth.

In passages which explicitly refer to heavenly bodies, Origen is always of the opinion that they neither cause events below the moon nor are a source of woe to humanity. Origen is familiar with the tradition which makes the heavenly bodies wrongdoers, and strongly opposes it. Several times he quotes Psalm 72 (73): 9 against Basilidean and Valentinian opponents: 'they have set their mouths against heaven.'[158] The Gospel of Matthew itself links the moon with the demonic possession that causes epilepsy (17: 15), but Origen, citing this passage, goes to great lengths to show that this is not in fact due to the heavenly body but to the cunning of demons who observe the movements of the moon and also of the stars and plan their own evil deeds accordingly:

---

[157] *In Jesu Nave* Hom. 4. 1 (7. 308. 9–17 B.).
[158] *In Matth.* Comm. Ser. 28 (11. 51. 8–11 K1.), *In Titum* (*PG* 14. 1305a), cf. *In Rom.* 2. 14 (*PG* 14. 916d), *In Gen.* Hom. 3. 5 (6. 46. 18–23 B.). The Matthew passage singles out the followers of Basilides. The Titus passage refers to those who believe in various types of soul, which suggests the Valentinians.

And all those who claim that the cause of all disasters upon earth (whether generally or individually) correlates with the position of the stars say that 'there is injustice on high.' And such people truly 'have set their mouth against heaven' by saying that some of the stars are harmful and others are beneficent, when no star has been made by the God of the universe to do evil, at least according to Jeremiah as it is written in Lamentations [3: 38], 'Evils and good do not come from the mouth of the LORD.'

It is probable that this unclean spirit which causes what is called epilepsy (σεληνιασμός) observes the configurations of the moon in order to work upon the person who has been handed over to it for certain reasons and who has not made himself worthy of angelic protection. In precisely the same way other spirits and demons attend to the configurations of the other stars, so that not only the moon but also the other stars are reviled by those who claim 'there is injustice on high.'[159]

The heavenly bodies are not intrinsically evil, but can be used for evil purposes by demonic powers. In this manner also the devil at the end of days will transform himself into an angel of light (2 Corinthians 11: 14) and deceive many by pretending to be the sun.[160]

Origen thus denies the important contemporary belief that the planets or stars were malevolent. As part of the divine creation their nature is good. He also opposed the common astrological assumption that their 'effluences' (ἀπόρροιαι)[161] cause affairs beneath the moon. Since one of the charges made against Origen by later opponents was that he believed in astrology,[162] it is important to note that Origen frequently refers to this discipline and its practitioners and always denies their claims.[163] In addition to a series of philosophical arguments drawn from Academic

[159] *In Matth.* 13. 6 (10. 194. 13–195, 10 Kl.), from the Greek, cf. Jerome *In Matth.* 1 (*PL* 26. 33c); already Tatian *Or.* 9 (10. 3–10 Schwartz). For the view that the moon causes epilepsy see Franz Cumont, *L'Égypte des astrologues* (Brussels: Fondation égyptologique Reine Élisabeth, 1937) 169 n. 1.

[160] *In Matth.* Comm. Ser. 49 (11. 103. 7–15 Kl.), interpreting Matt. 24: 29.

[161] See ps.-Thessalus of Tralles 1 (61. 7 f. Friedrich); Porphyry *Introductio* 12 (*CCAG* 5. 4. 199); the 'Sacred Book of Hermes to Asclepius', ed. Ruelle in *RPh* 32 (1908) 250. 7; *CH* frag. 23. 64 (4. 20. 27 f. N/F); *PGM* 12. 254; etc.

[162] So Theophilus of Alexandria in Jerome *Ep.* 92, and one anonymous citing another ap. Photius *Bib.* 117. K. quotes both passages in his edition of *Prin.* at 3. 3. 3.

[163] *In Gen.* Hom. 14. 3 (6. 124. 8 f. B.), *In Exod.* Hom. 7. 2 (6. 207. 17–19 B.), *In Num.* Hom. 12. 4 (7. 106. 5–7 B.), *In Jesu Nave* Hom. 7. 4 (7. 331. 12–15 B.), *In Ezech.* Hom. 1. 10 (8. 333. 27 f. B.)., *In Jer.* Latin Hom. 3. 4 (8. 314. 3–21 B.) *In Matth.* 13. 6 (10. 195. 13–16 Kl.).

sources which questioned the plausibility of astrological claims,[164] Origen says that belief in astrology destroys the free will and so eliminates any possible merit or blame for actions, and so any belief in a righteous judgement of God.[165] The determinism presupposed by astrology would empty all meaning out of Christ's Redemption, the efforts of the apostles, human endeavour, and prayer, and would make God unjust.[166]

The stars, however, had too strong a position both in contemporary philosophy and in the popular imagination to play no role whatsoever in shaping the life below. Connections between the moon and the movements of tides, or between the positions of stars and the seasons, had long since been made, and this lent much credibility to astrological claims. The belief that one could foretell the future by studying the heavens was common wisdom in Alexandria, the home of such influential astrologers as Nechepso/Petosiris and Ptolemy. And even later when he preached in Caesarea, Origen was aware that many in his congregation consulted astrologers routinely.[167] Among both intellectuals and the unlearned, complete disbelief in astrological theory was scarcely credible in the third century.

A middle course, however, was available. Following Philo, Clement, and the Platonic tradition,[168] Origen believed that the stars could act as signs of future events without causing them. He Christianizes this view, saying that the stars were signs of all that happens in accordance with Genesis 1: 14, 'let them be for signs,' and Jeremiah 10: 2, 'be not dismayed at the signs of heaven.'[169] This was combined with his conviction that all things in this world were traceable, not to Fate, but to free will or to the dictates of Providence. We saw above that Origen believed that demons watched the phases of the moon in order to plan their own misdeeds and so malign the moon, and this was possible because there was a relationship (the Stoics would say a 'sympathy') between events in heaven and the position of the stars. Incidents occurring on earth have regular counterparts in

[164] See *Philocalia* 23. 16 f. (204. 16–207. 23 R.).
[165] Ibid. 23. 1 (187. 24–188, 29 R.) and 23. 2 (189. 18–22).
[166] Ibid., and frag. 49 *In Jer.* to verse 36: 8 (3. 223. 13 Kl.).
[167] *In Jesu Nave* Hom. 7. 4 (7. 331. 12–15 B.). See also *Philocalia* 23. 1 (187. 20–4 R.).
[168] See ch. 5, n. 10 and ch. 7 n. 7.
[169] *Philocalia* 23. 15 (204. 8–213 R.).

heaven and vice-versa—not because one causes the other but because each is part of a single whole. This is the explanation for Jacob's reference to 'reading the pages of the sky':[170] the stars are 'heavenly writings' which angels and divine powers can read.[171] This is also probably the meaning of Origen's obscure reference to the good deeds recorded on 'the Gospel written on heavenly tablets' which can be read by all who are worthy to know all things.[172] Astrology is the mistaken use of this correlation between heaven and earth; one which (following *1 Enoch* and Clement) is abetted by fallen angels.[173]

There is a proper use for the signs of the heavens, and that is to refer to them in order to keep track of the change of seasons. In response to Celsus, Origen defended the Stoic idea that the whole universe had been made for the benefit of humanity,[174] and he thought that this was also true for the physical heavens. Along with earth, sea, winds, and rain, so too heaven, sun, moon, and stars were given by God to serve mankind.[175] Like most of his pagan contemporaries, Origen assumed that the association of different stars in the sky with different seasons meant that the stars caused the seasons and the changes in the weather that they brought. This also meant that the heavenly bodies produce all of the fruits of the earth for the human race to enjoy.[176] Thus the stars had a central role in daily human affairs, though only in regulating the natural world and not in our moral and spiritual life. Other Christian writers had the same idea,[177] but for Origen this service was the result of an immanent and conscious act, and not simply of Providence working directly through the stars. Origen believed that the universe was full of rational beings who were either well-disposed to humanity (angels) or hated it (demons), and the starry heavens were among the beneficent

---

[170] Ibid. 23. 15 and 19, quoting a lost Jewish apocalyptic work, the *Prayer of Joseph*, see J. Z. Smith ap. Charlesworth, *Pseudepigrapha*, 2. 699–712.

[171] Ibid. 23. 20 (209. 23–6 R.); cf. Plotinus 2. 3. 7. 4–13, 3. 1. 6. 18–24.

[172] *In Jo.* 1. 11. 68 (4. 16. 31–4 P.). For precedent in Jewish apocalyptic see Cécile Blanc's note in *Origène: Commentaire sur Saint Jean*, i, SC 120 (Paris: du Cerf, 1966), 95.

[173] *Philocalia* 23. 6 (193. 31–194. 4 R.), see ch. 7 n. 9.

[174] *CCel.* 4. 74 (1. 343. 14–344. 16 K.).

[175] *In Num.* Hom. 24. 2 (7. 229. 28–230. 2 B.).

[176] *In Rom.* 7. 4 (*PG* 14. 1111c), *In Jesu Nave* Hom. 23. 3 (7. 444. 5–13 B.); pagan: Varro frag. 26 (Cardauns), Celsus ap. Origen *CCel.* 5. 6 (2. 6. 3–5 K.).

[177] See W. Gundel, 'Astronomie', *RAC* I (1950), 835.

powers. They carried out (literally) mundane tasks, helping to preserve order and continuity in the world so that life could prosper and the opportunity could be present for those who were mortal and fleshly to strive after that which was higher and better.

At this point we see that three of Origen's innovative speculations on the stars were: (1) they were sinners who are now doing penance for pre-existent vices, (2) their bodies are the heavier and more material consequence of sin, and (3) their maintenance of the correct progression of the seasons through the rational movement of their bodies was their conscious service to humanity. All three are repeatedly referred to in Origen's exegesis of Romans 8: 20, 'the creation was subjected to vanity, not of its own will, but because of him who subjected it in hope.' Origen cites this passage in discussions of the function of heavenly bodies many different times, in works both early and late in his career.[178] The following passage is representative:

For indeed 'the creation was subjected to vanity, not willingly, but by reason of him who subjected the same in hope', so that sun, moon, stars, and the angels of God should fulfil an obedient service for the world; and it was for those souls which on account of their excessive spiritual defects required these grosser and more solid bodies and also for the sake of those others for whom this arrangement was necessary that the visible world was instituted.[179]

Elsewhere Origen suggests that the 'vanity' to which creation is subjected is a reference to the bodies which the stars have to put on.[180] Only at the moment of the 'revelation of the sons of God' (Romans 8: 19), i.e. the Redemption, will the heavenly bodies be freed from this task.[181]

Origen's opinion on this is not fixed. He once again prefaces one of these discussions with the admission that this is only his

---

[178] *De Mart.* 7, *Prin.* 1. 7. 5, 2. 9. 7, 3. 5. 4, *In Rom.* 7. 4, *CCel.* 5. 13, cf. *In Rom.* 9. 41, *In Num.* Hom. 28. 2. *De Mart.* is an early work, *CCel.* a late one. See further Paul Lebeau, 'L'Interprétation origénienne de Rm. 8. 19–22', *Kyriakon*, FS Johannes Quasten, ed. Patrick Granfield and Josef A. Jungmann (Münster: Aschendorff, 1970), 1. 336–45.

[179] *Prin.* 3. 5. 4. 116–22 (C/S); trans. Butterworth (slightly adapted). Cf. Jerome *Contra Jo.* 17 (*PL* 23. 385bc); Augustine *Comm. Orosii* 3 (162. 121–5 Daur).

[180] *Prin.* 1. 7. 5. 155–7 (C/S).

[181] Ibid. 164–75 (C/S), *De Mart.* 7 (1. 9. 10–14 K.).

opinion,[182] and it is perhaps significant that none of these discussions occurs in a homily: though the doctrinal differences between the homilies and his more esoteric works have been exaggerated in the past, it is true that Origen is somewhat more reserved in his public addresses than in his more private writings.[183] He keeps returning to this interpretation, and yet clearly it is an issue which he is still weighing.

One mark of how flexible Origen was in his interpretation of Romans 8: 20 is that at one point he appears to suggest that the service rendered by the stars and planets was not penance but a noble sacrifice:

for antecedent causes a different position of service is prepared by the Creator for each one in proportion to the degree of his merit, which depends on the fact that each, in being created by God as a mind or rational spirit, has personally gained for himself, in accordance with the movements of his mind and the disposition of his heart, a greater or less share of merit, and has rendered himself either lovable or it may be hateful to God. We must also note, however, that some beings who are of higher merit are ordained to suffer with the rest and to perform a duty to those below them, in order that by this means they themselves may become sharers in the endurance of the Creator, according to the Apostle's own words, 'The creature was made subject to vanity . . .' [etc.].[184]

This would suggest that the labours of the heavenly bodies were not a penance imposed on them by God, but a freely chosen service. Origen remarks that this might be specifically true of the sun, commenting on Philippians 1: 23:

For I consider that the sun might say that it was a finer thing to be dissolved and be with Christ; for it is much better. And whereas Paul adds: 'But to abide in the flesh is more needful for your sakes,' the sun might say: 'To abide in this heavenly body is more needful for the sake of the revealing of the children of God.' And the same may be said of the moon and the rest of the heavenly bodies.[185]

---

[182] *Prin.* 1. 7. 5. 155 (C/S).

[183] Exaggerated: Erich Klostermann, 'Formen der exegetischen Arbeiten des Origenes', *ThL* 72 (1947), 205; reserved: Franz Heinrich Kettler, *Der ursprüngliche Sinn der Dogmatik des Origenes*, BZNW 31 (Berlin: Alfred Töpelmann, 1966), 9, R. P. C. Hanson, *Origen's Doctrine of Tradition* (London: SPCK, 1954), 77.

[184] *Prin.* 2. 9. 7. 245–56 (C/S), trans. Butterworth.

[185] *Prin.* 1. 7. 5. 183–91, Greek fragment (almost identical) in C/S, *Principes*, 2. 112, trans. (from the Greek) Butterworth.

Such an interpretation again suggests that the stars are not sinners, and (here as we saw earlier) that they are ontologically superior to humanity. This very different understanding of how the usefulness of the stars has come about shows how ready Origen was to entertain completely new speculations. His method was not to create a cosmological system, but in matters of cosmology to leave no idea which scripture would allow to go unexplored. Origen's usual position is that stars have the place they do in temporal life because of their own pre-existent sin, but it was a matter in which he was ready to try out new speculations. Origen's cosmology is thus hard to pin down, which is why he has been so often misunderstood by both friend and foe.

Origen's understanding of the resurrected human soul is another aspect of his cosmology where his general drift is clear but his final positions are not fully worked out. His theories on the nature of the life after death are once again subtle and controversial, and once again his views are explicable in terms of the life already possessed by the stars. This is one of Origen's most important appropriations of speculations on the life of the heavens, and will form the subject of the next chapter.

9

STARS AND THE RESURRECTION BODY

As we have seen, Origen does believe that the stars are alive, and in fact his view is one of a series of Origenist views that is formally anathematized by the emperor Justinian.[1] But Origen was innovative—and so controversial—in a wide range of cosmological problems, and his views on the stars figure in many of them. Above all, his discussion of the resurrection body was an extraordinarily difficult subject in which his speculations were often closely interrelated with his discussions of the nature and life of the heavenly bodies.

The doctrine of the resurrection of the body is not put forward either consistently or clearly in the New Testament. While some passages suggest that the body we now possess will be resuscitated on the Last Day, others have a different perspective.[2] This other view is evident in 1 Corinthians 15: 34–54, a very important passage for Origen, where Paul says that the resurrected body is new and spiritual, and stands in relation to our present body as a seed does to its fruit. Against the claim that the resurrected body would be simply identical to the physical body we now have, Origen cites Paul's words that the body after death would not be the same as our body, 'for flesh and blood cannot inherit the kingdom of God; neither does corruption inherit incorruption' (1 Corinthians 15: 50).[3] The body we receive at death will not need food and drink but will be what Paul called a

---

[1] Anathema 6 from Justinian's *Ep. ad Mennam* of 543 (ACO 3. 213. 27 f.), and anathema 3 of his letter to the council of 553 (ACO 4. 1. 248, 14–16). On the other hand, the charge that Origen taught that the resurrection body would be spherical like the stars is based on a later misunderstanding, see A. J. Festugière, 'De la doctrine "origéniste" du corps glorieux sphéroïde', *RevSciPhilTheol* 43 (1959) 81–6.

[2] Resuscitated: Matth. 27: 52 f., John 11: 44. In John 20: 27 Jesus' resurrected body, like the ghost of Hector in Aeneas' dream, still bears the wounds he received in life. See on the other hand Luke 23: 43, 2 Cor. 5:8, Phil. 1: 23 f.

[3] *CCel.* 5. 19 (2. 20. 14–16 K.), and often, see *Biblia Patristica*, ed. J. Allenbach *et al.* (Paris: Centre national de la recherche scientifique, 1980), 3. 406 f.

'spiritual body' (1 Corinthians 15: 44).[4] From an early point a wide variety of Christian writers who were subsequently accused of heresy denied a physical resurrection and affirmed spiritual interpretations of this doctrine.[5] By Origen's day the tension between a physical and an entirely spiritual concept of resurrection had not been fully worked out,[6] but the latter view as it had been formulated by various groups (mostly 'gnostic') had been repeatedly condemned by developing ecclesiastical Christianity, of which Origen viewed himself as a loyal son.

Origen's most searching investigations of this problem were undertaken in his role as a Christian apologist, since the anti-Christian polemicist Celsus delighted in pointing out the difficulties entailed by the doctrine of a physical resurrection.[7] It was the sort of challenge that Origen could not resist. Acknowledging that this was one of the most perplexing Christian doctrines,[8] Origen attempted to steer a middle course between the views of 'simple' Christians that the resurrected body was no different from our physical body (his opposition to Chiliasts was a factor here), and the beliefs of a number of groups accused of heresy who had a purely spiritual or figurative interpretation of this doctrine.[9] Origen thought that both sides were wrong. Thus he accepted many of the criticisms of the idea of a purely physical resurrection, and yet also rejected the spiritualism of various Christian heresies.[10] He suggested that what would be raised on the resurrection at the Last Day would not be the physical body (which is always in a state of flux), but its form or principle

[4] *Prin.* 2. 11. 2. 27–36 (C/S).

[5] The *Gospel of Philip* 21 (NH 2. 56. 26–57. 22), *The Testimony of Truth* (NH 9. 36. 29–37. 5); opposed already in 2 Tim. 2: 18, and frequently thereafter in the heresiologists. See further H.-M. Schenke, 'Auferstehungsglaube und Gnosis', *ZNW* 59 (1958), 123–6.

[6] Tertullian suggested that the martyr rose immediately to heaven, while ordinary believers slept until the Last Day. See Henri Crouzel, 'Mort et immortalité selon Origène', *BLE* 79 (1978), 188.

[7] *CCel.* 5. 14 (2. 15. 4–7 K.); cf. Methodius *De Res.* 1. 20 (242 ff. Bonwetsch).

[8] *CCel.* 7. 32 (2. 182. 20–3 K.).

[9] See Jon F. Dechow, 'Dogma and Mysticism in Early Christianity', Ph.D. dissertation (University of Pennsylvania, 1975), 322, J. N. D. Kelly, *Early Christian Doctrines* (5th edn., San Francisco: Harper & Row, 1978), 471; chiliasts: see C/S, *Principes*, 2. 228–30.

[10] Accepted: see Henry Chadwick, 'Origen, Celsus, and the Resurrection of the Body', *HTR* 41 (1948), 83–102; rejected: see Leonhard Atzberger, *Geschichte der christlichen Eschatologie innerhalb der vornicänischen Zeit* (Freiburg im Breisgau: Herder, 1896), 431.

($εἶδος$).[11] This principle is the content of the soul (particularly the rational soul), and it is this and not the body which is both made in the image of God and granted eternal life.[12] The body as a merely physical entity passes into corruption, but its principle (which is identified with what Paul calls the 'seed' of the resurrected body, 1 Corinthians 15: 38) becomes the foundation of its new life.[13] Thus Origen could affirm that he believed in the resurrection of the body we now have,[14] since this principle would be the essence of all that our body truly is, lacking only that which is subject to growth or decay.

It was a subtle explanation, and its debt to Platonism is obvious. Unfortunately for Origen, his later opponents would demand plainer teachings which were less philosophically orientated and further removed from gnostic spiritualism. They insisted that the resurrected body be seen as identical to our present material body,[15] and their work was very influential in later controversies over Origen's theology. The resurrected body was not a spiritual or heavenly body, but the same material one which had sensation and suffered pain in the present life. This later view, which was formulated in conscious opposition to Origen and his admirers, follows the first tendency in New Testament theology, exemplified by Lazarus coming forth from the tomb, and does relatively little with the Pauline view. The proponents of this view, however, preferred facing the difficulties of teaching an entirely physical resurrection to the subtleties and dangers of a more spiritualizing interpretation.

Jerome and Justinian claimed that Origen taught a completely spiritual doctrine of the resurrection in which all souls would eventually revert to a state of complete incorporeality, but this is inaccurate. Origen does in fact refer to those who think that rational beings can live apart from the body,[16] but does not affirm

[11] *CCel.* 5. 23 (2. 24. 4–6 K.); Methodius ap. Eustathius *Engast.* 22, quoted by Dechow in Lothar Lies (ed.), *Origeniana Quarta* (Innsbruck: Tyrolia, 1987), 407; see also below n. 44.

[12] *CCel.* 8. 49 (2. 265. 2–6 K.).

[13] *CCel.* 5. 23 (2. 24. 1–3 K.), *In Rom.* 5. 10 (*PG* 14. 1050b), and often, see C/S, *Principes*, 2. 231 n. 14.

[14] *In Matth.* 17. 29 (10. 668. 9–24 K1.), *Prin.* 3. 6. 6. 203 f. (C/S). Christ rose 'cum ipso corpore quod susceperat ex Maria', *De Res.* 2 ap. Pamphilus *Apol.* 7 (*PG* 17. 595b); cf. Methodius *De Res.* 1. 20 (242. 5–7 Bonwetsch).

[15] Epiphanius *Anc.* 82. 3 (1. 103. 2–4 Holl).

[16] *Prin.* 2. 3. 3. 100–29 (C/S); for Jerome/Justinian see C/S, *Principes*, 2. 145 f.

their view. Elsewhere he raises the prospect of a completely incorporeal existence as one of the two possibilities of the state of the soul in the resurrection (along with the possession of an ethereal body and inheritance of a blessed life in a separate, superheavenly region), without ruling out this option.[17] Since as a Platonist he regarded the rational part of a human being as incorporeal, and since he thought the creation of the corporeal world was a consequence of sin,[18] it is easy to see how Jerome, Justinian, and many modern scholars could reach the conclusion that Origen believed that the soul was once completely incorporeal, fell into body because of sin, and would return to incorporeality at the soul's return to pre-lapsarian harmony, the ἀποκατάστασις.

But fundamentally this was not Origen's view, because he regarded it as an essential characteristic of any created rational nature that it exist in a body, and an essential aspect of the divine nature that it not exist in a body. Such a position is for Origen a theological necessity, enabling him to affirm simultaneously both his doctrine of the soul and the Christian doctrine of creation. His reasoning goes like this. Origen believes in typical Platonic fashion that diversity in the world does not exist apart from bodies.[19] It is only the presence of matter which enables things to be divided into classes.[20] Rational beings as such were therefore of one nature[21] and had no variation,[22] and would have none on that day 'when all are one'.[23] Taken to its logical conclusion this would necessitate a substantial identity between any form of rationality and the supreme rational being, God. And in fact Origen allows that there is a 'certain kinship' between the rational soul and God.[24] But he explicitly denies the identity of the two,[25] for God alone is completely simple while everything

[17] *Prin.* 2. 3. 7. 328–30 (C/S), and Völker, *Vollkommenheitsideal,* 128.
[18] See above ch. 8 nn. 14 and 145.
[19] *Prin.* 2. 1. 4. 93 f. (C/S).
[20] *Prin.* 3. 6. 4. 126–30 (C/S). See Clement *Exc. ex Theod.* 11. 3 (82 Sagnard).
[21] *Prin.* 3. 5. 4. 133 f. (C/S).
[22] *Prin.* 2. 9. 6. 185–90, 4. 4. 9. 350–9 (C/S), *In Jo.* 2. 23. 146 (4. 79. 21–3 P.), *In Cant.* Hom. 2 (8. 147. 21 f. B.).
[23] *Prin.* 3. 6. 4. 130–3 (C/S).
[24] *Exh. Mart.* 47 (1. 42. 29 f. K.), *Prin.* 1. 1. 7. 252–6 (C/S), cf. *In Lev.* ap. *Philoc.* 1. 30 (36. 5–8 R.); Clement *Protrep.* 2. 25 (1. 18. 29–19. 1 St.). For Philo see Runia *Philo* 341.
[25] *In Jo.* 13. 25. 149 (4. 249. 5 f. P.); cf. Clement *Strom.* 2. 16. 74 (2. 152. 6 f. St.). Even Origen's critic Augustine concedes this, *De Civ. Dei* 11. 23 (341. 8 f. Dombart/Kalb).

which exists as part of the created order is composite and multiple.[26] This includes rational natures, which do not exist from eternity but have been created *ex nihilo* by God.[27] God is an incorporeal unity, while rational creation is always a corporeal multiplicity. This is a fixed part of Origen's thought—so fixed that he (like Philo) uses the word 'incorporeal', not to refer to the soul's complete independence from body, but its independence from an earthly body.[28]

It is possible to separate mentally human rationality from its material setting (that is why there is a 'certain kinship' between our reason and the divine), but embodied existence is always the actual state for a rational creature.

But if it is impossible by any means to maintain this proposition, namely, that any being, with the exception of the Father, Son, and Holy Spirit, can live apart from a body, then logical reasoning compels us to believe that, while the original creation was of rational beings, it is only in idea and thought that a material substance seems to have been produced for them or after them, yet never have they lived or do they live without it; for we shall be right in believing that life without a body is found in the Trinity alone.[29]

This passage has been considered by some an interpolation by Rufinus, but Origen's view that the soul had an ethereal body is confirmed by his later enemy Methodius. Basing his opinion on Origen's work (now lost) *De Resurrectione*, Methodius cites Origen as writing that the soul at death has a material vehicle ($\check{o}\chi\eta\mu\alpha$) and garment ($\pi\epsilon\rho\iota\beta\omega\lambda\acute{\eta}$).[30] Like other Platonic contemporaries, Origen considered the possibility that the soul was placed in a vehicle which was akin to the bodies of stars. This was the only body of the soul before its incorporation and after its departure from the body of flesh.[31] Thus for Origen, even creatures with a

---

[26] *In Jo.* 1. 20. 119 (4. 119. 23–6 P.), *De Orat.* 21. 2 (2. 345. 17 K.).

[27] *Prin.* 1. 4. 5. 87 f., 1. 7. 1. 10–14; *ex nihilo*: 1. 3. 3. 56–68 C/S, *In Jo.* 32. 16. 187 (4. 451. 26–8 P., quoting the *Shepherd of Hermas*).

[28] See above ch. 8 n. 139; Philo: see Dillon, 'Angels', 201.

[29] *Prin.* 2. 2. 2. 24–32 (C/S), trans. Butterworth. See also 1. 6. 4. 175–82, 4. 3. 15. 481–96, *In Ex.* Hom. 6. 5 (6. 197. 8 B.), and Henri Crouzel, 'La Thème platonicien du "véhicule de l'âme" chez Origène', *Didask.* 7 (1977), 228, and Crouzel, 'Mort', 26.

[30] Methodius *De Res.* 3. 18 (415. 1–4 Bonwetsch), cf. *CCel.* 2. 60 (1. 183. 7–10 K.), 1 Cor. 15: 53, 2 Cor. 5: 2–4; for apocalyptic literature, see Cavallin, 'Leben', 302.

[31] Pre-existent body: see Crouzel, 'Véhicule', 232 f.

higher ontological status than humans in this life, such as the redeemed at the resurrection or angels, had bodies.

And here we see that the soul's body is understood in astral terms. For Origen, bodies ontologically superior to our earthly bodies were identified as ethereal, like the stars. Now, since the bodies of stars were regarded as a result of sin, this would pose a problem if Origen were truly 'systematic'. Presumably the resurrected human soul (or, for that matter, the souls of stars after they had finished their penance in this cosmos) would require a better body than an astral one if the astral body itself were a consequence of sin. But this difficulty apparently never occurred to Origen. The philosophical tradition which identified the stars as superior to humanity was so strong it was perhaps natural to speak of higher forms of life in these terms.

The exception to this of course was God. Origen writes that some (meaning the Stoics) say that God has a subtle and ethereal body, but that this is absurd. God is a completely incorporeal spirit (*pneuma*).[32] It is also incorrect to say this about the incarnate Christ: Origen writes that some heretics claim that Christ was incarnated in a body taken from the stars, but that this contradicts the prophecy of Zechariah (3: 3), who said that 'Joshua [i.e. Jesus—the names are the same in Greek] was clothed with filthy garments.'[33] 'Filthy garments' can only apply to the human body, not to an astral body, so on earth Christ's body had an earthly nature. Against his gnostic opponents, Origen thus insists that Christ took on true flesh in the Incarnation.[34]

On the other hand Christ's resurrection body, though it truly was a body, did not have an earthly nature but again an ethereal and divine one.[35] The destiny of this body is to dwell 'in ether and the realms above it'.[36] Origen interpreted Matthew's version of

[32] *In Jo.* 13. 21. 123–5 (4. 244. 19–245. 3 P.).
[33] *In Luc.* Hom. 14 (9. 86. 7–18 Ra.), *In Ps.* 18 (*PG* 12. 1242 f.), cited by Harnack, *Marcion*, 418* (who identifies it with either Apelles or Hermogenes). Cf. *In Rom.* 9. 2 (*PG* 14. 1210c), *Prin.* 1 Praef. 8. 167 (C/S), *In Gal.* (PG 14. 1295bc). See ch. 7 n. 26.
[34] *In Matth.* Comm. Ser. 92 (11. 208. 15–17 Kl.).
[35] *CCel.* 3. 41 (1. 237. 15–18 K.); cf. Clement of Alexandria *In Ep. Ioh. Prima* (3. 210. 13–15 St.). Both writers feel the weight of the criticism, which is later expressed in Porphyry, that Christ could not have entered heaven with a material body: *Contra Chr.* frag. 35 (Harnack, from Macarius Magnes).
[36] *CCel.* 3. 42 (1. 238. 1 K.).

Jesus' entry into Jerusalem (in which Jesus is said to ride both a colt and an ass into the city) as a reference to Jesus' reception into the spiritual Jerusalem together with his corporeal vehicle.[37] When he appeared to his disciples his body was in an intermediate stage and so had its physical wounds from the crucifixion.[38] In its fully resurrected state, however, Christ's body was not limited by the constraints of the life of this world: he has then, as Origen put it, 'the condition of a soul uncovered by any body'.[39] Christ in heaven has a body, but not one which interferes with his knowledge of God, and so he escapes that ignorance which is an inevitable consequence of materiality.[40]

Likewise angels are said to have luminous and heavenly bodies.[41] Even demons, depite their moral inferiority, lack the thicker bodies which we possess.[42] Since Origen suggested both that angels sin and that resurrected human souls might take the place of fallen demons in heaven,[43] he might have been expected to suggest that resurrected human souls inherited a body superior to that of demons, but this again never was regarded as a problem by Origen.

Instead, Origen simply assumes that any being which lives in heaven must have a heavenly body.

For it is necessary for the soul that is existing in corporeal places to use bodies appropriate to those places. Just as if we became aquatic beings, and had to live in the sea, it would no doubt be necessary for us to adopt a different state similar to that of the fish, so if we are to inherit the kingdom of heaven and to exist in superior places, it is essential for us to use spiritual bodies. This does not mean that the form ($\varepsilon\tilde{\imath}\delta o\varsigma$) of the earlier body disappears, though it may change to a more glorious condition, as did the form of Jesus, Moses, and Elijah, which did not differ in its transformation from what it had been before.[44]

[37] *In Matth.* 16. 19 (10. 538. 30 ff.), quoted by Crouzel, 'Véhicule', 230. See also *In Ps.* 15. 9 ap. Pamphilus *Apol.* 7 (*PG* 17, 600a).

[38] *CCel.* 2. 62 (1. 184. 11–17 K.).

[39] Ibid. (1. 184. 13), trans. Chadwick.

[40] *In Matth.* 13. 17 (10. 224 f. Kl.), cited by Cornélis, 'Fondements', 66.

[41] *In Matth.* 17. 30 (10. 671. 19–21 Kl.). Cf. Clement *Exc. ex Theod.* 12. 2 (82 Sagnard).

[42] *CCel.* 5. 5 (2. 5. 20 K.).

[43] Sin: see above ch. 8 nn. 116–18; take the place: *In Ezech.* Hom. 13. 2 (8. 444. 15–18 B.).

[44] Origen *In Ps.* 1. 5 ap. Methodius *De Res.* 1. 22. 4 f. (246, 3–11 Bonwetsch), trans. (up to 'glorious condition') by Chadwick in his *Contra Celsum* 420 n. 7. The authenticity of this is confirmed by a parallel in Pamphilus, *Apol.* 7 (*PG* 17. 599ab).

Origen is not quite sure about the nature of this body, but thinks it is some special type of matter, characterized by its subtlety and purity.[45] This resurrection body of human beings is not distinguished from the body of Christ, or angels, or demons, but once again is described as ethereal (αἰθέριος), heavenly (οὐράνιος), or luminous (αὐγοειδής)—terms which Origen uses interchangeably.[46]

We see here that while resurrection bodies are apparently not exactly stars, they are described as similar to them. Origen followed the tradition of contemporary Jewish literature in referring to souls shining after death. As there are different degrees of brightness in heaven so there are different states of righteousness, and he writes that he hopes to be compared only with a dimmer star and not with the moon or one of the brighter stars, since the latter comparison would make him look bad.[47] And yet it is only at the beginning of the blessed life that the redeemed shine with a different light, for in the end they shine with the same light, namely that of the sun, in accordance with Matthew 13: 43.[48] Thus commenting on this same verse elsewhere Origen can say:

In this life human nature is able to progress so far that at the Resurrection of the dead it may equal not only the glory of the stars but even the shining of the sun, as it is written 'the just will gleam like the sun in the kingdom of God' [Matthew 13: 43].[49]

At another point Origen speaks of the citizens of the heavenly Jerusalem as those who have ascended into heaven by their way of life and who have become a multitude of stars praising God.[50] He combines this with the Platonic view that the souls of the wicked remain visible and are murky and black, concluding that

---

[45] Unsure: *Prin.* 1. 6. 4. 182–7 (C/S); special: *CCel.* 4. 57 (1. 330. 7–11 K.), *De Orat.* 26. 6 (2. 363. 22 K.), *In Matth.* Comm. Ser. 50 (11. 109. 3 K1.); subtle: *Prin.* 2. 3. 3. 109–12, 3. 6. 4. 106 f. (C/S).

[46] See previous note, and also: heavenly: *In Num.* Hom. 15. 3 (7. 135. 23 f. B.); ethereal: *CCel.* 3. 42 (1. 238. 1 K.), *In Matth.* 17. 29 (10. 667. 12 f. K1.), *Prin.* 2. 3. 7. 336; luminous: *In Matth.* 17. 30 (10. 671. 17–21 K1.), *Prin.* 2. 10. 8. 267 (C/S), cf. Procopius of Gaza *In Gen.* 3. 21 (*PG* 87. 1. 221).

[47] *In Ezech.* Hom. 9. 4 (8. 412. 8–19 B.).

[48] *In Matth.* 10. 3 (10. 3. 18–4. 4 K1.).

[49] *In Num.* Hom. 2. 2 (7. 12. 17–21, cf. 13. 3–6), *De Res.* 2 ap. Pamphilus *Apol.* 7 (*PG* 17. 596b), *Prin.* 2. 3. 7. 337, 3. 6. 8. 240 f. (C/S).

[50] *In Ps.* 147 (*PAS* 3. 359).

as the souls of the righteous become more lucid, the souls of the wicked become darker.[51] Like the portrait of Dorian Grey, our physical condition always corresponds to the state of our moral life. In the future life as in this one, our ontological status is a reflection of our merits.[52]

This life and the life after death are a moral challenge and opportunity. They are a challenge because moral failure means ontological decline and the assumption of a thicker and more earthly body. It is also an opportunity, because the soul was able to learn more about what it should be like and so improve its own ontological state. Walther Völker, the great scholar of Alexandrian theology, entitled his book on Philo *Fortschritt und Vollendung*, 'Progress and Perfection', but the same words also summarize Origen's eschatology. The life of the soul is a journey in which it learns about God, and a completion in which it knows God. Seen in a different way, there are two journeys for the soul: one an inward journey in which it ascends through the different 'grades of perfection' that are part of this life (an important idea for later monasticism), and a second in which it traverses the 'many abiding places' (John 14: 12) of God, and is continually illumined by Wisdom at each stage, until it reaches the 'father of lights' (James 1: 17).[53] Concern with the first journey—that of the inward life and the moral decisions of the soul's free will—dominates Origen's theology, as Völker rightly emphasized in his monograph on Origen.[54] And yet Origen could not resist speculating on the soul's journey at death out of this cosmos and into the heavens. In fact the two were closely linked in his mind: the inward journey of ethical decision made it possible for the soul to cross the barriers which separated it from God, and the soul in heaven in turn learned more about God and about its own true destiny. If the soul was virtuous enough in this life, it had nothing to fear from the heavens, where indeed it would receive new opportunities to become like God. In this journey too there

[51] Plato: *Phaedo* 81c4–d4; Origen: *CCel.* 7. 5 (2. 156. 25–30 K.), *Prin.* 2. 10. 8. 265–73 (C/S); cf. Basil (*PG* 29. 372).
[52] *Prin.* 2. 10. 3. 110–16 (C/S), Henri Crouzel, 'L'Hadès et la Géhenne selon Origène', *Gregorianum* 59 (1978), 318, and id., 'Différences entre les ressuscités selon Origène', *Jenseitsvorstellungen in Antike und Christentum*, JAC suppl. 9, ed. Theodor Klauser *et al.* (Münster: Aschendorff, 1982) 108.
[53] *In Num.* Hom. 27. 6 (7. 264. 5–12 B.).
[54] *Vollkommenheitsideal* 15, and *passim*.

were different levels of achievement and so different levels of glory among those who ascended to heaven.[55] As the stars differed in their shining according to their merits, so too there was not one fixed destiny for the soul after death but many different ways in which it might travel.

As a first stage in this journey, the soul would go to 'paradise', which is located on earth. Origen describes this paradise as 'so to speak, a lecture room or school for souls' in which souls are taught about the future (i.e. about heaven) in a much clearer way than what is available to us in this life, where knowledge is only in part and we see through a glass dimly (1 Corinthians 13: 2).[56] Origen continues:

If anyone is pure in heart and of unpolluted mind and well-trained understanding he will make swifter progress and quickly ascend to the region of the air, until he reaches the kingdom of the heavens, passing through the series of these 'abiding places' [cf. John 14: 2], if I may so call them, which the Greeks have termed spheres, that is, globes, but which the divine scripture calls heavens. In each of these he will first observe all that happens there, and then learn the reason why it happens; and thus he will proceed in order through each stage, following him who has 'entered into the heavens, Jesus the Son of God', who has said, 'I will that, where I am, they also may be with me' [John 17: 24]. Further, he alludes to this diversity of places when he says, 'In my Father's house there are many abiding places.'[57]

This passage is obscure for a number of reasons. First, it is hard to see what Origen means when he says this paradise is on earth, especially since elsewhere he locates paradise in heaven.[58] Second, it is not clear exactly what relation the soul will have to the living spheres. In the section following this one, however, Origen says that perhaps the resurrected souls will learn if the heavenly bodies are alive or not,[59] so it is probable that Origen sees this ascent through the heavens as an opportunity for the

---

[55] *Prin.* 2. 10. 2. 67–72 (C/S).

[56] *Prin.* 2. 11. 6. 214–24 (C/S) trans. Butterworth, cf. *In Matth.* Comm. Ser. 51 (11. 114. 17 f. K1.).

[57] *Prin.* 2. 11. 6. 224–35 (C/S), trans. Butterworth.

[58] See Crouzel's note, C/S, *Principes*, 2. 250. This cannot be the 'true earth' located in the ninth sphere, since Origen says the soul goes from this paradise located on earth up through the spheres.

[59] Cf. above ch. 8 n. 56.

soul to learn about the life in the heavens, to which the
resurrected soul is now closely related by nature.

In one of the homilies he delivered on the Book of Numbers,
Origen addresses the issue of what the soul learns and where it
goes after death.

For the Lord spoke of the 'abiding places' which the soul would inhabit
when it put off the body, or rather when it put on again its own body,
when he said in the Gospel, 'In my Father's house are many abiding
places. Truly I would say to you, I go and prepare an abiding place for
you' [John 14: 2]. There are 'many abiding places' which lead to the
Father. What is the reason and profit for the soul to abide in each of
these places, and how much instruction or illumination it will receive,
only the 'Father of the age to come' [Isaiah 9: 6] knows. He says of
himself, 'I am the door, no one comes to the Father except by me' [John
10: 9]. Perhaps in each of these 'abiding places' he becomes a door for
each soul, so that the soul may 'enter' through him and 'leave' through
him, and 'find pasture' [John 10: 9], and again go into another, and then
another abiding place, until it comes to the Father himself.[60]

Here we see that entrance to the heavenly abiding places is
connected with the soul's release from its earthly body and its
assumption of an astral body. The soul is now fit for life in the
stars, which as in the *Timaeus* are seen as places of instruction.
Origen's debt to current speculations is particularly evident in the
imagery both here and in the *Contra Celsum* of a gate through
which the soul must pass, an idea also shared by Numenius,
Mithraists, and many gnostics.[61]

Origen differed from these groups, however, in stressing that
passage to a higher way of life was gained not through esoteric
knowledge but in accordance with individual moral effort. This is
evident in a rather dense passage in Origen's *Commentarium Series
in Evangelium Matthaei*. Here Origen discusses the difference
between Mark 13: 27, where the elect are gathered 'from the
peaks of earth to the peak of heaven', and Matthew 24: 31 where
the elect are gathered 'from the peaks of the heavens to their
limits'. He suggests that this process of gathering happens
sequentially. First the elect are gathered in accordance with their
way of life on earth, or rather, since they are not gathered simply

---

[60] *In Num.* Hom. 27. 2 (7. 258. 27–259. 8 B.); cf. Clement *Exc. ex Theod.* 26. 2
(112 Sagnard).
[61] *CCel.* 6. 23 (2. 93. 26 K.). See ch. 6 n. 40.

from the earth but 'from the peak of the earth', in accordance with their highest earthly achievements. If a person's attitude was not simply earthly but indeed a heavenly attitude had taken hold in him, this attitude did not come about from the 'peak of heaven' but from its 'peaks', since each heaven had both the beginning of an education and its perfections. So after the highest manner of living on earth, the manner of living of the first heaven took hold of a person. This happened with the second and third heavens as well. So the many beginnings of ways of living in the various heavens are also 'limits', i.e. perfections, and from these beginnings and limits God gathers his elect.[62] God's gathering is thus interpreted as closely linked to the exercise of free will and to ethical achievement. In each heavenly sphere there is a certain level of mind and understanding[63] to be attained, and once that is reached the soul is ready to enter the next heavenly sphere. The Christian promise of heaven is understood on analogy to Origen's own school, where students went through a programme of various studies on the way to their study of divine wisdom. It is a tribute to Origen's interest in education and to his own dedication to teaching that he could think of no better way of describing heaven.

Once the soul attained the heavens, what kind of life would it find there? It may seem odd now to talk about what the living stars were like, but the question was addressed by a writer as sophisticated as Origen's younger contemporary Plotinus.[64] Origen's views on this are not clearly stated, and it is likely that they are not entirely worked out. There are, however, some hints that Origen thought of the stars as heavenly cities. In a homily on Joshua, Origen quotes Hebrews 12: 22, 'you have come to Mount Zion and to the city of the living God, the heavenly Jerusalem', and writes that the earthly Zion and Jerusalem are only a type and image of the celestial places which have these names in their truest sense. This also holds true for the 'cities of Judaea' which will be the dwellings of the servants of God (Psalm 68: 36 (69: 35)). And then Origen refers to these cities as the 'many abiding

---

[62] Comm. Ser. 51 (11. 115. 3–23 Kl.).
[63] *Prin.* 2. 11. 7. 261 f. (C/S), cf. 1. 6. 3. 131–49. In good Platonist fashion Origen does not distinguish between intellectual and moral achievement: spiritual knowledge of God is the same as love, *In Prov.* 6 (*PG* 17. 176d).
[64] Plotinus 4. 3. 18. 13–19; 4. 4. 5. 15–22; 4. 4. 30; 4. 4. 41.

places' of John 14: 2.[65] Since elsewhere he refers to the 'abiding places' as heavenly spheres, it seems that he thought of the heavenly Jerusalem as in some sense related to the stars. A belief that the visible heavens are in some sense identifiable with heavenly cities also appears to be behind a train of thought in his homilies on Numbers. Here after some earlier remarks about the soul's ascent through the 'many abiding places' of heaven, Origen interprets Psalm 146 (147): 4, which says that the Creator has given the stars their names, to mean that at some future point we might know the true names of the stars and constellations, of which our present knowledge is but a shadow and copy (cf. Hebrews 5: 8, 1 Enoch 82: 10–20). A little later he adds that the question of whether the stars and constellations can be called a city in heaven was one about which he did not dare speak with certainty.[66] As so often Origen holds something back, but he at least seems to have pondered the idea that the stars were not simply abiding places in the soul's ascent but, comparable to the views of Heraclides Ponticus, were celestial habitations.

The soul passes through the visible heavens, and yet every soul ultimately has a higher destiny. Earth, heaven, sun, and visible light cannot be 'that which eye has not seen' (1 Corinthians 2: 9), and so it is necessary for the soul to press on to still higher heavens.[67] The end of the righteous soul is likened to Plato's myth in the *Phaedrus* in which the soul passes out of this world and contemplates the superheavenly realities.[68] In this super-heavenly realm 'God is keeping and storing in himself far greater wonders than are seen by sun, moon, and the choir of stars, and even by the holy angels.'[69] As usual Origen leaves room for differences in achievement and speaks of two superheavenly goals. Those who ascend above the visible heavens but whose adherence to that which is intelligible and incorporeal is not first-rate will receive the 'land of the living' (Psalm 26 (27): 13) or the 'earth of heaven' which is located in the ninth, starless sphere.[70]

[65] *In Jesu Nave* Hom. 23. 4 (7. 444. 20–446. 9 B.).
[66] *In Num.* Hom. 28. 2 (7. 281. 34–282. 6; 283. 21–3 B.).
[67] *In Num.* Hom. 9. 8 (7. 65. 31–66. 4 B.), *In Rom.* 7. 5 (PG 14. 1117c); these are nos. 998 and 999 in Balthasar, *Origen*.
[68] *CCel.* 6. 59 (2. 129. 27–130. 6 K.).
[69] *Exh. Mart.* 13 (1. 13. 23–30 K.), trans. Chadwick.
[70] *In Num.* Hom. 21. 1 (7. 200. 11–22 B.), *Prin.* 2. 3. 6. 274–89, 2. 3. 7. 337–48 (C/S). See above ch. 8 nn. 28 and 45.

Elsewhere Origen also refers to this inferior destiny as 'the kingdom of the heavens', and contrasts it with the 'kingdom of God' which is for those who have achieved perfection.[71]

In either event the resurrected soul has a higher goal than the mere physical heavens, whose glory is de-emphasized in comparison to that of redeemed humanity. Thus even though Origen speaks of the soul as having an ethereal body, he explicitly denies that it receives the form of sun, moon, or stars.[72] The soul's destiny is higher than that of the visible bodies, and so it will have an even more glorious body.[73] Humanity is, in the end, more important than the stars, and it is probably for this reason that Origen did not feel the need to explain what the destiny of the living heavenly bodies would be. Presumably once they had finished their service of marking the times and seasons they too would rise to a better condition, but Origen does not provide any more information on this.

Or at least any more information which we know about, for much of Origen's corpus is lost. In his *De Principiis* Origen says that he writes more about the 'earth of heaven' in his commentary on Genesis,[74] but the passage is no longer extant. It is even more discouraging to read Jerome's letter to Vigilantius where he advises his friend to discard Origen's commentary on Job (again no longer extant) since in that work Origen has opinions about the stars and the heavens which are unacceptable to the Church.[75] And yet enough has survived to provide the main points of Origen's teachings on the life of the stars and their relationship to humanity.

The stars and planets are each living and rational creatures, whose bodies are ethereal and made of light. They are self-moving beings, spherical, of vast size, and located far from the earth and yet still within our own cosmos. Origen agrees with earlier philosophical traditions that their precise movement is a tribute both to their own intelligence and to divine providence. Scriptural references to heavenly bodies worshipping God and

---

[71] *In Ps.* 36 Hom. 5. 7 (*PG* 12 1365d–1366a).
[72] Origen *De Res.* 2 ap. Pamphilus *Apol.* 7 (*PG* 17. 596c–597a).
[73] *Prin.* 3. 6. 4. 106–10 (C/S).
[74] *Prin.* 2. 3. 6. 289–91 (C/S).
[75] *Ep.* 61. 2. 4 (1. 578. 4–6 Hilberg).

praying are not just metaphors, since like all rational creatures they are part of God's creation and subordinate to his will.

And yet they too are sinners and stand in need of divine redemption. Their presence in bodies is linked to pre-existing sins, and this also affects both the brightness with which they now shine and their particular place in the sky. Satan and his evil angels are stars which had sinned especially badly and fallen into even lower types of bodies, but the planets and stars visible in the evening sky did not sin as much. In contrast to the demons, now they are doing penance for their sins by providing the times and seasons for the earth, and they will do so until the end of time. They certainly do not cause events on earth, but they can serve as signs of the future, and this and the cunning of demons has lent credence to astrology.

When human beings rise from the dead, they ascend through the heavens. The resurrection body is ethereal and luminous, like the bodies of stars, and resurrected humanity visits heavenly bodies, to which they (it would seem) have a physical kinship. The heavenly spheres are places of instruction for human souls, and are also tentatively likened to cities. Resurrected souls, however, have a higher destiny, and eventually go beyond the fixed sphere ('the firmament') and ascend to a higher earth, the 'earth of heaven', or even above that to the true heaven. Since stars only measure out the seasons until the Last Day, and since they too are included in the Redemption of Christ, their destiny is probably thought of in the same way, though Origen does not address this point.

CONCLUSION

Examination of the starry heavens is usually regarded as impractical use of the intellect. The ancient story of Thales stumbling into a well as he looked upon the stars sums up the judgement of popular pre-Socratic opinion. But the study of the impractical and the unlikely often has far-reaching implications, and the astronomical advances of a few sophisticated Ionians had a profound philosophical and religious impact in their day. Plato recognized that their astronomical discoveries had been a source of intellectual and social chaos, and by an impressive *tour de force* made a new interpretation of astronomy part of the quest for true wisdom. Correctly understood, the stars were proof of a higher design in the cosmos; they were worthy of awe, and perhaps even of devotion.

The impact of this approach on subsequent Greek philosophy and religion was enormous, and lasted down to Origen's day. Plato's influence in discussing that which was unseen in terms of that which was visible in the night sky is evident in the attention which philosophy gave to the heavens in the Hellenistic period. The difficulty was that there were already contradictions in Plato's philosophical understanding of the stars. Later thinkers in different schools came up with different solutions to the problem of the relationship of observable heavenly phenomena to religion and the soul, but by this point it was a case of pouring new wine into old skins. After Plato, the problems inherent in an astral theology were not so much solved as jumbled.

Origen's assessment of the stars' proper place in the world was complicated by his interest in traditions outside of the traditional Hellenistic schools. He selectively used a broad assortment of ideas on the stars in response to a number of pressing theological controversies. The visible heavens had an important place in Origen's theodicy, which was designed to offset the attacks made against the Creator of the world by Marcionites and others. The stars were examples of the importance of free moral decisions, and proof that the same divine laws held true not only across the whole human race but even across all rational beings. While agreeing with pagan thought that the stars had a significant impact on terrestrial life, he limited this influence to the regulation of the natural order, a duty which they performed in their penance for pre-existent sins.

One of his most controversial decisions was to adopt the old idea that there was a relationship between the astral soul and the human soul together with contemporary discussions of the soul's body to help explain the knotty Christian doctrine of the resurrection of the dead. Here he combined Pauline views on the spiritual nature of the resurrection with speculations on the star's body and on the role of the heavenly bodies in instructing the soul after death. Although the relative lack of interest in the visible heavens in scripture limited his speculations on the soul's heavenly journey to a certain degree, he thus also fit Platonic ideas on the soul's return to the stars into a Christian eschatology.

Ambrose of Milan carries on Origen's view that the stars are alive,[1] but the idea is rejected even by such admirers of Origen as Basil the Great and Didymus the Blind,[2] and this hostile attitude was not unusual among later writers, especially in the East.[3] The most intellectually rigorous criticisms were made by the sixth-century Alexandrian Christian John Philoponus, who both denied the life of the stars and claimed (against Aristotle) that heavenly events were governed by the same physical principles as those on earth.[4] His insights, however, did not have much influence. Instead, the resurgence of Aristotelian philosophy in the Middle Ages put intelligences back in the spheres for a time, and no less a thinker than Thomas Aquinas believed that the heavenly bodies had (in a restricted sense) a rational soul.[5] Only gradually were the heavens emptied of life and their movements analysed in purely mechanical terms,[6] science as it were returning to the Ionians.

---

[1] *PL* 16. 1121 f.

[2] Basil *Hex.* 3. 9 (*PG* 29. 75a); Didymus *Trin.* 1. 32 (214. 1–8 Hönscheid); cf. Gregory Naz. *Orat.* 38. 9, 45. 5 (*PG* 36. 320cd, 629b).

[3] Cyril of Alex. (*PG* 74. 952b); Sophronius (PG 87. 3501cd); John of Damascus (*PG* 94. 885ab).

[4] Denied: *Opif.* 6. 2 (233. 13 f. Reichardt); claimed: see S. Sambursky, *The Physical World of Late Antiquity* (London: Routledge & Kegan Paul, 1962), ch. 6.

[5] See Wolfson, 'Souls', 48.

[6] See Richard C. Dales, 'Medieval De-Animation of the Heavens,' *JHI* (1980), 531–50. I owe many of the references in nn. 2 f. of the conclusion to this article.

The ancient assumption that the stars are living beings has now passed away, but just as the sea retains its fascination even though Poseidon no longer dwells in it, so too the celestial regions without their ancient gods. Kant declared his awe at the starry heavens above and the moral law within, recognizing in each case that we are in the presence of something great. The modern age no longer believes that the stars have souls, but astronomical progress has not robbed them of their power. The farthest created things, our own nearest self, these two remain mysteries to us. Observing both we are indeed on the boundary of another land.

APPENDIX A

RUFINUS AS A TRANSLATOR

It is impossible to discuss any aspect of Origen's cosmology without addressing the textual problems associated with his *De Principiis*, which is extant in a Latin translation made by Origen's admirer Rufinus in 398 (roughly 175 years after the treatise was first written). Over the years much good evidence has been excluded and many doubtful assertions have been accepted because of the way the critical text of *De Principiis* has been assessed in modern scholarship. This appendix intends to justify the use that has been made of Rufinus' translation in the present work.

Origen has always had a penchant for attracting both powerful friends and powerful enemies. Among modern scholars he has had virtually no enemies and among medieval ones he had very few friends, but opinion in antiquity was sharply divided. In his own day he was supported against charges of heresy by bishops in Palestine, Arabia, Phoenicia, and Achaia,[1] and was also driven from his native city of Alexandria and was under attack throughout much of his life.[2] In the two centuries after his death many composed apologies on his behalf,[3] but he remained the target for charges of heresy. After he was strongly criticized by the influential heresiologist Epiphanius, Origen was once again the focus of a great theological debate at the end of the fourth century. Indeed, the period was marred by an *odium theologicum* so intense that even St Augustine (no gentle campaigner in doctrinal disputes) voiced his misgivings.[4]

The controversy began when a friend of Rufinus asked him to translate *De Principiis* into Latin to help him refute the arguments of astrologers. Origen's detailed attacks on astrology (based mostly on earlier Academic criticisms) were of unassailable orthodoxy—in fact a long anti-astrological extract from his commentary on Genesis is preserved in two fourth-century anthologies.[5] Even though *De Principiis* in fact says little about astrology, Rufinus agreed, and made the work a

---

[1] Jerome *Ep.* 33. 5 (1. 259, 6–8 Hilberg).
[2] *In Jo.* 6. 2. 8–10 (4. 107. 24–108. 13 P.), *In Luc.* Hom. 25 (9. 151. 7–14 Ra.).
[3] Pamphilus/Eusebius, see also Photius *Bib.* 92 B 5–7 (2. 90 Henry).
[4] *Ep.* 73. 6 (2. 2. 271. 1–10 Goldbacher).
[5] In Eusebius' *Praeparatio Evangelica*, and Basil and Gregory's *Philocalia*.

counter-attack in the attempt to prove Origen's orthodoxy. Rufinus had recently argued in a work entitled *De Adulteratione Librorum Origenis* that heretics had interpolated errors into the text of Origen, and in his preface to *De Principiis* he claimed that this is especially true in this work.[6] He added that wherever he had found in the text anything contrary to the faith he had omitted it, referring specifically to teachings on the Trinity— perhaps the single most damaging charge against Origen at the time was that he was a proto-Arian.[7] Rufinus judged such passages to be interpolations and substituted views from elsewhere in Origen's corpus. Rufinus also wrote that he attempted to clarify Origen's more obscure passages, and so added a few things to the text—not of his own, but again from other works of Origen.[8]

After Rufinus' translation appeared, Jerome complained that Rufinus' version was inaccurate. He said that Rufinus (once his friend but now his bitter enemy) had added things of his own and had suppressed things offensive to the faith.[9] Jerome accordingly made a new, 'more literal' translation (no longer extant) which he gave to a friend.[10] He also cites extracts from *De Principiis* in his various attacks on Rufinus (he found that attacking Origen was the most effective way of injuring his contemporary opponent).

These reports together with charges later made by Justinian and other enemies of Origen have often been seen by modern scholars as correctives to Rufinus' work and as providing the key to Origen's true beliefs.[11] Since Origen's opponents often single out the *De Principiis* as a heretical work,[12] and since these opponents accuse Origen of having views which are not found in Rufinus' edition of the *De Principiis*, increasingly scholars came to question the integrity of Rufinus' translation. The prevailing scholarly opinion until recently has been that

---

[6] Praef. 3. 42–8 (C/S).

[7] Epiphanius *Pan.* 64. 4. 2–4 (2. 410. 3–7 Holl, see his note), Jerome *Ep.* 84. 4 (2. 125. 21–126. 2 Hilberg). One purpose of Basil/Gregory's *Philocalia* was to clear Origen on this point, Socrates *HE* 4. 26 (*PG* 67. 529b).

[8] Praef. 2. 36 f., 3. 54–64 (C/S).

[9] Jerome *Apol. Contra Ruf.* 1. 7 f. (6–8 Lardet).

[10] *Ep.* 83 (2. 120 f. Hilberg) and *Ep.* 85. 3 (2. 136. 14–137. 4 Hilberg).

[11] So Hans Jonas concludes 'daß der unverfälschte spekulative Origenes nicht in dem uns erhaltenen *De Principiis*, d. h. dem Rufinschen Texte, sondern in den verstreuten haeresimachischen Fragmenten und Lehrtexten zu finden ist, denn eben das Spekulative war zugleich das Heterodoxe', *Gnosis* 2. 78, cited here from Ulrich Berner, *Origenes*, Erträge der Forschung 147 (Darmstadt: Wissenschaftliche, 1981), 49.

[12] For Epiphanius' and Theophilus' use of *De Prin.* see Dechow, 'Dogma', 258 and 426. Marcellus of Ancyra was also offended by *Prin.*, see ap. Eusebius *Contra Marc.* 1. 4 (4. 22. 29–23. 13 Kl.), as was Justinian, who includes numerous extracts from *Prin.* in his formal attack on Origen, the *Ep. ad Mennam* (*PG* 86. 1. 945d—990d).

Rufinus himself interpolated Origen's text and suppressed and rewrote controversial passages—Rufinus' translation is 'ein Werk absoluter Willkür' according to Grützmacher, who is quoted with approval by Koetschau.[13] The original sense of the cosmology set forth in *De Principiis* had to be reconstructed by piecing together the charges of Origen's various fourth- and sixth-century opponents and forming a coherent system (it was presumed that Origen had one). The crowning achievement of this effort is Koetschau's edition of *De Principiis* (GCS 22, 1913), which prints along with the text of Rufinus a wide variety of sources which either explicitly or (in Koetschau's view) implicitly refer to teachings allegedly once in *De Principiis* but suppressed by Rufinus.

The impact of this edition was enormous. Many scholarly works in this century have made claims about Origen's teachings based on the Koetschau edition, and when one looks up the passage in question one discovers that it is not written by Origen but by one of his opponents, or even by someone who does not refer to Origen at all but is assumed to oppose a view that Origen once had. Koetschau's deservedly high reputation as a philologist and the status of the GCS series in scholarly circles ensured the widespread influence of these editorial decisions. The impact of this new text in English-speaking circles was furthered by a translation of this edition into English by G. W. Butterworth, who retained Koetschau's collection of the fragments and (if anything) even strengthened its strong editorial bias against Rufinus. Radical scepticism about Rufinus' text had become a widespread scholarly assumption.

The first major challenge to this assumption was Gustave Bardy's *Recherches sur l'histoire du texte et des versions latines du De Principiis d'Origène* in 1923.[14] Bardy investigated Rufinus' work as a translator against extant Greek passages (mostly in the *Philocalia*), and noted that there was little evidence to support Koetschau's radical conclusions. Rufinus' work is often periphrastic, 'but in the end he translates, and on the whole it is very much Origen's thought that he expresses'.[15]

After the Second World War, an extensive Greek portion of Origen's commentary on Romans was published. This work too had previously

---

[13] Praef., p.cxxx. Koetschau himself says that Rufinus' translation 'ist im einzelnen so wenig zuverlässig, daß sie stets der controlle bedarf, um benutzbar zu werden', p.cxxviii; so too Eugène de Faye, *Origène: Sa vie, son œuvre, sa pensée*, BEHE. R 37 (Paris: Ernest Leroux, 1923) 1. 227.

[14] MemTravFacCath 25 (Paris: Edouard Champion, 1923).

[15] *Recherches*, 206. More recently Görgemanns/Karpp write concerning Rufinus' translation of *Prin.*: 'Dennoch scheint die Theologie des Origenes im ganzen nicht verfälscht zu sein, nur ihre kühnsten Formulierungen sind beseitigt oder umgebogen', *Prinzipien*, 43. See also Völker, *Vollkommensheitsideal*, 17. Annie Jaubert writes concerning Rufinus' translation, 'Dans l'ensemble, elle donne l'impression d'une longue paraphrase, mais non d'une paraphrase inexacte', *Origène: Homélies sur Josué*, SC 71 (Paris: du Cerf, 1960), 82.

only been available in Rufinus' Latin translation, and so should have contained at least some evidence of his allegedly radical textual alterations, but again this was not found to be so.[16] Another important event was the publication in 1958 of Evagrius Ponticus' *Kephalaia Gnostica* (in Syriac translation).[17] This text and the renewed study of fourth- and sixth-century Origenist monasticism led many to conclude that Origen's opponents in this later period were in large part directing their criticisms against contemporary followers of Origen rather than against Origen himself.[18] It would appear that later Origenists did make his work more systematic, and were at times much more adventurous in their cosmological speculations. Their opponents tended to read these tendencies into Origen's writings, often without justification. As with so many other controversial figures in history, Origen is frequently associated with views that are a caricature of his real position, because this is what his enemies saw or wanted to see.

Increasingly scholars (with some exceptions) have concluded that Rufinus' work, though not a strict translation by modern standards, has suppressed little for doctrinal reasons, and is generally a more reliable guide for Origen's cosmology than the fragments in the Koetschau edition. It would appear that Rufinus has changed some of Origen's language to bring it into line with later views of the Trinity (as Rufinus himself admits), but there is little reason to think that major changes have been made in his cosmology. Jerome's complaints about the translation must be viewed in light of his bitter hatred of Rufinus, and his less than scrupulous treatment of theological opponents. His evidence cannot be dismissed, and indeed is often of great value,[19] but should only be used with due caution. Charges made by other opponents also must be examined in light of both their theological settings (often polemical), and the reliability of the source.[20]

Henri Crouzel has been a leader in this approach to Rufinus' text of *De Principiis*, and together with Manlio Simonetti has edited a new edition of the text with these presuppositions. I chose to use their edition (which

---

[16] See Henry Chadwick, 'Rufinus and the Tura Papyrus of Origen's Comment-ary on Romans', *JThS* NS 10 (1959), 10–42; Éric Junod, *Origène: Philocalie 21–27* (Paris: du Cerf, 1976), 91. See already von Balthasar, *Origen*, 366 n. 1.

[17] A. Guillaumont, *Les Six Centuries des 'Kephalaia gnostica'*, PO 28. 1 (Paris: Firmin-Didot, 1958).

[18] See A. Guillaumont, *Les 'Kephalaia Gnostica' d'Évagre le Pontique*, PatSor 5 (Paris: du Seuil, 1962). Already Bardy *Recherches* 79.

[19] See appendix B.

[20] Setting: for the fourth-century controversy see Dechow 'Dogma'; for both eras see Guillaumont, *Les 'Kephalaia'*. Even a literal correspondence between Jerome and Justinian is not a sure indication that a teaching stems from Origen, see Crouzel, 'L'Apocatastase chez Origène', in Lothar Lies (ed.), *Origeniana Quarta* (Innsbruck: Tyrolia, 1987), 284, against Kettler, *Sinn*, 28.

is in the *Sources chrétiennes* series), though I have continued to use the other standard GCS editions, which cover a large portion (but not all) of Origen's corpus. Koetschau was a great scholar and editor, and his Latin text of Rufinus, though updated, has not been radically emended by Simonetti in the C/S edition. For this reason it was possible to continue to use the (excellent) Butterworth translation, though in each case it has been compared to Görgemanns/Karpp's German and Crouzel's French translation, and has in a few cases been modified (as signalled in the notes). The use of the C/S edition is mainly intended to indicate a different attitude toward Rufinus' translation and the fragments collected by Koetschau than the one that has been dominant in much of this century's discussions of Origen's cosmology.

APPENDIX B

A NOTE ON ORIGEN'S USE OF THE TERM 'ANTIZONE'

In his letter to Avitus[1] Jerome reports the following as one of Origen's three conjectures in the *De Principiis* about the possible destiny of the soul. The fixed sphere and everything in it will be dissolved, and that by which the antizone itself is contained and surrounded will be called the 'good earth' (Matthew 13: 8). The other sphere which surrounds this same earth in its circuit and which is called 'heaven' will be the home of the saints.

The fixed sphere is the eighth sphere, the ninth is apparently both Hipparchus' starless sphere and also the 'celestial earth',[2] and the tenth is the higher and greater of the two heavens. What is puzzling here is the 'antizone' beneath them. As Crouzel notes, the word ἀντιζώνη is nowhere else attested in Greek literature. It is apparently an 'anti' zone because it moves in a direction opposite that of the ninth sphere. Crouzel says that the antizone is either the fixed sphere, moving from East to West, or the fixed sphere and the planets, which have this same overall direction despite their additional West-East movement.[3]

A passage in Origen's *Commentariorum Series in Evangelium Matthaei* throws some light on this question. Here Origen says that the 'middle zone' is the area between the earth and the planetary region.[4] This probably indicates that the planets are part of the antizone. There are evidently three zones beneath the celestial earth and so in the world of becoming:[5] the topmost is an antizone which encompasses the planets and the fixed sphere; the second is a middle zone which includes the area between the earth and the planetary region (i.e. the air and the ether). I know of no reference to the third zone, which must be beneath

---

[1] *Ep.* 124. 5 (3. 102. 26–103. 6 Hilberg). Rufinus omitted this passage, probably because he found it irrelevant or puzzling (or both).
[2] See ch. 8 n. 28 and 45.
[3] *Principes*, 2. 157 n. 43.
[4] 11. 102. 21 f. Kl.
[5] Following the Stoics it is common to say that the world consists of heaven and earth (since they did not admit anything beyond them), Posidonius frag. 334 (Theiler), Philo *Aet.* 4.

the 'middle zone', nor what such a zone would be called. Presumably it would include the earth and underworld.

In Greek science 'zones' (ζῶναι) refer both to regions on earth and to their counterparts on the celestial sphere.[6] Heavenly zones refer to the intervals between the planets,[7] and are commonly used to denote one of the seven planetary spheres.[8] In Origen's passage in the *Commentariorum Series*, the Greek word ζώνη (which must lie behind the Latin *zona*) refers to one of only three regions. The question then is the background of this otherwise unattested word ἀντιζώνη (which Origen probably did not coin) and its unusual usage.

The ultimate background may well be astrological, for Origen had a good knowledge of astrological vocabulary. Hippolytus attributes a division of the universe into three parts to 'the astrologers'. First is the region of the signs of the zodiac, called an immovable world, presumably not only because it is the 'fixed' sphere but also because it is above Fate. Second is the planetary region, which extends as far as the moon, and below this is our world.[9] Here the seven planets are treated as one entity, which is not unusual in astrology or magic.[10] The division of the universe is different from that in Origen, but one could see how the planetary region might be called an ἀντιζώνη, since it moves in a direction opposite that of the fixed sphere. The same word then perhaps was applied by Origen to the antizone's relationship to the ninth sphere when he too divided the cosmos into three parts.

Such a division may have been adopted by Origen because it could be used in exegesis of 2 Corinthians 12: 2. At a few other points Origen talks about the three parts of the universe under highest heaven, but he describes its sections differently,[11] and he evidently was uncertain how to describe these heavens. This indecision no doubt was due in part to the relative novelty[12] of such a teaching, since a threefold division of the cosmos conflicted with the more familiar division of the cosmos into seven planetary regions and the fixed sphere.

[6] Geminus *Elem.* 16. 12 (78 Aujac); Strabo 2. 5. 3 (1. 2. 81. 15–17 Aujac); Philo *Her.* 147.

[7] Achilles *Isag.* 29 (62. 20–3 Maass).

[8] So Porphyry *De Phil. ex Orac.* 141; Vettius Valens 1. 10 (25. 19 f. Pingree); Zosimus of Panopolis *On the Letter Omega* 1 (16. 2). 9 (28, 10 Jackson); J. Lydus *De Mens.* 3. 12 (54. 10–12 Wünsch); etc.

[9] Hippolytus *Ref.* 5. 13. 1 (174. 1–175. 8 Marcovich).

[10] *PGM* 13. 213–26; Vettius Valens 6. 7 (245. 25 f. Pingree).

[11] In *In Gen.* Hom. 2. 5 he divides the cosmos into subterranean, earthly, and heavenly (6. 36. 2–5 B.); see further the sources in ch. 8 n. 66.

[12] Though this is not unheard of in pagan circles, see Lewy *Chaldaean* 137. 376, and at a later date Theodore of Asine test. 30 (Deuse).

SELECT BIBLIOGRAPHY

ALEXANDRE, MONIQUE, 'La Culture profane chez Philon', in Roger Arnaldez *et al*, (eds.), *Philon d'Alexandrie* (Paris: Éditions du Centre national de la recherche scientifique, 1967), 105–30.

ANZ, WILHELM, *Zur Frage nach dem Ursprung des Gnostizimus*, TU 15. 4 (Leipzig: J. C. Hinrich, 1897).

APELT, MATHILDA, *De Rationibus quibusdam quae Philoni Alexandrino cum Posidonio intercedunt* (Leipzig: Teubner, 1907).

ARMANTAGE, JAMES WALTER, 'Will the Body be Raised? Origen and the Origenist Controversies', Ph.D. Dissertation (Yale University, 1971).

ATZBERGER, LEONHARD, *Geschichte der christlichen Eschatologie innerhalb der vornicänischen Zeit* (Freiburg im Breisgau: Herder, 1896).

BALTES, MATTHIAS, 'Zur Theologie des Xenokrates', in R. van den Broek *et al*. (eds.), *Knowledge of God in the Graeco-Roman World*, EPRO 112 (Leiden: E. J. Brill, 1988), 43–68.

BALTHASAR, HANS URS VON, *Origen: Spirit and Fire*, trans. Robert J. Daly, SJ (Washington, DC: Catholic University, 1984).

BARBEL, JOSEPH, *Christos Angelos*, Theoph 3 (Bonn: Peter Hanstein, 1941). Note: a much abbreviated edition of the same work was published in the same year by Wilh. Postberg.

BARDY, GUSTAVE, *Recherches sur l'histoire du texte et des versions latines du De Principiis d'Origène*, MémTravFacCath 25 (Paris: Édouard Champion, 1923).

BECK, ROGER, 'Mithraism since Franz Cumont', *ANRW* 2. 17. 4 (1984), 2002–115.

—— *Planetary Gods and Planetary Orders in the Mysteries of Mithras*, EPRO 109 (Leiden: E. J. Brill, 1988).

BERCHMAN, ROBERT M., *From Philo to Origen: Middle-Platonism in Transition*, Brown Judaic Studies 69 (Chico, Calif.: Scholars Press, 1984).

BERNER, ULRICH, *Origenes*, Erträge der Forschung 147 (Darmstadt: Wissenschaftliche Buchgesellschaft, 1981).

BETTENCOURT, STEPHANUS TAURES, *Doctrina Ascetica Origenis*, StAns 16 (Vatican City: Libreria Vaticana, 1945).

BEUTLER, RUDOLF, 'Numenios', *PW* Suppl. 7 (1940), 664–78.

BLANC, CÉCILE, 'L'Angélologie d'Origène', *StPatr* 14 (1971), 79–109.

—— *Origène: Commentaire sur Saint Jean*, SC 120, 157, 222, 290 (Paris: du Cerf, 1966–82).

BORRET, MARCEL, SJ, *Origène: Homélies sur le Lévitique*, SC 286–7 (Paris: du Cerf, 1981).

BOSTOCK, GERALD, 'The Sources of Origen's Doctrine of Pre-Existence', in Lothar Lies (ed.), *Origeniana Quarta* (Innsbruck: Tyrolia, 1987), 259–64.

BOUCHÉ-LECLERCQ, A., *L'Astrologie grecque* (Paris: Ernest Leroux, 1899).

BOUSSET, WILHELM. 'Gnosis, Gnostiker', *PW* 7. 2 (1912), 1502–47.

—— 'Die Himmelreise der Seele', *ARW* 4 (1901), 136–69 and 229–73.

—— *Jüdisch-christlicher Schulbetrieb in Alexandria und Rom* (Göttingen: Vandenhoeck & Ruprecht, 1915).

—— 'Zur Daemonologie der späteren Antike', *ARW* 18 (1915), 134–72.

BOYANCÉ, PIERRE, 'Études philoniennes', *REG* 76 (1963) 64–110.

—— *Études sur le Songe de Scipion* (Paris: A. Bontemps, 1936).

—— 'La Religion astrale de Platon à Cicéron', *REG* 65 (1952) 312–49.

BÜCHLI, JÖRG, *Der Poimandres: Ein paganisiertes Evangelium*, WUNT 27 (Tübingen: J. C. B. Mohr, 1987).

CADIOU, RENÉ, *Introduction au système d'Origène* (Paris: Les Belles Lettres, 1932).

—— *La Jeunesse d'Origène* (Paris: Gabriel Beauchesne, 1945).

CAPELLE, PAULUS, *De luna, stellis, lacteo orbe animarum sedes* (Halis Saxonum: E. Karras, 1917).

CAVALLIN, HANS C., 'Leben nach dem Tode im Spätjudentum', *ANRW* 2. 19. 1 (1979), 240–345.

CHADWICK, HENRY, *Early Christian Thought and the Classical Tradition* (Oxford: Clarendon, 1966).

—— 'Origen, Celsus, and the Resurrection of the Body', *HTR* 41 (1948), 83–102.

—— *Origen: Contra Celsum* (Cambridge: Cambridge University, 1965).

—— 'Philo and the Beginnings of Christian Thought', in A. H. Armstrong (ed.), *The Cambridge History of Later Greek and Early Medieval Philosophy* (Cambridge: Cambridge University, 1970), 137–57.

—— 'Rufinus and the Tura Papyrus of Origen's Commentary on Romans', *JThS* NS 10 (1959), 10–42.

—— 'St Paul and Philo of Alexandria', *BJRL* 48 (1966), 286–307.

CHARLESWORTH, JAMES, H., (ed.), *The Old Testament Pseudepigrapha* (Garden City, NY: Doubleday, 1983).

CHERNISS, HAROLD, *Aristotle's Criticism of Plato and the Academy* (Baltimore: Johns Hopkins University, 1944).

—— *The Riddle of the Early Academy* (Berkeley: University of California, 1945).

—— *Selected Papers*, ed. Leonardo Tarán (Leiden: E. J. Brill, 1977).

CHROUST, ANTON-HERMANN, *Aristotle* (London: Routledge & Kegan Paul, 1973).

CORNÉLIS, H., 'Les Fondements cosmologiques de l'eschatologie d'Origène', *RevSciPhilTheol* 43 (1959), 32–80 and 201–47.

CORNFORD, FRANCIS MACDONALD, *Plato's Cosmology* (New York: Harcourt, Brace & Co., 1937).

COURCELLE, P., 'Flügel (Flug) der Seele', *RAC* 8 (1972), 29–65.

CROUZEL, HENRI, SJ, *Bibliographie critique d'Origène*, IP 8 and 8a (The Hague: Martinus Nijhoff, 1971, 1982).

—— 'Différences entre les ressuscités selon Origène', *Jenseitsvorstellungen in Antike und Christentum*, JAC suppl. 9, ed. Theodor Klauser *et al.* (Münster: Aschendorff, 1982), 107–16.

—— 'L'Hadès et la Géhenne selon Origène', *Gregorianum*, 59 (1978), 291–331.

—— 'Mort et immortalité selon Origène', *BLE* 79 (1978), 19–38, 81–96, 181–96.

—— *Origen*, trans. A. S. Worrall (San Francisco: Harper & Row, 1989).

—— *Origène et la 'connaissance mystique'*, ML. T 56 (Toulouse: Desclée de Brouwer, 1961).

—— *Origène et la philosophie* (Paris: Éditions Montaigne, 1962).

—— 'La Thème platonicien du "véhicule de l'âme" chez Origène', *Didaskalia* 7 (1977), 225–37.

—— and SIMONETTI, MANLIO, *Origène: Traité des principes*, SC 252, 253, 268, 269 (Paris: du Cerf, 1978–80).

CUMONT, FRANZ, 'Les Anges du paganisme', *RevHistRel* 72 (1915), 159–82.

—— 'Le Mysticisme astral dans l'antiquité', *BCLAB* (1909), 256–86.

—— 'Les Noms de planètes et l'astrolatrie chez les Grecs', *AnCl* 4 (1935), 5–43.

—— 'La Théologie solaire du paganisme romain', *MAIBL. E* 12. 2 (1913), 447–80.

DALES, RICHARD C., 'Medieval De-Animation of the Heavens', *JHI* 41 (1980), 531–50.

DANIÉLOU, JEAN, *Philon d'Alexandrie* (Paris: Arthème Fayard, 1958).

—— *Primitive Christian Symbols*, trans. Donald Attwater (Baltimore: Helicon, 1964).

—— 'Les Sources juives de la doctrine des anges des nations chez Origène', *RSR* 38 (1951), 132–7.

DECHOW, JON F., 'Dogma and Mysticism in Early Christianity', Ph.D. Dissertation (University of Pennsylvania, 1975). Now a monograph from Mercer University Press (Atlanta, 1988), in the NAPS Monograph Series.

DE LEY, HERMAN, *Macrobius and Numenius*, ColLat 125 (Brussels: Latomus, 1972).

DES PLACES, ÉDOUARD, *Études platoniciennes, 1929–1979*, EPRO 90 (Leiden: E. J. Brill, 1981).

DES PLACES, ÉDOUARD, *Numénius: Fragments* (Paris: Les Belles Lettres, 1973).
—— *Syngeneia*, EeC 51 (Paris: C. Klincksieck, 1964).
DEVREESSE, ROBERT, *Les Anciens Commentateurs grecs des Psaumes*, SeT 264 (Vatican City: Apostolica Vaticana, 1970).
DICKS, D. R., *Early Greek Astronomy to Aristotle* (Bristol: Western Printing, 1970).
DILLON, JOHN, 'Looking on the Light: Some Remarks on the Imagery of Light in the First Chapter of the *Peri Archon*', *Origen of Alexandria: His World and his Legacy*, in Charles Kannengiesser and William L. Petersen (eds.), (Notre Dame, Ind.: University of Notre Dame, 1988), 215–30.
—— *The Middle Platonists* (London: Duckworth, 1977).
—— 'Philo's Doctrine of Angels', in David Winston and John Dillon (eds.), *Two Treatises of Philo of Alexandria*, Brown Judaic Studies 25 (Chico, Calif.: Scholars Press, 1983).
DODDS, E. R., *The Greeks and the Irrational* (Berkeley: University of California, 1951).
—— *Pagan and Christian in an Age of Anxiety* (Cambridge: Cambridge University, 1965).
—— *Proclus: The Elements of Theology.* (2nd edn., Oxford: Clarendon, 1963).
DÖLGER, FRANZ, 'Zur Symbolik des altchristlichen Taufhauses', *AuC* 4 (1934), 153–87.
DORIVAL, GILLES, 'Origène et la résurrection de la chair', in Lothar Lies (ed.), *Origeniana Quarta* (Innsbruck: Tyrolia, 1987), 291–321.
DÖRRIE, HEINRICH, *Platonica Minora*, Studia et Testimonia 8 (Munich: Wilhelm Funk, 1976).
DRACHMANN, A. B., *Atheism in Pagan Antiquity* (London: Gyldendal, 1922).
DUPUIS, JACQUES, SJ, *L'Esprit de l'homme: Étude sur l'anthropologie religeuse d'Origène*, ML. T 62 (Toulouse: Desclée de Brouwer, 1967).
DÜRING, INGEMAR, 'Aristoteles', *PW* Suppl. 11 (1968), 159–336.
EASTERLING, H. J., 'Homocentric Spheres in *De Caelo*', *Phron.* 6 (1961), 138–53.
—— 'Quinta Natura', *MH* 21 (1964), 73–85.
EDELSTEIN, LUDWIG, 'The Philosophical System of Posidonius', *AJPh* 57 (1936), 286–325.
EFFE, BERND, *Studien zur Kosmologie und Theologie der aristotelischen Schrift Über die Philosophie'*, Zet. 50 (Munich: Beck, 1970).
ELDERS, LEO, *Aristotle's Cosmology* (Assen: van Gorcum & Co., 1966).
ELFERINK, M. A., *La Descente de l'âme d'après Macrobe*, PhAnt 16 (Leiden: E. J. Brill, 1968).
ELSAS, CHRISTOPH, *Neuplatonische und gnostische Weltablehnung in der Schule Plotins*, RGVV 34 (Berlin: Walter de Gruyter, 1975).
FESTUGIÈRE, A. J., 'De la doctrine "origéniste" du corps glorieux sphéroïde', *RevSciPhilTheol* 43 (1959), 81–6.

—— *L'Idéal religieux des grecs et l'Évangile* (2nd edn., Paris: Librairie Lecoffre, 1981).

—— *La Révélation d'Hermès Trismégiste*: vol. 1. *L'Astrologie et les sciences occultes* (Paris: Librairie Lecoffre, 1950); vol. 2. *Le Dieu cosmique'* (1954); vol. 3. *Les Doctrines de l'âme* (1953); vol. 4. *Le Dieu inconnu et la gnose* (1954).

FLAMANT, J., 'Sotériologie et systèmes planétaires', in V. Bianchi and M. J. Vermaseren (eds.), *La soteriologia dei culti orientali nell' impero romano* EPRO 92 (Leiden: E. J. Brill, 1982), 223–42.

FLASHAR, HELLMUT, 'Aristoteles', in Hellmut Flashar (ed.), *Die Philosophie der Antike* (Basle/Stuttgart: Schwabe, 1983), 3. 175–457.

FOERSTER, WERNER, " Ἀστήρ, Ἄατρον", trans. Geoffrey W. Bromiley, *TDNT* 1 (1964), 169–71.

FRANK, ERICH, *Plato und die sogenannten Pythagoreer* (Halle: Max Niemeyer, 1923).

FRITZ, KURT VON, 'Philippos von Opus', *PW* 19. 2 (1938), 2351–66.

GERSH, STEPHEN, *Middle Platonism and Neoplatonism: The Latin Tradition* (Notre Dame, Ind.: University of Notre Dame, 1986).

GIROD, ROBERT, *Origène: Commentaire sur l'Évangile selon Matthieu*, SC 162 (Paris: du Cerf, 1970).

GÖGLER, ROLF, *Zur Theologie des biblischen Wortes bei Origenes* (Düsseldorf: Patmos, 1963).

GOLDSCHMIDT, V., *Platonisme et pensée contemporaine* (Aubier: Éditions Montaigne, 1976).

GÖRGEMANNS, HERWIG, and KARPP, HEINRICH, *Origenes vier Bücher von den Prinzipien* (Darmstadt: Wissenschaftliche Buchgesellschaft, 1976).

GOTTSCHALK, H. B., *Heraclides of Pontus* (Oxford: Clarendon, 1980).

GRÄSER, ANDREAS, 'Zu Aristoteles *Peri Philosophias* (Cicero, *Nat. deor.* II 16, 44)', *MH* 27 (1970), 16–27.

GRY, LÉON, 'Séjours et habitats divins d'après les Apocryphes de l'Ancien', *RSPhTh* 4 (1910), 694–722.

GUILLAUMONT, A., *Les 'Kephalaia Gnostica' d'Évagre le Pontique*, PatSor 5 (Paris: du Seuil, 1962).

GUNDEL, WILHELM, and GUNDEL, HANS GEORG, *Astrologumena*, Sudhoffs Arch. Suppl. 6 (Wiesbaden: Franz Steiner, 1966).

—— 'Planeten', *PW* 20. 2 (1950), 2017–85.

GUTHRIE, W. K. C., 'Introduction', *Aristotle: On the Heavens* (Cambridge, Mass.: Harvard University, 1939).

HAHM, DAVID E., 'The Fifth Element in Aristotle's *De Philosophia*: A Critical Re-examination', in John P. Anton and Anthony Preus (eds.), *Essays in Ancient Greek Philosophy* (Albany, NY: SUNY, 1983), 2. 404–28.

—— *The Origins of Stoic Cosmology* (Columbus: Ohio State University, 1977).

Harl, Marguerite, 'Cosmologie grecque et représentations juives dans l'œuvre de Philon d'Alexandrie', in Roger Arnaldez *et al.* (eds.) *Philon d'Alexandrie* (Paris: Éditions du Centre national de la recherche scientifique, 1967), 189–205.

—— 'Introduction', *Philo d'Alexandrie: Quis rerum divinarum heres sit* (Paris: du Cerf, 1966).

—— *Origène: Philocalie 1–20*, SC 302 (Paris: du Cerf, 1983).

Harnack, Adolf von, *Der kirchengeschichtliche Ertrag der exegetischen Arbeiten des Origenes*, TU 42. 3–4 (Leipzig: J. C. Hinrich, 1918).

Heath, Thomas L., *Aristarchus of Samos* (Oxford: Clarendon, 1913).

Heine, Ronald E., *Origen: Homilies on Genesis and Exodus*, FaCh 71 (Washington, DC: Catholic University, 1982).

Heinze, Richard, *Xenokrates* (Leipzig: Teubner, 1892).

Huet, Pierre, *Origeniana*, in C. H. E. Lommatzsch, *Origenis Opera Omnia* (Berlin: Haude & Spener, 1846), vols. 22–4.

Husson, Pierre, and Nautin, Pierre, *Origène: Homélies sur Jérémie*, SC 232, 238 (Paris: du Cerf, 1976–7).

Jaeger, Werner, *Aristotle: Fundamentals of the History of his Development*, trans. Richard Robinson (2nd edn., Oxford: Clarendon, 1934).

Jaubert, Annie, *Origène: Homélies sur Josué*, SC 71 (Paris: du Cerf, 1960).

Jonas, Hans, *Gnosis und spätantiker Geist*, FRLANT 51, 63 (Göttingen: Vandenhoeck & Ruprecht, 1934, 1954).

Junod, É., *Origene: Philocalie 21–27 (Sur le libre arbitre)*, SC 226 (Paris: du Cerf, 1976).

Kahn, Charles H., *Anaximander and the Origins of Greek Cosmology* (New York: Columbia University, 1960).

Kehl, Alois, 'Gewand (der Seele)', *RAC* 10 (1978), 945–1052.

Kelly, J. N. D., *Early Christian Doctrines* (5th edn., San Francisco: Harper & Row, 1978).

Kerschensteiner, Jula, *Platon und der Orient* (Stuttgart: W. Kohlhammer, 1945).

Kettler, Franz Heinrich, *Der ursprüngliche Sinn der Dogmatik des Origenes* (Berlin: Alfred Töpelmann, 1966).

Klostermann, Erich, 'Formen der exegetischen Arbeiten des Origenes', *ThL* 72 (1947), 203–8.

Koch, Hal, 'Origenes', *PW* 18. 1 (1942), 1036–59.

—— *Pronoia und Paideusis*, AKG 22 (Berlin: Walter de Gruyter, 1932).

Krämer, Hans Joachim, 'Die ältere Akademie', in Hellmut Flashar (ed.), *Die Philosophie der Antike* (Basle/Stuttgart: Schwabe, 1983) 3. 1–150.

Kroll, Josef, *Die Lehren des Hermes Trismegistos*, BGPhMA 12 (Münster: Aschendorff, 1914).

Kroll, Wilhelm, *Die Kosmologie des Plinius* (Breslau: Marcus, 1930).

Kübel, Paul, *Schuld und Schicksal bei Origenes, Gnostikern und Platonikern* (Stuttgart: Calwer, 1973).

LAPIDGE, MICHAEL, 'Stoic Cosmology', in John M. Rist (ed.), *The Stoics* (Berkeley: University of California, 1978), 161–86.

LEBEAU, PAUL, 'L'Interprétation origénienne de Rm. 8. 19–22', *Kyriakon*, FS J. Quasten, ed. Patrick Granfield and Josef A. Jungmann (Münster: Aschendorff, 1970), 1. 336–45.

LEWY, HANS, *Chaldaean Oracles and Theurgy*, ed. Michel Tardieu (2nd edn., Paris: Études augustiniennes, 1978).

LILLA, S. R. C., *Clement of Alexandria* (London: Oxford University, 1971).

LUBAC, HENRI DE, *Histoire et esprit* (Paris: Aubier, 1950).

MAAS, ERNST, *Die Tagesgötter in Rom und den Provinzen* (Berlin: Weidmann, 1902).

MANSFELD, J. *The Pseudo–Hippocratic Tract Peri Hebdomadon ch.1–11 and Greek Philosophy* (Assen: van Gorcum, 1971).

MAU, GEORG, *Die Religionsphilosophie Kaiser Julians* (Leipzig: Teubner, 1906).

MEHAT, ANDRÉ, *Origène: Homélies sur les Nombres* SC 29 (Paris: du Cerf, 1951).

MERKELBACH, REINHOLD, *Mithras* (Königstein: Anton Hain, 1984).

—— *Weihegrade und Seelenlehre der Mithrasmysterien* (Opladen: Westdeutscher, 1982).

MERLAN, PHILIP, *Kleine philosophische Schriften*, ed. Franciszka Merlan (Hildesheim: Georg Olms, 1976).

MICHL, J., 'Engel I–IV', *RAC* 5 (1962), 53–200.

MILLER, JAMES, *Measures of Wisdom* (Toronto: University of Toronto, 1986).

MOLLAND, EINAR, *The Conception of the Gospel in the Alexandrian Theology* (Oslo: Jacob Dybwad, 1938).

MÖLLER, WILHELM, *Geschichte der Kosmologie in der griechischen Kirche bis auf Origenes* (Halle: 1860, repr. Frankfurt am Main: Minerva, 1967).

MORAUX, PAUL, *Der Aristotelismus bei den Griechen* (Berlin: Walter de Gruyter, 1984), vol. 2.

—— 'Einleitung', in P. Moraux (ed.), *Frühschriften des Aristoteles*, WdF 224 (Darmstadt: Wissenschaftliche Buchgesellschaft, 1975).

—— 'Introduction', *Aristote: Du Ciel* (Paris: Les Belles Lettres, 1965).

—— 'Quinta Essentia', *PW* 24 (1963), 1171–263.

MOREAU, JOSEPH, *L'Âme du monde de Platon aux stoïciens* (Paris: Les Belles Lettres, 1939).

NAUTIN, PIERRE, *Origène: Sa vie et son œuvre* (Paris: du Cerf, 1976).

—— and NAUTIN, MARIE-THÉRÈSE, *Origène: Homélies sur Samuel*, SC 328 (Paris: du Cerf, 1986).

NILSSON, MARTIN P, *Geschichte der griechischen Religion*, HAW 5. 2. vols. 1, 2 (2nd edn., Munich: C. H. Beck, 1961).

NOCK, ARTHUR DARBY, *Essays on Religion and the Ancient World*, ed. Zeph Stewart (Cambridge, Mass.: Harvard University, 1972).

NOCK, ARTHUR DARBY, *Sallustius: Concerning the Gods and the Universe* (Hildesheim: G. Olms, 1966).

PEASE, ARTHUR STANLEY, 'Caeli Enarrant', *HTR* 34 (1941), 163–200.

—— *Ciceronis De Natura Deorum* (Cambridge, Mass.: Harvard University, 1955).

PÉPIN, JEAN, *Idées grecques sur l'homme et sur Dieu* (Paris: Les Belles Lettres, 1971).

—— *Théologie cosmique et théologie chrétienne* (Paris: Presses universitaires de France, 1964).

PÉTREMENT, SIMONE, *Le Dieu séparé* (Paris: du Cerf, 1984).

PFEIFFER, ERWIN, *Studien zum antiken Sternglauben*, Stoicheia 2 (Leipzig: Teubner, 1916).

POHLENZ, MAX, *Die Stoa* (Göttingen: Vandenhoeck & Ruprecht, 1959).

PRAECHTER, KARL, *Kleine Schriften*, ed. Heinrich Dörrie (Hildesheim: Georg Olms, 1973).

RECHEIS, P. ATHANAS, *Engel, Tod und Seelenreise*, TeT 4 (Rome: Edizioni di storia e letteratura, 1958).

REINHARDT, K., 'Poseidonios von Apameia', *PW* 22. 1 (1953), 558–826.

REITZENSTEIN, RICHARD, *Poimandres* (Leipzig: Teubner, 1904).

RIEDINGER, UTTO, *Die heilige Schrift im Kampf der griechischen Kirche gegen die Astrologie* (Innsbruck: Wagner, 1956).

RONDEAU, MARIE-JOSÈPHE, 'Le Commentaire sur les Psaumes d'Évagre le Pontique', *OCP* 26 (1960), 307–48.

ROSS, W. D., *Aristotle's Metaphysics* (Oxford: Clarendon, 1924).

—— *Fragmenta Selecta* (Oxford: Clarendon, 1955).

ROUGIER, LOUIS AUGUSTE PAUL, *L'Origine astronomique de la croyance pythagoricienne en l'immortalité céleste des âmes* (Cairo: Institut français d'archéologie orientale, 1933).

RUNIA, DAVID T., *Philo of Alexandria and the Timaeus of Plato*, PhAnt 44 (Leiden: E. J. Brill, 1986).

RÜSCHE, FRANZ, *Blut, Leben und Seele*, SGKA. E 5 (Paderborn: Ferdinand Schöningh, 1930).

SAMBURSKY, S., *The Physical World of Late Antiquity* (London: Routledge & Kegan Paul, 1962).

SCHWEIZER, EDUARD, 'Slaves of the Elements and Worshipers of Angels: Gal. 4: 3, 9 and Col. 2: 8, 18, 20', *JBL* 107 (1988), 455–68.

SKEMP, J. B., *The Theory of Motion in Plato's Later Dialogues* (Amsterdam: Adolf M. Hakkert, 1967).

SMITH, ANDREW, 'Porphyrian Studies Since 1913', *ANRW* 2. 36. 2 (1987), 717–73.

SOLMSEN, FRIEDRICH, *Aristotle's System of the Physical World*, CSCP 33 (Ithaca, NY: Cornell University, 1960).

—— 'Cleanthes or Posidonius? The Basis of Stoic Physics', *MNAW* 24. 9 (1961), 265–89.

—— *Plato's Theology*, CSCP 27 (Ithaca, NY: Cornell University, 1942).

—— 'The Vital Heat, the Inborn Pneuma and the Aether', *JHS* 77 (1957), 119–23.

SORABJI, RICHARD, *Time, Creation and the Continuum* (Ithaca, NY: Cornell University, 1983).

SVOBODA, KAREL, *La Démonologie de Michel Psellus* (Brno: Filosofická fakulta, 1927).

TARÁN, LEONARDO, *Academica*, MAPS 107 (Philadelphia: MAPS, 1975).

TAYLOR, A. E., *A Commentary on Plato's Timaeus* (Oxford: Clarendon, 1928).

THEILER, WILLY, *Forschungen zum Neuplatonismus*, QSGP 10 (Berlin: Walter de Gruyter, 1966).

—— *Poseidonios: Die Fragmente*, TK 10 (Berlin: Walter de Gruyter, 1982).

—— *Untersuchungen zur antiken Literatur* (Berlin: Walter de Gruyter, 1970).

TORJESEN, KAREN JO, *Hermeneutical Procedure and Theological Method in Origen's Exegesis*, PTS 28 (Berlin: Walter de Gruyter, 1986).

TURCAN, ROBERT, *Mithras Platonicus*, EPRO 47 (Leiden: E. J. Brill, 1975).

TUROWSKI, EDMUND, *Die Widerspiegelung des stoischen Systems bei Philon von Alexandreia* (Borna-Leipzig: Robert Noske, 1927).

ULANSEY, DAVID, *The Origins of the Mithraic Mysteries* (New York: Oxford University, 1989).

VAN DEN BROECK, R., 'The Creation of Adam's Psychic Body', *Studies in Gnosticism and Hellenistic Religions*, FS Gilles Quispel, EPRO 91 (Leiden: E. J. Brill, 1981) 38–57.

VAN DER HORST, PIETER WILLEM, *Chaeremon, Egyptian Priest and Stoic Philosopher*, EPRO 101 (Leiden: E. J. Brill, 1984).

VERBEKE, G., *L'Évolution de la doctrine du pneuma du stoïcisme à S. Augustin* (Paris: Desclée de Brouwer, 1945).

VERDENIUS, W. J., 'Plato and Christianity', *Ratio* 5 (1963), 15–32.

—— 'Platons Gottesbegriff', *Entretiens sur l'antiquité classique* 1 (Geneva: fondation Hardt, 1954), 241–92.

—— 'Traditional and Personal Elements in Aristotle's Religion', *Phron* 5 (1960), 56–70.

VLASTOS, GREGORY, *Plato's Universe* (Seattle: University of Washington, 1975).

VOGEL, C. J. DE, *Greek Philosophy*, vol. 2 (Leiden: E. J. Brill, 1967).

—— 'Was Plato a Dualist?', *Rethinking Plato and Platonism*, MnSuppl 92 (Leiden: E. J. Brill, 1986), 159–212.

VÖLKER, WALTHER, *Fortschritt und Vollendung bei Philo von Alexandrien*, TU 49. 1 (Leipzig: J. C. Hinrichs, 1938).

—— *Das Vollkommenheitsideal des Origenes*, BHTh 7 (Tübingen: J. C. B. Mohr, 1931).

—— *Der wahre Gnostiker nach Clemens Alexandrinus*, TU 57. 2 (Berlin: Akademie, 1952).

WALLACE-HADRILL, D. S, *The Greek Patristic View of Nature* (Manchester: Manchester University, 1968).

WASZINK, J. H., 'Aether', *RAC* 1 (1950), 150–8.

—— 'Bemerkungen zum Einfluß des Platonismus im frühen Christentum', *VigChr* 19 (1965), 129–62.

—— *Tertulliani De Anima* (Amsterdam: J. M. Meulenhoff, 1947).

WENDLAND, PAUL, *Die hellenistisch–römische Kultur in ihren Beziehungen zu Judentum und Christentum*, HNT 1. 2 (Tübingen: J. C. B. Mohr, 1912).

—— *Philos Schrift über die Vorsehung* (Berlin: K. Gaertners, 1892).

WHITTAKER, J., 'Platonic Philosophy in the Early Centuries of the Empire', *ANRW* 2. 36. 1 (1987), 81–123.

WINSTON, DAVID, *Logos and Mystical Theology in Philo of Alexandria* (Cincinnati: Hebrew Union College, 1985).

WOLFF, GUSTAVUS, *Porphyrii de Philosophia ex Oraculis Haurienda* (Berlin: Iulii Springeri, 1856).

WOLFSON, HARRY AUSTRYN, *Philo* (Cambridge, Mass.: Harvard University, 1947).

—— 'The Problem of the Souls of the Spheres from the Byzantine Commentaries on Aristotle through the Arabs and St. Thomas to Kepler', in Isadore Twersky and George H. Williams (eds.), *Studies in the History of Philosophy and Religion* (Cambridge, Mass: Harvard University, 1973), 1. 22–59.

ZELLER, E., *Die Philosophie der Griechen* (5th edn., Leipzig: O. R. Reisland, 1922).

INDEX OF SCRIPTURAL REFERENCES

GENERAL INDEX